# CLASSIC WORLD WAR II
# AIRCRAFT CUTAWAYS

# CLASSIC WORLD WAR II
# AIRCRAFT CUTAWAYS

BILL GUNSTON

Bounty
Books

First published in Great Britain in 1995 by Osprey
Reprinted 1997, 1998

This edition first published in 2011 by Bounty Books,
A division of Octopus Publishing Group Ltd
Endeavour House
189 Shaftesbury Avenue
London WC2H 8JY
www.octopusbooks.co.uk
Reprinted 2012, 2013

This edition of *Classic World War II Cutaways* is published
by arrangement with Osprey Publishing Ltd

www.octopusbooks.co.uk

An Hachette UK Company
www.hachette.co.uk

ISBN: 978-0-753722-88-6

A CIP catalogue record for this book is available from the British Library

Printed and bound in China

# CONTENTS

# RICHARD RIDING

I was born during an air raid on Hayes, Middlesex, in 1942, just down the road from the Fairey Aviation Company's factory where my dad worked in the AID department signing out Albacores. Dad was also an accomplished aeromodeller, photographer and draughtsman; thus I was brought up in a totally aviation household. Copies of *Beano* and *Chick's Own* were forsaken for back issues of the defunct *Popular Flying*, edited by Biggles creator Capt W E Johns, and copies of *The Aeroplane* liberated from Faireys; I still have copies bearing the company stamp on their covers! In addition, the skies overhead were permanently busy with aircraft and even at the tender age of $2^1/2$ I could recognise most of 'our' aircraft – 'their' aircraft being those that often woke me up at night!

Highlights from mid-1944, by which time we had moved to the end of one of Hendon's runways, were 'Mr Hitler's' V1s; their distinctive and spine-chilling approach would send me gleefully toddling into the garden, shouting to all and sundry, 'Here comes another ruddy Doodlebug!'. Each time, I was quickly bundled into the air raid shelter under the stairs to pore over my treasured copies of *Popular Flying* and *The Aeroplane*. I recall marvelling over Clark's magical cutaway drawings, particularly those of the big bombers. Even at that tender age I knew that I wanted to be with aeroplanes. Little did I realise that 30 years later I would become custodian of much of Clark's original artwork, including the magnificent drawings of those big bombers which had so captured my youthful imagination. Many of these classic wartime cutaways have been reproduced in *The Aeroplane*'s successor, *Aeroplane Monthly*, which I started in 1973.

So popular have they remained that *Aeroplane Monthly* has used them time and again as promotional posters and free give-aways. Many, but not all, of the original Clark cutaway drawings are in the safe keeping of *Quadrant* Picture Library at Sutton, in Surrey, where they rub shoulders, so to speak, with cutaways produced by *Flight*, the 'opposition'.

Many of the postwar *Flight* cutaways were produced by Frank Munger, who worked in their studio for 40 years until his retirement in 1985. Fifty years after joining *Flight*, Frank is still producing cutaway drawings; not of the latest aircraft, but of machines that were in the frontline in his youth, commissioned and published by *Aeroplane Monthly* for its long-running series on pre-war RAF biplane bombers. These exquisite drawings are not clinical, computer-generated stereotypes, but hand-crafted works of art, with character and style in the tradition of Clark and his generation.

This book will appeal not only to the generation of readers of *The Aeroplane*, *Aeroplane Spotter* and *Flight*, but to everyone, young and old, whose interests in aeroplanes is more than skin deep.

RICHARD RIDING • EDITOR • *AEROPLANE MONTHLY* • LONDON

# ALLAN WINN

For over 60 years, our cutaway drawings have formed an essential part of our coverage of aviation technology. If any picture can be worth a thousand words, it must be one of these, laying bare the bones of aircraft and their engines in a way in which no mere written description or set of photographs ever could. As such they form an essential part of aviation journalism's record of technical advance – a combination of art and science which has served us, and our readers, proud.

The history of this descriptive form has been well-told elsewhere – from its beginnings as little more than ghosted illustration, to its current incarnation as computer-aided draughtsmanship – as has the story of the people like Millar, Clark, Bowbeer, Munger and Marsden who drew that history. What may be less well-known or understood (or appreciated) is the significance of these drawings to their time.

The drawings in this book were all completed in the run-up to, during and in the aftermath of, probably the most violent and far-reaching conflict this world has ever seen. It was a time in which security was tight and restrictions on reporting great, yet the *Flight* and *The Aeroplane* artists continued to describe and dissect the machines of war in almost incredible detail. It is difficult to imagine *Flight International* artists being allowed to cut away the Lockheed F-117 in the middle of the Gulf War of 45 years later, yet in the middle of the 1939-45 conflict, there we were exposing the details of the Boeing B-17.

Almost as remarkable as the access these artists were allowed was the extraordinary progress in aviation which they chronicled in these few years. In 1937, they were still cutting away fabric to reveal welded-steel and wood structures, and cutting away simple, air-cooled cylinders to reveal nothing more exotic or complex than a couple of valves fed by a carburettor. Less than 10 years later, they were cutting away stressed monocoques powered by jet engines – an entire generation of ultra-highly stressed fuel-injected piston engines having come and gone in the meantime – and were having to pick up details like powered controls.

That progress in technology was mirrored by a progress in the art (or is its science?) of the cutaway itself. The great pre-war and wartime practitioners were artists first and foremost – many of those who joined and then succeeded them postwar had worked on the design, construction or maintenance of aircraft, and brought an intimate insight with them which showed up in their work.

That which Millar and Clark began is something of which we are enormously proud. They began a tradition which has been carried through into the present, in which *Flight International* is now the only aerospace magazine in the world to maintain its own staff of full-time cutaway artists. As this book shows, we owe those early artists, and their art, a great deal.

ALLAN WINN • EDITOR • *FLIGHT INTERNATIONAL* • SURREY

# TIM HALL

The cutaway illustrations of *Flight* and later *Flight International* have evolved over a number of years, their roots being traced back to the work of two technical artists, Max Millar and James 'Jimmy' Clark. Max Millar was the 'founding Father' of the cutaway in the technical journals of Illiffe Associated Press. Although his real interest lay in the subjects portrayed in Autocar, he had an unquenchable enthusiasm for drawing anything of a technical nature.

Millar's cutaways of aircraft started in 1934 with the illustration of the Hawker Hardy, and his style of drawing was noted for its clarity, strength of line and treatment and mastery of drawing in perspective. His drawings had more of an artistic content than Clark's, and a fair number of his aeronautical cutaways were finished in wash with pictorial backgrounds.

James Clark worked as a freelance technical artist for *Flight*'s competitor *The Aeroplane*, a Temple Press publication. Clark's drawings were more the work of a draughtsman than an artist, and this was shown in his attention to detail in both his main drawings and his details. Clark's work did not, however, have the artistic presentation and perspective accuracy of Max Millar's drawings. Nevertheless, he was easily the most prolific and better known of the two artists producing aeronautical cutaways during this period.

In the late 1940s and into the 50s names like John Palmer, Arthur Bowbeer, John Ferguson, Dick Ellis, Frank Munger and John Marsden appeared. These artists, under the leadership of 'the Father', began a standard of cutaway drawing which combined the styles of both Millar and Clark work, and which has led to the cutaways of today. Max Millar's way of

setting an example to 'His boys' as manager was to continue working on the board, and he created an office environment in which enthusiasm in engineering and drawing was encouraged above all else.

One story about Max typifies this. Frank Munger and Arthur Bowbeer brought a model diesel engine into work one day and were feverishly trying to start it when Max walked in. Instead of asking them to put it aside and get on with their work, he rolled up his shirt sleeves and helped them spend most of an afternoon trying to get it running!

The cutaway drawing from its inception until the late 1960s changed very little. The artist would visit a factory with a blank piece of board and leave a week later with a fully finished pencil drawing. The job entailed sketching accurately the subject matter from the components and available technical information. For example, when producing an engine illustration the artist would ask for the crankshaft and connecting rods to be set up on blocks. He would then sit and draw the assembled parts and finish the illustration by sketching the other components and crankcase into place around his original sketch, with the aid of engineering drawings.

The task was similar for an aircraft. The subject would be laid out on the board with the use of station point drawings of the aircraft's structure. The artist would walk around the shop floor putting 'the meat on the bones' of the geometric layout. The drawing would then be taken back to the office and inked and finished, with the written key being added last.

As the cutaway entered the 1960s the subject matter was becoming more complicated, and manufacturers were becoming reluctant to play host to the

artist for durations of longer that two or three days. The journal also became international in its coverage. Gradually the artists began to visit the manufacturers only to gather the material – they did this by gathering engineering drawing material, taking photographs and talking to engineers. They then returned to the office to do the drawing, using the material they had collected. With this new working practice, it was important that the artist made sure that he had enough material and information to complete the job when he left the manufacturer's premises.

In the 1980s computer aided design (CAD) technology began to transform the drawing office, and we began to encounter difficulties in accessing information in the form to which we were accustomed. This has led us to the position we are in today. We take CAD information from the manufacturer on tape and then use CAD to lay out the geometry of the aircraft or engine. Once the perspective geometry is plotted out, we sketch in the detail from photographs and engineering data, and then ink it in the time honoured way. The big advantage of CAD technology is that it allows easy access to manufacturers' layout and assembly drawings, and therefore saves time in the early stages of the cutaway.

As we near the end of the century the present team of technical artists – myself, David Hatchard and Joe Picarella – carry on the tradition of the 'cutaway' and with it, a form of pictorial journalism which is becoming increasingly unique.

TIM HALL • TECHNICAL ARTIST • *FLIGHT INTERNATIONAL* • SURREY

*Flight* artists John Marsden (foreground), David Hatchard (centre) and Tim Hall (right) are seen here in 1993 when the magazine's technical art department was awarded a plaque by the American Aviation and Space Writers Association for 61 years of excellence in cutaway drawings *(Flight)*

# INTRODUCTION

This volume collects together cutaway drawings of aircraft of World War 2. The selection is predominantly British, with a leavening of German, because the artists worked for the weekly magazines *The Aeroplane* and *Flight*, and could only draw what they had access to.

Apart from showing how the technique of such drawings progressed, over 50 years ago, these illustrations remind me that even in those days aircraft were quite complicated. Bearing in mind that no artist could put in all the engineering detail, one is left with a feeling of regret that so much effort was devoted at that time to designing and constructing over 600,000 aircraft, virtually all of which were soon destroyed.

The cutaway drawing has always been a special art form, but it comes in limitless variations. Those prepared by architects are usually different in style from those of aeroplanes, while ship artists often draw deck plans or a series of bow-to-stern chunks, like slicing a baguette. Instructional books often contain so-called 'exploded' drawings, while traditional engineering drawings may include isometric (perspective) views, but always provide front, side and plan elevations, in what is strictly called a GA (general arrangement) drawing, but is popularly known as a three-view.

My old employer, *Flight*, published the occasional cutaway drawing from its very first year, 1909, but in those days you could see almost everything from the outside anyway. Between the World Wars aircraft cutaways varied enormously from one periodical to another. Most artists or editors thought that the right thing to do was to draw, or rather paint, a picture of the aircraft, often complete with landscape or sky background, and then cut bits away to show such things as the engine(s), fuel tanks, bombs and, invariably, the crew at work. Advertisements for Imperial Airways, PanAm and Air France were often based on colourful cutaways in which passengers and sacks of mail were more in evidence than details of structure.

My old journal was published by Iliffe & Sons, in Dorset House south of the river. Here, were also to be found many other magazines, with titles as diverse as *Autocar*, *Amateur Photographer*, *Yachting World*, *Iron & Steel*, *Farmer & Stockbreeder*, *British Plastics* and *Nursing Mirror*. These, and many others, made varying demands on the in-house Artists Department. North of the Thames in Rosebury Avenue, later in Bowling Green Lane, was the deadly rival, Temple Press. They published such titles as *The Aeroplane*, *The Motor*, *The Oil Engine*, *Light Metals* and *The Motor Ship*. All made use of cutaway drawings.

As a boy I often noticed the initials 'J P' on drawings in *Flight* and, later,

its supplement *The Aircraft Engineer*. Despite his Polish-sounding name, Janusz Prochazka was a Dane, who joined *Flight* in 1910 and became its chief artist. He was able to draw aircraft throughout Europe, and when he retired, the issue of 4 October 1945 said 'No artist has ever "dissected" aircraft structures more successfully . . . in many drawing offices his sketches of structural details were filed for reference'.

Max Millar ran the art department at *Flight* for many years, and although his real passion was for engines, he proved extremely skilled at drawing aircraft cutaways

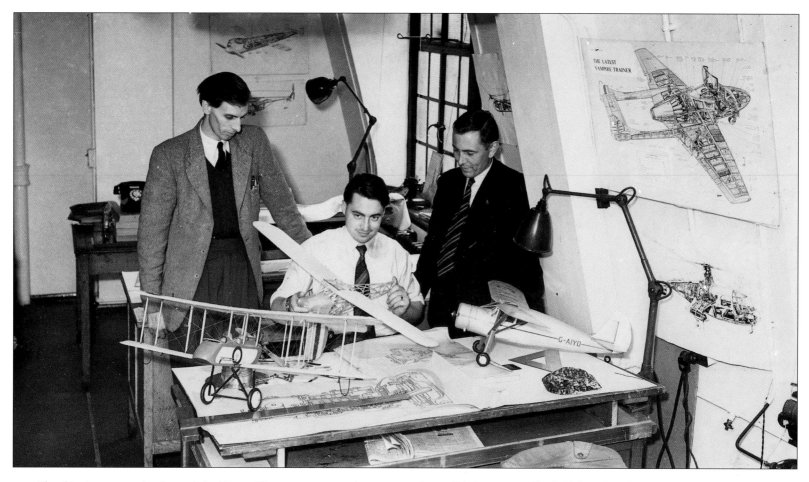

Some of Max's postwar staff in the *Flight* studio at Dorset House in Stamford Street in the 1950s. John Marsden is flanked by Frank Munger (left) and Arthur Bowbeer (right)

After his departure, the dean of the Dorset House cutaway artists was Max Millar. Though often required to do 'pretty' drawings, almost like photographs with bits cut open, his preference was for clear black-line work with a mapping pen and Indian ink. In the 1930s he refined this style of technical art. It was acceptable to use various kinds of hand-drawn shading, or even solid black in places, but the essence was to draw everything accurately in the finest possible detail. Various parts would be labelled, at first using capital letters with serifs throughout. If necessary, items might be labelled with a mere letter or number, and explained in a key alongside which was hand-lettered on the same piece of art board as the drawing. This established a style which endured until, in some major publishing houses, it is now computerised.

Max's particular love was engines; he had been an RFC Captain instructing on aero engines in World War 1. His engines were usually more detailed and comprehensive than his aircraft. He loved nothing better than to be told (for example) there was a new kind of Rolls-Royce Merlin with a two-stage supercharger and intercooler. He had a particularly free rein in such matters, because of the parallel existence in the same house of a very serious industry magazine, *Aircraft Production*. Though published only monthly, instead of weekly as was *Flight*, I think Max had more drawings in *Air Prod* in the course of a year than in *Flight*.

I did not join the team until 1951, so before writing this introduction I sought the advice of former Head Artist, Arthur Bowbeer. He recalls 'At the start of the war all Max's "boys" went away. This left him with R E Poulton,

13

Frank Beak (who graduated to technical subjects from illustrating touring articles for the motoring journals) and John Palmer. When the authorities weeded out "reserved occupation" men, Frank went to Farnborough and Palmer to Short Brothers. I joined as "the boy" and did two years before being sent off to fly RAF aeroplanes, but in that time didn't graduate beyond a spate of aircraft-recognition charts.

'So Max did *Flight*'s main aircraft and engine drawings during the War. His aircraft began as pictures, with camouflage and roundels, but settled down as black-line work, at first usually with lots of solid black. They were a rapidly done, clear statement of the main technical features, but often with the

Fairey Battle I K7558 – the first production-standard aircraft built – is seen on the wing in early 1937. A further 2418 Battles were delivered to the RAF up to 1941

crew in place, together with bombs (big, black, shiny ones!), and with emphasis on the engines.

'In the 1930s Max had trained an intended successor, James 'Jimmy' Clark, but Clark left to draw for the opposition. He developed his own distinctive style whilst working as a retained freelance, and became the artist beloved of the small boys of the time because "he seemed to put everything in". Perhaps predictably, in view of his joining the competition, our own artists took a jaundiced view of "Clark drawings", and claimed that he was usually inaccurate, but the fact remains that he swiftly became the pre-eminent aircraft-cutaway artist. This was largely because his enormous output received virtually weekly exposure not only in *The Aeroplane* but also in the mass-circulation *Aeroplane Spotter*.' Thank you for that bit of background, Arthur.

When you look at one of these wartime cutaways it is usually obvious whether or not the artist knew what he was about. It seems only common sense to suggest that an artist should never draw an aircraft that he knows little about, but many cutaways were drawn when the artist knew little except the external shape, and invented most of what went inside. Clark sometimes did this with German aircraft in 1939-40, before the British landscape was littered with them, and it was supremely unhelpful. Sometimes he even got the shape wrong, as for example when in November 1939 he did what purported to be the latest version of He 111 bomber. He gave it the elliptical wings of previous versions, and drew the interior structure in convincing detail. Only much later did I discover that, quite apart from having a wing of incorrect shape, all the beautifully drawn structure, with bold zig-zag internal ribs, was pure fiction, bearing not the slightest resemblance to anything designed by the Günter brothers!

In my view this is unforgivable. The reader has to have confidence in the artist, just as he needs to feel he can believe the non-fiction writer.

On the other hand, Sir Peter Masefield, who was the wartime Technical Editor of *The Aeroplane* and overworked Editor of *The Aeroplane Spotter*, believes my criticisms may be too harsh. He recalls 'One has to remember that the chief objective of *The Aeroplane* and *Flight* was to inform – as far as was possible and as far as was permitted – a much less-professional readership than these magazines had enjoyed before the war. The information had to be produced "in the fog of war". That accounts for the fact that in the early days of the conflict Clark got the shape and detail of the He 111 wrong, and also its internal structure. But when he was let loose for a day upon a heavily damaged He 111 at Farnborough he got it pretty well right, though he was allowed only a short time on the job'. Thank you Sir Peter.

I am still unconvinced of the value of a cutaway that is pure fiction, however. I have also frequently been exasperated by what I consider to be another heinous crime: throwing away the opportunity to impart information. There is a saying 'Reading maketh a full man, speech a ready man and writing an exact man', and to the last bit you can certainly add cutaway drawings. Perhaps a thousand times I have wondered where I could check a particular item of technical detail and, having found nothing in the relevant Jane's or Putnam, and often nothing in books dealing specifically with the type of aircraft concerned (it's astonishing how people can write big books without mentioning crucial technical details!), I have suddenly recalled that a cutaway

exists. Today, I doubt if anyone would draw an aircraft cutaway without drawing attention to all the major technical features, but there are drawings and drawings.

Time after time I have looked up a cutaway to find out how a wing was made, only to find that the relevant key item read 'Wing structure'. I wish to discover whether the flaps are driven electrically, hydraulically or whatever, and the key says 'Flap mechanism'. I felt that as the artist at the time probably knew the answers, to write informative words would cost no more. In 1981 I ventured to suggest as much to Bill Green, then managing director of Pilot Press. My bleat stirred a hornet's nest. Bill wrote an astonishingly long reply, saying in part:

B-17E *YANKEE DOODLE* (41-9023) of the Eighth Air Force's 414th Bomb Squadron, 97th Bomb Group is seen undergoing maintenance at Grafton Underwood in September 1942

'Our cutaways have never been presented as engineering drawings, and are not intended as such. Do you seriously believe that one in a thousand of our readers is really interested to know if bleed air or combustion heaters serve for de-icing purposes? When you say "What we wish to know", are you not identifying the vast majority with you personally? The drawings are not intended to be used as a technical reference, nor are they for posterity as you suggest. They are purely commercial drawings created for a specific market, and their cost must be commercially viable! Personally, I am not sure that I care what people may think in 2081. I certainly will not be around to worry if the undercarriage of an aircraft built 150 years earlier was cranked up by hand or was hydraulically actuated.'

Bill was explaining the factors governing drawings produced for Pilot Press, but precisely the same arguments apply to those from any other commercial publisher. This being so, one begins to appreciate the way the quality and general standard of drawings progressed during World War 2, leading to the outstanding results produced by the end of that conflict. This is especially reinforced by the fact that these wartime drawings were often done under almost impossible conditions – in a freezing hangar, a badly lit Nissen hut or a hotel bedroom – and almost always under the unyielding pressure of the publishing deadline. And woe betide the artist who inadvertently included an item that he could see on the aircraft but which had not yet been cleared for publication. Considerations of security account for many apparent omissions from the drawings of Allied aircraft in this book.

Collecting the material for this album was not easy. Very few of the original drawings exist. The quality of reproduction in *The Aeroplane Spotter* was unacceptable by today's standards, and it is impossible to copy from bound volumes of *Flight* and *Aeroplane* without losing the central part of the drawing along the spine. Many drawings were photographed from an unbound copy original issue, and then doctored to eliminate the staples!

Today we are used to cutaways with key items numbered up to 500. This reflects the growing complexity of aircraft, a process that was well under way by 1939. Clark's Stirling and Lancaster, for example, give a pretty good indication of what these aircraft were like, and stand out in sharp contrast to those of, say, the Wellington and Whitley which were from the previous generation.

An anonymous flight of Anson Is patrol the southern English coastline near Gosport in late 1939. Note the variation in the national markings applied to each aircraft

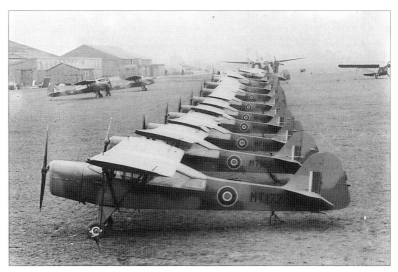

Factory-fresh and awaiting their first frontline postings, an impressive line-up of Taylorcraft Auster IVs sit on the grass at Rearsby in early 1944. MT177 later served with No 659 Sqn

Despite this, had security allowed it, he could have added to either of the later aircraft about 30 additional items of equipment, mainly of an electronic nature.

Today, producing a cutaway is made that bit easier by the use of special software. An artist can insert the geometrics of his subject, in colour if that helps, spin it around on the screen to study it in detail from any aspect, and finally pick the best viewpoint. He can then get to work knowing that, for a

Hampden I P1333 of No 49 Sqn is readied for a mission in July 1940 from Scampton. This machine was lost during a raid performed by the unit on Essen on 17 August

start, his overall shape is absolutely correct, though he may choose to distort it slightly for clarity. In World War 2 he had to do it all 'the hard way', often later wished he had chosen a different viewpoint, and on not a few occasions got propellers, landing gear or other parts visibly wrong!

A fine Vickers-Armstrongs press shot of a quartet of then brand new Wellington Is of No 9 Sqn out on a daylight navigation exercise from Honington in the spring of 1939

Having completed his drawing, the artist then had to point out various parts. In 1939 just a few labels might suffice. As aircraft became more complicated, and the accepted standards of drawing were raised, it must have taken many hours to write in dozens of labels. In Clark's case, for no better reason than pure fashion, these were invariably written entirely in letters with serifs! After 1939 he used capital letters only, but retaining the serifs. I just asked a highly literate friend to copy one of Clark's shorter labels – it said 'METAL FIN' – and not only did it take him over two minutes, but it wasn't nearly as neat as the one done 50 years previously. It's all a matter of practice.

On the other hand, there is a certain almost childish naiveté about many of the classic wartime drawings, especially with those of Clark. Time after time he was under such pressure that he would begin a word and find that he couldn't get it into the available space. His cutaway Tempest (which is in this book) had a huge 'hole' drilled through the engine to show the rear engine mounts! Sometimes words were mis-spelt, and on one occasion he drew an arrow to an aperture in a captured aircraft and labelled it 'THINGS SEEN THROUGH GAP'!

I have harped on Jimmy Clark, because he has by far the lion's share of the drawings in this book. He individually must have been worth a sizeable fraction of the circulation of *The Aeroplane* during the war years. Incidentally, for most of the war, while *The Aeroplane* and *Flight* were published on Fridays, the eagerly awaited *Aeroplane Spotter* came out a day earlier.

This newspaper-style weekly was launched by Temple Press on 2 January 1941 to meet an unfilled need that literally could mean life or death. Despite this need, stringent paper rationing forced it from November 1941 to appear

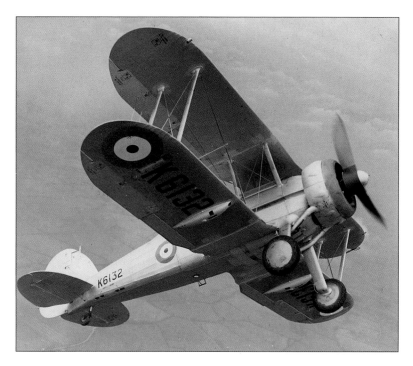

The fourth production Gladiator I built by Glosters, K6132 enjoyed a long career serving firstly with No 72 Sqn, then No 13 Gp's Communication Flight, and finally the RAE

only on alternate Thursdays. It reprinted many of Clark's cutaways, bringing them to a far wider audience, but usually had to squeeze them into a smaller space which, combined with the poor quality of wartime newsprint, lost much fine detail. In my view this was work of national importance. Quite apart from reducing the many tragic 'own goals' by anti-aircraft gunners and even fighter pilots, it helped hundreds of thousands of former clerks, shop assistants and window-cleaners who suddenly found themselves making, maintaining or flying aircraft, to feel that they understood a little about these complex creations. Beyond doubt, this not only helped them to tell friend from foe (the immediate task), but also gave them an all-important psychological lift. Without cutaways, except to the few enthusiasts, aircraft would have remained total enigmas.

Today, most of us are clerks, shop assistants and window-cleaners, and telling one aeroplane from another is seldom a matter of life or death. But many thousands of silver-haired chaps will no doubt enjoy poring over these drawings, once again threading their way over the wing spars of a Lancaster to wherever they used to sit. Probably their grandsons will find these drawings of interest also.

Uniformly sprayed up in Training Command yellow, these early-build Oxford IIs lack the dorsal turret of the Mk I, thus denoting their exclusive use as pilot trainers

# WHITLEY III

In starkest contrast to Clark's pure-black pen drawing of the Armstrong Whitworth bomber published in *The Aeroplane* on 5 June 1941, this is one of the best of Max's pen and wash productions. One can imagine the camouflage, officially called dark green and dark earth, with the roundels surrounded by yellow rings. The underside would have been soot-black.

The subject is a Whitley III, visibly identified from the Mk I externally by having increased dihedral on the outer wings. When extended, the ventral turret was another feature which distinguished the Mk III from all other Whitleys. Of course, when the later Merlin-engined Whitleys were making their long raids over the Alps to northern Italy, there were no enemy night-

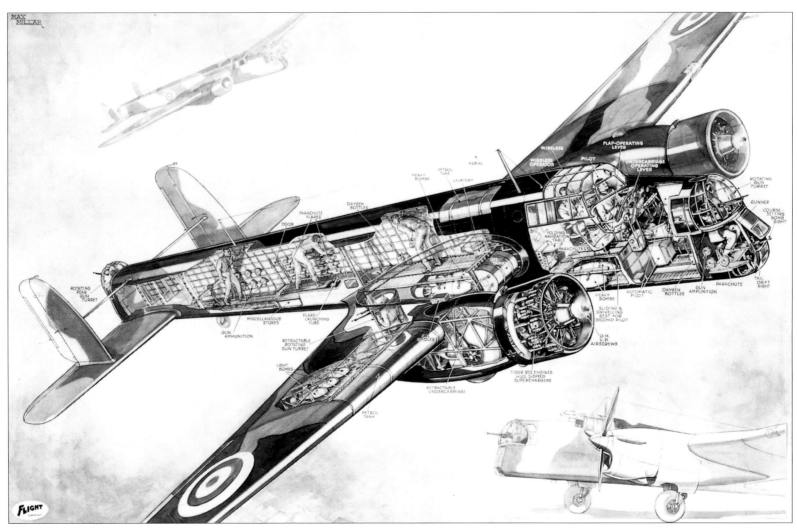

fighters with upward-firing guns, so removal of ventral turrets from these later versions was of little consequence.

The first three marks of Whitley had defensive armament which in the mid-1930s seemed very modern, but by the start of the War was woefully inadequate. In the Whitley I the turrets at the nose and tail were of the Armstrong Whitworth manually operated type, a related version being fitted to the first Ansons. The gun was the Mk IIIA Lewis, fed from 97-round drum magazines. In the Mk III the nose turret was usually the hydraulically powered Nash and Thompson FN16, equipped with a single Vickers K gas-operated gun, the drum magazines for which can be seen. The tail gunner had seven drums, which can be seen clipped to the left wall of the fuselage. One can imagine the unfortunate gunner having to scramble out of his turret each time he ran out of ammunition and make his way to a fresh drum, the Whitley meanwhile possibly performing violent evasive manoeuvres!

In contrast, the ventral turret was a modern hydraulically powered design by Nash and Thompson, the FN17. This could be raised or lowered by twin rams, and the guns were two Brownings, fed by 500-round belts. It was omitted from the Mk IV and subsequent Whitleys mainly because of its installed weight of 715 lb (325 kg) complete with ammunition, and also because of its high drag when extended. Sadly, the Air Staff got it into their heads that all a bomber needed were nose, mid-upper and tail turrets, when by 1943 these were precisely the turrets it didn't need.

Unlike Clark, Max took care to draw the engines. He could easily also have drawn attention to the simple oil coolers, which projected into the airstream above the highest point of each nacelle. Several standard books state that the Whitley II and III were 'the first aircraft in RAF service with a two-stage supercharger'. Max knew his engines, and correctly described the Tiger VIII as having a 'two-speed' supercharger.

This did at least give better power at high altitude, though the two-position bracket-type DH Hamilton propellers were limited in pitch range, and in any case by later standards these aircraft were underpowered. This state of affairs was to some degree rectified by switching to Rolls-Royce Merlin engines in the Mk IV. Max drew the front end of a Mk IV as an inset to the cut-away, but was perhaps unaware that this mark introduced a welcome improvement to the bomb-aiming position. In the Tiger-engined aircraft the nose comprised a hinged door containing a window, which when open provided a mounting for the course-setting bomb sight.

In the Merlin-engined aircraft a permanent projecting balcony or chin was provided incorporating an optically flat window, but Max did not show this in his inset of the new version.

Normal crew of all Whitley bomber versions was five, four of whom were usually ahead of the wing. It is strange that Max drew three chaps apparently busily engaged in the normally empty rear fuselage. I am not sure what he meant by 'heavy bombs'. The biggest bomb that could be carried by a Whitley from the Mk III onward was the 2000-lb armour-piercing type, and the usual load was made up of 250-lb or, on occasion, two of 500 lb. The maximum load was two 500-lb and 12 of 250-lb.

Tiger-engined aircraft had wood-framed bomb doors, with aluminium skin, which could be opened by the weight of the released bombs and closed by strong bungee cords. These cords were disconnected during the loading of bombs. The Mk III introduced hydraulically operated doors, which obviously improved bombing accuracy.

Clearly, Max was under no restrictions when he did this drawing, though not long afterwards it became usual practice to omit any reference to armament in most aircraft cutaways. Max did not indicate that there were no fewer than 14 cells for small bombs in the wings, both inboard and outboard of the nacelles. The maximum permissible bomb load was 7000 lb, which at that time was a very respectable figure. During the frantic and costly attacks on the barges which were intended to bring the victorious *Wehrmacht* to Britain, in July/September 1940, Whitleys actually carried this maximum.

As explained in the text accompanying Clark's Whitley drawing, when the bomber's wing was flying straight and level, the fuselage was tilted steeply nose-down. This explains the apparent upward tilt of the engines in Max's drawing. In a typical cruising attitude the engine thrust lines were horizontal.

# LYSANDER I

Utterly unlike anything else in the RAF, the 'Lizzie' flew as a prototype in June 1936. It had the look of a dragonfly about it, because of its long and slender wings seemingly about to part company with the tubby fuselage hanging underneath. People who were useless at aircraft recognition used to divide up flying machines into two groups – aeroplanes and Lysanders.

A fundamental requirement of an army co-operation aircraft was the ability to operate from any reasonable field near frontline troops. The wings were the key to how the 'Lizzie' met this STOL (short take-off and landing)

No 16 Sqn replaced its five-year-old Hawker Audaxes with brand new Lysander Is at Old Sarum in June 1938. By the summer of the following year they were flying the modestly improved Mk II. This trio were photographed over Wiltshire in the autumn of 1938

demand, whilst still having far higher all-round performance than the Hawker biplanes it replaced. A two-seater, it also had to have outstanding all-round vision for such roles as artillery spotting and frontline reconnaissance. To preserve radio silence written messages could be thrown from the cockpit, or picked up from the ground by a very long hook which could be pivoted down under the right side of the fuselage.

The US Army used the Piper L-4 Grasshopper and similar types with 65 hp. The British Army used Austers with 130 hp. The Germans used the Storch, which was about the same size as the Lysander (its wing area was significantly greater), with 240 hp. In contrast, the Lysander was powered by either a Bristol Mercury poppet-valve engine of 870 or 890 hp or a Bristol Perseus sleeve-valve engine of 905 hp. This gave it a higher performance, and enabled it to carry heavier loads and fly missions not dreamed of when it was designed.

It had a light-alloy structure with fabric covering. In the cockpit the pilot sat 10 feet off the ground. The wings had maximum profile at the attachment of the bracing struts, tapering from this point inboard as well as to the tip. This gave both crew an outstanding view in virtually all directions, especially as one's entire torso was elevated in the cockpit thanks to a superior seating position. Max Millar's traditional-style drawing showed this, and the location of some of the important items of equipment, particularly well.

On the other hand, as was commonly the case with this type of drawing, he didn't worry very much about the airframe structure. He ignored the construction of the wings and tail. He even failed to show any interest in the mechanism powered by a hydraulic jack which drove the slotted flaps, as well as four interconnections, with long torque tubes outboard, which simultaneously drove the inboard slats. He didn't explain that the outboard slats moved freely under air loads.

When this drawing was published on 9 June 1938 security restrictions on the armament had been relaxed. By then it was common knowledge that a fixed Browning machine gun was normally mounted in the top of each spat, fed from a 500-round box in the fuselage. At first the observer had a Vickers K or even a Mk III Lewis, as depicted here, but by 1942 these had often been replaced by twin Brownings with belt feed. Also, by this stage the inner and outer spat side-plates were commonly left off. Max could have noted that this modest aircraft featured the biggest Elektron (magnesium-alloy) extrusion ever made at that time, a single giant arch inside the landing gear strut fairings carrying both wheels.

The first unit to receive Lysander Is was No 16 Sqn at Old Sarum, near

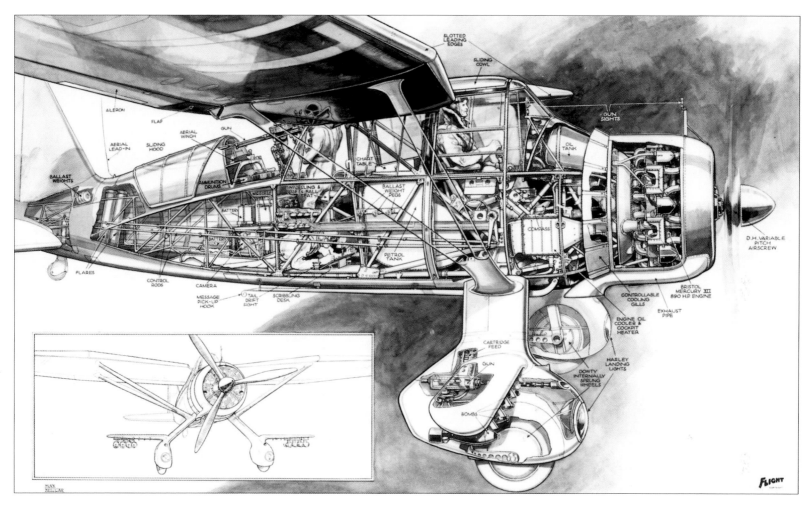

SLOTTED LEADING EDGES
SLIDING COWL
GUN SIGHTS
OIL TANK
D.H. VARIABLE PITCH AIRSCREW
BRISTOL MERCURY XII 890 H.P. ENGINE
EXHAUST PIPE
CONTROLLABLE COOLING GILLS
ENGINE OIL COOLER & COCKPIT HEATER
HARLEY LANDING LIGHTS
DOWTY INTERNALLY SPRUNG WHEELS
GUN
CARTRIDGE FEED
BOMBS
AILERON
FLAP
AERIAL WINCH
GUN
AERIAL LEAD-IN
SLIDING HOOD
CHART TABLE
BALLAST WEIGHTS
AMMUNITION DRUMS
SWIVELLING & RISE & FALL SEAT
BALLAST WEIGHT PEGS
COMPASS
BATTERY
BATTERY
PETROL TANK
FLARES
CONTROL RODS
CAMERA
TAIL DRIFT SIGHT
SCRIBBLING DESK
MESSAGE PICK-UP HOOK

MAX MILLAR
FLIGHT

Salisbury, in June 1938 –exactly two years later this outfit were one of five Lysander squadrons tasked with both dropping supplies to the remnants of the British Expeditionary Force (BEF) defending Calais, and bombing the Germans surrounding them. Nos 2, 4, 13 and 26 Sqns had flown across to France in September 1939 as part of the Air Component of the BEF, whilst No 16 Sqn had joined their ranks the following April.

The last 100 Lysanders were built as target tugs, and many others were converted for this role. Four squadrons were specially equipped for the air/sea rescue role, six more were specially equipped for the Middle East and India, and the most heroic missions of all were flown by Nos 138 and 161 Sqns using the overloaded black-painted Mk III(SD) with a 150-gal external tank and a

ladder with rungs indicated by luminous paint. Few other aircraft had the range, toughness and STOL capability to fly from Tempsford, in Bedfordshire, to tiny rough fields in southern France, on moonless nights, with no navigation gear whatsoever. They carried 101 agents into Hitler's Europe, and brought 128 out. These missions also said something about the pilots, who flew alone. Behind them were anything up to four passengers

Many Lysanders were subjected to extraordinary modifications. Even the first prototype was rebuilt with tandem wings mounted on a stubby fuselage with a four-gun tail turret. Altogether 1449 of these distinctive aircraft were built at Yeovil and Doncaster, plus a further 225 by National Steel Car in Canada. Fortunately, several have been preserved today.

# OXFORD I

It is only to be expected that aircraft used for training should tend to disappear into the background more quickly than fighters and bombers, but I am sure thousands of wartime veterans will agree with me that it is sad that not many of today's aviation enthusiasts know much about the Oxford. It is sad because 8586 were built, and there must be very few RAF multi-engined wartime pilots who did not qualify on the 'Ox-box'. But, unlike almost all other countries, we in Britain are vandals when it comes to preserving famous aeroplanes, and while you can see plenty of Harvards, you won't be able to fly an Oxford.

To fill in the background first, Airspeed (1934) Ltd caused raised eyebrows when, in 1932, they built the Courier, a trim six-seat cantilever monoplane with retractable undercarriage. Next came the bigger twin-engined Envoy, which even added split flaps. This was then the basis of the Oxford multi-role crew trainer built to Specification T.23/36. The 8586 were built by Airspeed at Portsmouth (total 4411) and at Christchurch (550), de Havilland at Hatfield (1515), Percival Aircraft at Luton (1356) and Standard Motors at Coventry (750). After the War a few Oxfords found civil customers, while 150 aircraft on the production line were completed by Airspeed as civil transports called Consuls.

The prototype Oxford flew on 19 June 1937. Apart from the nose, which was aluminium and Perspex, the light-alloy cowlings and nacelles (which were mainly above the wing) and the fabric-skinned control surfaces, the structure was entirely wooden, and extremely strong. Though there were other versions, the vast majority of Oxfords were powered by the Armstrong Siddeley Cheetah X 7-cylinder radial, rated at 355/370 hp and with direct drive to a Fairey-Reed fixed-pitch metal propeller. Despite this, the central pedestal in the cockpit always had a lever which had to be moved from 'COARSE' to 'FINE' before entering the landing circuit, because that was part of the all-important drill in the training process. In some Oxfords the manipulation of the lever actually had some effect!

The engines were hand-cranked for starting, and drew fuel from a 49-gal tank on each side, to which could be added auxiliary fuel from 29-gal tanks beyond the nacelles. This total of 156 gal meant you could fly for nearly six hours without having to refuel. The starboard engine drove a hydraulic pump for the narrow-chord split flaps and retractable main undercarriage. The latter varied, depending on who made the aircraft, some having a single fairing attached to the twin legs instead of the more common two doors hinged to the nacelle.

The prototype was fitted with an Armstrong Whitworth manually controlled turret with a Lewis gun, while various light bombs (8½, 11½ and 20-lb) could be carried in a shallow bay between the centre-section spars. As the drawing shows, equipment was also carried for complete crew training, for a

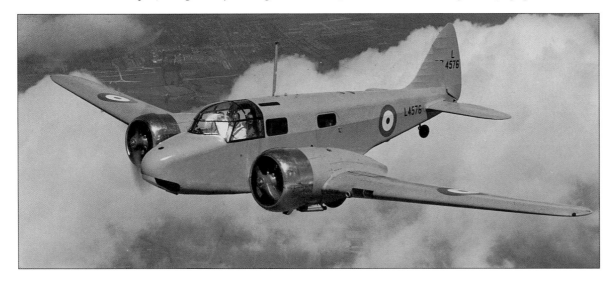

Part of the initial order for 136 aircraft, L4576 was completed at Portsmouth in early 1938 without an Armstrong Whitworth dorsal turret

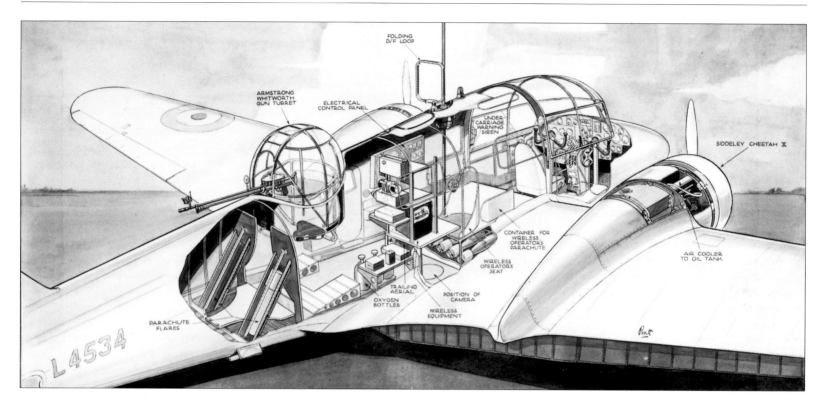

Labels on the illustration:

FOLDING D/F LOOP

ARMSTRONG WHITWORTH GUN TURRET

ELECTRICAL CONTROL PANEL

UNDER CARRIAGE WARNING SIREN

SIDDELEY CHEETAH X

CONTAINER FOR WIRELESS OPERATOR'S PARACHUTE

AIR COOLER TO OIL TANK

WIRELESS OPERATOR'S SEAT

TRAILING AERIAL

POSITION OF CAMERA

OXYGEN BOTTLES

WIRELESS EQUIPMENT

PARACHUTE FLARES

L4534

Pratt

for a pilot, navigator, bomb-aimer, radio operator, camera operator or gunner. In practice about 98 per cent of Oxfords had no armament, and were employed night and day passing out twin-engined pilots, navigators and radio operators principally for streaming into Bomber Command. They were also used as ferry-pilot transports, ambulances, radar-calibration aircraft, and for many other tasks.

The door was on the left above the trailing edge. The cockpit was most agreeable, with an almost perfect view except where blocked by the seemingly big cowlings. The pilot (or pupil, in a dual aircraft) naturally sat on the left, to force him to fly with the left hand whilst getting used to a stack of throttle, mixture, propeller, undercarriage and flap controls on his right. The engine-speed indicators were vertical, as they usually were on wartime RAF aircraft, and the control wheels were simple two-handed yokes with a thumb-operated brake lever.

I could never understand why the Oxford always yawed in flight. Watching the left wingtip, it would proceed along the horizon, slow to a stop or go backwards, and then accelerate forward again. There was absolutely no way you could stop this, even by trying to move throttles a thousandth of an inch at a time. In contrast, the Anson, with virtually the same engines and propellers, just flew straight. Like all Oxford pilots I was left in no doubt that, if you let it divert as much as a degree or two from the straight and narrow on landing, no amount of frantic full rudder and maximum braking would prevent a ground loop. I think most Oxford drivers, if they were allowed to, just did 'wheelers', flying the aircraft gently on in a level attitude.

This drawing was done by a relatively unknown *Flight* freelance artist named Pratt, who obviously borrowed much of his style from Millar's wash artworks of the time. It shows the original prototype, and whilst giving an excellent idea of the training equipment, made little effort to tell us about the aircraft (though it did show the flaps down). I think the annotation 'air cooler to oil tank' actually shows the oil cooler.

The artist drew a line across the cabin in line with the leading edge, but of course it should have been in line with the front spar. This was a favoured place for ATC (Air Training Corps) cadets on air experience flights. Incidentally, my own ATC school squadron, No 628, suffered one of the ATC's very few wartime casualties in an Oxford, on a flight from Kidlington (today, appropriately, Oxford airport).

# BLENHEIM I

One gets the impression from this drawing that Max Millar was more interested in engines than in aircraft. This was undoubtedly true, but on the other hand from the aspect Max selected, the Blenheim I was dominated by its engines. The fuselage was particularly cramped, and by later standards not very interesting, though I am surprised Max did not choose a viewpoint looking obliquely down from above in order to show far more than was possible from the same level.

As explained in the text accompanying James Clark's totally different drawing of the Mk IV aircraft, the Bristol 142M Blenheim was a fast day bomber derived from the even faster Bristol 142 executive transport. This was the first high-power high-speed aircraft in Britain to have an all-metal stressed-skin structure. It also had a retractable undercarriage, flaps and, except during its first few flights, variable-pitch propellers. In Britain all these things were innovations.

Despite Max's drawing, production Blenheims had a fixed tailwheel. In an inset he showed the gear extended, and the split flaps fully down. The main wheels were carried on twin shock struts on which was mounted a single arched fairing. In the retracted position this filled in the underside of the nacelle, except where part of the wheel projected. This sometimes reduced damage in belly landings, and despite the use of a warning horn triggered by closing both throttles with the wheels up, pilots often forget to lower the gear.

In the original Bristol 142 transport the wheels were fully faired in, but wheels-up landings could have been made with no damage at all, except to the propellers. In the Blenheim this was no longer possible, because the wing had to be raised to make room for the bomb bay, which normally carried four bombs of 250 lb or two of 500 lb. As was common practice at that time, the bomb doors were pushed open by the weight of the released ordnance, closing again under the pull of elastic bungee cords. This crude arrangement reduced bombing accuracy because there was no way the bomb-aimer could judge how long the bombs would tarry in pushing past the spring-loaded doors.

With so restricted a space, the pilot's cockpit had to fit precisely into the left half of the nose. This was just wide enough for the RAF standard 'basic six' blind-flying panel, with the two middle instruments nicely obscured behind the control column and the rest pretty well hidden behind the pilot's gloved hands. The vertical-scale engine-rpm indicators, and oil pressure and temperature dials, had to be put above the panel, where they effectively spoilt the pilot's view of the airfield when landing. Everything else had to be arranged along the left wall, or put behind the pilot or arranged along the centreline beside the seat. When climbing away, to change the DH Hamilton propellers from fine pitch to coarse you reached round behind, located two plungers by feel, and pulled them both. Before landing, you took care to bang them in again. Wartime aircraft made pilots quite familiar with instruments and controls in incredibly ill-designed locations.

Max indicated the thing like an elevator trim wheel which worked the engine cooling gills, and also the odd vertical plungers which managed the hydraulics controlling the landing gear and flaps. The tail trimmers were indeed small wheels, but further forward. The aileron control was a neat two-handed yoke with a lever for the wheel brakes and a firing button for the Browning gun far out in the left wing, not mentioned by Max. Both these had to be operated by the pilot's right thumb, which had to be fully serviceable!

Max took care to show the twin ram inlets which fed air to the oil cooler behind each engine. He also showed how the exhaust from the nine cylinders

A quartet of weary Blenheim Is sit dispersed on the perimeter of an unknown airfield in late 1942. These aircraft all wear Type C1 roundels and revised fin flashes as introduced in May of that year. Judging by the numeral codes on the fuselage and lack of gun armament in the dorsal turrets of each machine, these Blenheims are probably assigned to an Operational Training Unit

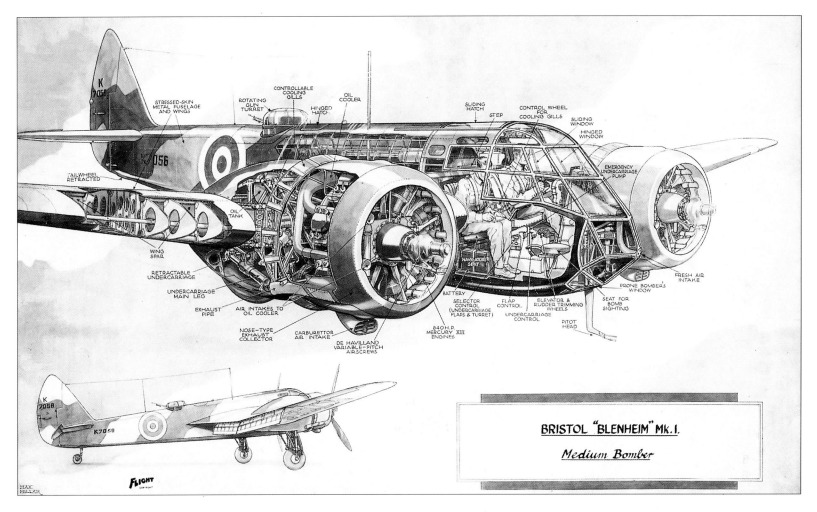

STRESSED-SKIN METAL FUSELAGE AND WINGS

ROTATING GUN TURRET

CONTROLLABLE COOLING GILLS

HINGED HATCH

OIL COOLER

SLIDING HATCH

STEP

CONTROL WHEEL FOR COOLING GILLS

SLIDING WINDOW

HINGED WINDOW

EMERGENCY UNDERCARRIAGE PUMP

TAILWHEEL RETRACTED

WING SPAR

OIL TANK

RETRACTABLE UNDERCARRIAGE

UNDERCARRIAGE MAIN LEG

EXHAUST PIPE

AIR INTAKES TO OIL COOLER

NOSE-TYPE EXHAUST COLLECTOR

CARBURETTOR AIR INTAKE

DE HAVILLAND VARIABLE-PITCH AIRSCREWS

840 H.P. MERCURY XIII ENGINES

BATTERY

SELECTOR CONTROL (UNDERCARRIAGE FLAPS & TURRET)

NAVIGATORS SEAT

FLAP CONTROL

UNDERCARRIAGE CONTROL

ELEVATOR & RUDDER TRIMMING WHEELS

SEAT FOR BOMB SIGHTING

PITOT HEAD

PRONE BOMBER'S WINDOW

FRESH AIR INTAKE

MAX MILLAR

FLIGHT

BRISTOL "BLENHEIM" Mk.I.

*Medium Bomber*

was piped to the steel collector ring round the front of the cowling and expelled through a pipe on the right side. In some ways the Mk I Blenheim made life easier, compared with the old fabric-covered biplanes, in that there was plenty of power if both Mercuries kept going. The problem was, if either engine cut on take-off you might be in trouble. Soon, the concept of single-engined safety speed was invented. If you had reached it, and I believe for most Blenheims it was 115 mph, you could keep going on one. So pilots got into the absolutely never-broken habit of holding the Blenheim down on takeoff to reach this speed as quickly as possible. Only then was it safe to climb away. Safety speed was always increased if the propeller could not be feathered, as was the case with the two-pitch units on the Blenheim.

Max wrote K7056 on his Blenheim. This was the 23rd aircraft to come off the production line. Later very large numbers of Blenheims were made by the Rootes Group at Speke (Liverpool) and at Blythe Bridge in Staffordshire, and also by A V Roe at Manchester. It is curious how de Havilland's idea of a bomber so fast it did not need defensive guns (the Mosquito) was almost universally derided as complete nonsense, whilst at the same time Blenheims were pouring off the assembly lines that were 100 mph slower and had a single Lewis gun for defence. A bonus with the Mosquito is that, if you lost an engine on take-off, at below safety speed, you could still keep going, provided you were alert, feathered quickly and gave it a bootful of rudder. With the Blenheim you had no option but to put it down as directly in front as possible.

# SPITFIRE IX

Max Millar's cutaway of the Spitfire was subjected to almost as many modifications as the Spitfire itself. He did it in November 1938, and it first appeared in *Flight* for 1st December. Of course at that time only the original Mk I aircraft exisited, with a Merlin II engine with three ejector exhaust pipes on each side (each served by two cylinders), driving a two-blade fixed-pitch propeller carved by the Airscrew Company from laminated wood.

Other features included an engine coolant radiator under the starboard wing only, a flat-topped cockpit hood and provision for eight 0.303-in Browning machine guns in the wings. Like many of Max's drawings, this one was dominated by the engine. He made virtually no attempt to show construction of the wing or tail.

During the war this drawing was repeatedly modified, by Max himself of course. As reproduced here, it is meant to depict the Mark IX aircraft, which entered RAF service in July 1942. Max couldn't do much about the propeller, which he left as it was. He couldn't do much about the engine either, though he gave it individual exhaust pipes (six on each side), and removed the original reference to a hand starter socket because later Merlins did not have one. Early Spitfires had a hand turning crank socket on the right side of the cowling only, unlike the the Hurricane's engine which could be cranked on both sides. This was real y a provision against a flat battery, or unavailability of a 'trolley acc.' It soon disappeared from the Spitfire, later Merlins relying entirely upon the electric starter, while Seafires and all versions with the big Griffon engine had a Coffman multi-breech cartridge starter.

He also altered 'Merlin II 1,000 H.P.' to 'Merlin LXI 1,620 H.P.' What he did not attempt was to lengthen the whole nose, which he should have done because the Spitfire IX was powered by one of the first versions with a two-stage supercharger which made the engine 7 inches longer.

Max had previously changed the flat-topped canopy (seen here in the second aircraft in the lineup of 19 Sqn below left) for a bulged one, which made life easier for tall pilots. He had also previously drawn in a thick bulletproof windscreen, and given the pilot an oxygen mask. In his original drawing he showed a crude ring and bead sight; as modified he made the ring look like a reflector sight, but he forgot to remove the bead post above the cowling just to the left of the label describing the engine!

Apart from the six exhaust stubs the most prominent modification to the drawing was to do just as Supermarine had done and replace the inboard pair of machine guns in each wing with a 20-mm Hispano cannon, though for some reason he omitted to give these guns a label. Curiously, in 1940 this drawing had the starboard wing partly cut away to show the Browning guns and their ammunition boxes, whereas here the wing is skinned over again, as it was in 1938.

There are several other odd features. The original drawing was of course not in colour, but it showed green/brown camouflage with roundels above the wings with yellow outer wings. This scheme followed the short-lived use of Type B roundels (red/blue only) on wings and fuselage as seen in the photograph. As modified, Max drew strange overwing roundels which appear to be red/white/blue. He should also have added a three-colour 'flash' to the fin. Even stranger, his original drawing showed the fin/rudder of the prototype (not even the Mk I). All production aircraft had a 90° angle forming the horn balance.

Max's other modifications included tapering off the antenna mast and adding a slipper-type drop tank behind the carburettor air intake. This was also added in the inset drawing, which I imagine Max did in order to show the extended landing gear, radiator (which in the Mk IX was partnered by

Charles E Brown was one of a number of photographers invited to Duxford on the morning of 4 May 1939 to view a full line up of No 19 Sqn's new Spitfire Is for the first time. At this stage in the fighter's career it was still fitted with a two-bladed fixed-pitch wooden prop

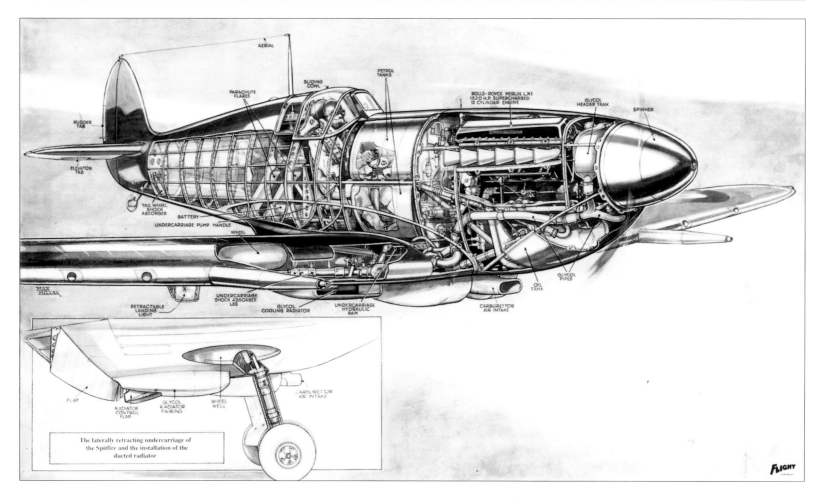

AERIAL

PETROL
TANKS

PARACHUTE
FLARES

SLIDING
COWL

ROLLS-ROYCE MERLIN LXI
1520 H.P. SUPERCHARGED
12 CYLINDER ENGINE

GLYCOL
HEADER TANK

SPINNER

RUDDER
TAB

ELEVATOR
TAB

TAIL WHEEL
SHOCK
ABSORBER

BATTERY

UNDERCARRIAGE PUMP HANDLE

WHEEL

MAX
MILLAR

RETRACTABLE
LANDING
LIGHT

UNDERCARRIAGE
SHOCK ABSORBER
LEG

GLYCOL
COOLING RADIATOR

UNDERCARRIAGE
HYDRAULIC
RAM

CARBURETTOR
AIR INTAKE

OIL
TANK

GLYCOL
PIPES

FLAP

RADIATOR
CONTROL
FLAP

GLYCOL
RADIATOR
FAIRING

WHEEL
WELL

CARBURETTOR
AIR INTAKE

The laterally retracting undercarriage of
the Spitfire and the installation of the
ducted radiator

FLIGHT

another under the port wing) and the split flaps. These were extended pneu-matically to no less than 90°, being selected by a simple switch on the panel. (The prototype's 60° flaps were judged insufficiently powerful, and the increased deflection was easier to incorporate than the alternative of making them bigger.) One Spitfire, R6718, a Southampton-built Mk I, was tested with slotted flaps. These showed some advantages, but not enough to warrant dis-rupting the hectic production lines.

In the earliest batches of Mk I aircraft the landing gear had to be worked by a hydraulic hand-pump. It was virtually impossible, flying with the left hand, not to work the stick in opposition to the pump, so even in the hands of

an experienced pilot the aircraft would perform a roller coaster flight path after taking off.

One feature incorporated very early on in production was an oval panel let into the left side of the hood. In emergency, the pilot could hit this hard enough to knock it out of its rubber frame. This equalised the air pressures inside and outside the hood, making it much easier to wind it back should the pilot wish to bail out.

Finally, Max originally signed the drawing in the tight space in the extreme bottom left corner. Here he has moved his 'logo' to just below the starboard wing.

# GLADIATOR I

Last survivor of the so-called 'stick and string' biplane era in the Royal Air Force, the Gloster Gladiator was the eventual winner of an Air Ministry specification issued in 1930. In those days Britain had an aircraft industry, and to meet the very important F.7/30 specification no fewer than 16 fighter designs were proposed by eight companies, and in the end nine contrasting prototypes were built. The whole programme was marked by indecision and delay, a major problem being difficulties with the preferred engine, the steam-cooled Rolls-Royce Goshawk.

In September 1934 Gloster Aircraft had flown a prototype called the SS 37, and in July 1935 the Air Ministry in desperation simply ordered it as their next fighter, naming it the Gladiator. It met most of the F.7/30 demands, such as carrying four machine guns at 250 mph, but in most respects it was merely a more powerful version of the fighters that had fought in World War 1.

The structure was mainly aluminium, braced by wires and skinned in fabric. The engine was the excellent Bristol Mercury, a refined short-stroke version of the Jupiter and thus a very close relative of the Pegasus. Rated at 840 hp, it was enclosed in a short cowling which incorporated an exhaust collector ring at the front, and drove a two-blade fixed-pitch wooden propeller. The single fuel tank had a capacity of 84 gallons, which compares well with the 85 gallons of most early Spitfires, which had a much bigger engine. The oil cooler, indicated in the drawing, was an unusual arrangement of parallel tubes forming the entire top decking of the fuselage between the cabane struts (the struts

supporting the upper wing). Mounted on top of the oil cooler on the centreline were the simple ring and bead forming the gunsight.

The F.7/30 specification demanded radio and oxygen bottles, and new features for the RAF included a sliding transparent hood over the cockpit, four small split flaps on the upper and lower wings driven down for landing by a cockpit hydraulic hand-pump, and George Dowty's patented wheels which had shock-absorbing springs inside them, and so could be attached to neat cantilever legs.

The first Gladiators came off the assembly line at the end of 1936, armed with two belt-fed Vickers Mk V machine guns in the sides of the fuselage, their firing synchronised to avoid the propeller, and two Lewis machine guns in blisters under the lower wings each with a 97-round drum. Some replaced the Lewis by Vickers, with 400-round belts, but from the 71st aircraft the standard armament was four of the American Brownings, converted to take rimmed 0.303 in ammunition, made under licence.

Whereas the requirements of F.7/30 had been adequate (no more than that) for 1930, when the first Gladiators reached the RAF's No 72 Sqn in February 1937 the aircraft was already obsolescent. By that time early versions of the Messerschmitt Bf 109 were in service with the Luftwaffe, and it was obvious that when the Bf 109 got an engine in the 1000 hp class and 20 mm cannon, even the manoeuvrability of the biplane would be unable to save it. The Gladiator's single advantage – apart from being simple and able to use

A splendid photograph of No 65 Sqn Gladiator Is taken at the time the unit was transitioning over from another Gloster biplane fighter, the Gauntlet, in June 1937

Labels on the drawing:

AERIAL
FOLDING AERIAL STRUT
PILOT'S OXYGEN MASK
MAIN OIL COOLER
SLIDING COWL
WIRELESS TUNING
TWO-WAY WIRELESS UNIT
PETROL TANK
OXYGEN BOTTLE
VICKERS GUN IN FUSELAGE
ELECTRIC GENERATOR
COMPRESSED AIR BOTTLE FOR BRAKES
OXYGEN CONNECTION FOR PILOT
AMMUNITION BOXES
BRISTOL SUPERCHARGED MERCURY ENGINE
OUTBOARD VICKERS GUN
SPENT AMMUNITION BOXES
OIL COOLER AND COCKPIT HEATER

small fields – was that it was agile, and it could turn inside most monoplane fighters. However, Air Commodore Allen Wheeler said 'My one criticism was that you no longer felt part of the aircraft. Fighters were beginning to get big'.

Altogether Gloster delivered 747 Gladiators, of which substantial numbers went to export customers. Those for Finland and Latvia often operated on streamlined skis. The RAF used them in Britain, Norway and throughout the Middle East, while the Sea Gladiator, with an arrester hook, catapult attachments and a dinghy carried in a blister between the landing gears, served with the Fleet Air Arm. It is part of war time legend that four Sea Gladiators borrowed by the RAF formed the sole defence of Malta in June 1940.

Max Millar's drawing is a good example of its era, with cloud background and the pilot in the cockpit. The serial number is that of the original SS 37 prototype, with a spatted tailwheel and, when first built, an open cockpit.

It is interesting to see that Max drew a belt-fed Vickers in the underwing blister, annotating the ammunition boxes which were inside the wing on the inboard side, reloaded through the usual type of removable upper skin panel. When he did the drawing the prototype was still fitted with racks to carry eight 20-lb Cooper bombs, but these were absent from production aircraft. Production aircraft also differed in having no radio mast, the antenna wire being bifurcated into a Y-shape and attached to the left and right upper wings.

# ANSON I

It is remarkable how one's perceptions of aircraft change, often in quite a short period. By the time the author got into the cockpits of RAF aircraft immediately after the War the Avro Anson was universally regarded as 'Faithful Annie', a sort of old lady, a gentle lumbering vehicle which anyone could use when they wanted a hack to take them from one place to another. Because to retract the landing gears required prolonged manual effort one often just left them down, reducing a happy cruising speed from about 155 mph to maybe 125. Who cared?

It requires quite a mental effort to recall that when Max Millar did this drawing the Anson was almost the 'hottest ship' in the RAF. The idea of a cantilever monoplane with retractable wheels was almost breathtaking, and one spoke of the claimed speed of 188 mph with astonished pride!

As the future general-reconnaissance aircraft of the newly formed Coastal Command, it was roughly 50 mph faster than anything previously used for that purpose, and 45 mph faster than the Heyford used by Bomber Command. The pilot had a fixed Vickers Mk V on the left of the nose, the gunner had a Lewis Mk IIIA in a manually-driven Armstrong Whitworth turret, and cells in the centre wing could carry two 100-lb and eight 20-lb bombs, aimed by a Wimperis course-setting sight in the extreme nose, where there was also a searchlight.

The immensely strong airframe was of mixed construction, the wings and tailplane being of spruce, covered with Bakelite-impregnated plywood. The fuselage and fin were welded steel tube covered in fabric, except along the sides of the cabin where the entire skin was transparent Rhodoid or Perspex sheet giving a view all round. The door was on the right at the trailing edge.

The usual crew comprised pilot, navigator/bomb aimer and radio operator/gunner.

Altogether, the Avro Type 652M – the suffix indicating it was the military version of the 652 airliner – promised to be a modern high-speed battlewagon. Indeed, in the opening weeks of the War it was just that. On the third day of the War an Anson scored a 'probable' on a U-boat, and in June 1940 an amazing encounter took place between three Ansons and nine Bf 109Es which, partly because the Ansons throttled right back, resulted in a score 2-0 in the Ansons' favour! By July Ansons had claimed a Do 18, He 111, He 115 and a Bf 110.

However, the 'Annie' was to find its true niche as the most important crew trainer of the RAF and Commonwealth air forces. Ansons in many versions poured off the assembly lines at Chadderton, Newton Heath and Yeadon, soon followed by yet other versions built by Canadian firms with assembly by Federal Aircraft in Montreal. While the Oxford trained twin-engined pilots, the Anson trained navigators, bomb-aimers and gunners, the latter often using a power-driven Bristol Mk VI turret with twin Brownings. In Britain the most common version was the Mk I in its training forms, usually with no turret.

At the end of the War completely new Ansons emerged from A V Roe Ltd, with a different structure, more power, constant-speed propellers, hydraulically operated landing gear and far more room inside. Production of these continued until 1952, the total number built being 11,020. Among British multi-engined types this was second only to the Wellington.

By the time the author reached the RAF he had flown as an ATC cadet 21

Undercarriages locked down, three early production Anson Is cruise sedately along the south coast of England in June 1937

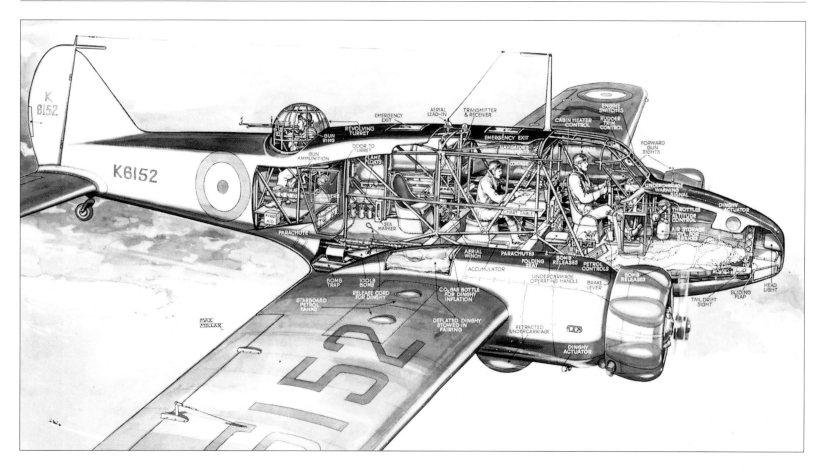

times in Ansons, the Oxford and Dragon Rapide coming next with only nine each. Later he was to fly Ansons on countless occasions. It never occurred to him either that, like any other aircraft, the Anson could turn and bite if mishandled, nor that anything might go wrong. The engines were seven-cylinder 350 hp Armstrong Siddeley Cheetah IXs, started by groundcrew inserting a big handcrank into the right side of the nacelle just behind the helmeted cowling. They drove two-blade fixed-pitch Fairey-Reed propellers made of solid Duralumin. The oil coolers were simple multi-plate radiators on the lower left side of the nacelle, unseen in the drawing.

Max's drawing bears the serial number of the production prototype, first flown at Woodford on 31 December 1935. He signed it in the corner, and then clearly had to sign it again to allow it to be used with the lower part cut off. Like other drawings of the period, it gives an excellent idea of the general interior layout. Probably nobody at that time had even considered what might

later be done with a fine pen and black ink to give far greater technical detail. You don't get much for nothing, and the clarity of the 'picture' approach mitigated against any detail of structure and systems, and incidentally required much of the annotation to be in white on black. How this was done is outlined in the Introduction.

The very first production Ansons were some of the few RAF aircraft to have large black serial numbers on the upper surface of the wings, as well as the underside. Later Mk Is also could have a different turret, or no turret, and also might have two radio masts, an astro dome, direction-finding loop and many other visible changes. All, however, had the little folding crank beside the pilot's seat which ATC cadets actually enjoyed turning laboriously to bring the wheels up. The number of turns required was 140, and via cycle-type chains the crank rotated screwthreads on each landing gear. With new aircraft, especially, it was very hard work.

# SUNDERLAND I

This drawing was probably the most complicated James Clark had done up to that time. It appeared in *The Aeroplane* for Wednesday, 25 June 1939. On the following day the rival, *Flight*, came out with one by Max Millar. Predictably, Max's was much more of a picture, showing the whole of the great flying boat, with all the crew at their stations and roundels on the aircraft's wings. I suspect that, while technically illiterate cabinet ministers would have preferred Millar's rendering, which was much easier to follow and almost ignored airframe structure, anyone with a real wish to know the aircraft would have preferred the black pen-work of Clark. Another point of interest is the number of items shown in one drawing but not the other, but we do not have room here for both.

I shall never forget going to the cinema in about 1942 and seeing the epic film Coastal Command. Of all the stars of this film the Sunderland was the

greatest, and its sheer majesty held me spellbound. To be on the flight deck as the captain of aircraft firmly moved forward the four long throttles, to hear the sound of the Pegasus engines and watch the four rpm indicators move up their vertical scales to 2600, and then pan back to the fast-receding wake, was the kind of thing calculated to make a 15-year-old impatient to do likewise.

On board it was quite a community. On the lower deck were domestic items ranging from an anchor, bunks and a galley, to a tool-chest near the bow and a workbench near the stern. Clark could have added the three spare propeller blades strapped to the right wall. At the upper level were the operational areas, which in the Mk I aircraft included two dorsal hatches for hand-aimed Vickers K machine guns. These were also useful lookout stations, but in all subsequent marks they were replaced by a power-driven turret.

This leads to a comment made with regard to several drawings of this period. Though it had been described in general terms, Clark had obviously been instructed not to show any detail whatsoever of the armament. In fact, the main defence was the Nash and Thompson FN13 tail turret, with four 0.303 in Brownings fed from 500-round belts. Luftwaffe pilots soon learned to avoid getting behind the flying boat they called the 'Flying Porcupine'! The FN11 nose turret, with a single Vickers K, could retract backwards on rails as shown, and its floor could hinge down for mooring operations. Both turrets were specially designed to give the gunner the best possible view for searching the ocean. The later Sunderland III and V had the front turret rearmed with twin Brownings. A beam hatch was added on each side, immediately aft of the trailing-edge fillet, with either a Vickers K or, by 1943, one or even a pair of 0.5 in Brownings aimed as in a B-17, while two Vickers K were added firing

ABOVE One of the first Sunderland Is delivered to No 204 Sqn lifts off from Plymouth harbour in July 1939, just a month after the unit had become the third UK-based squadron to receive the Shorts flying boat. Based at Mount Batten until a mid-1940 move to Reykjavik, No 204 flew the Sunderland throughout World War 2

RIGHT The ultimate Sunderland (the Mk IV) wasn't a Sunderland at all – it was a Seaford! Considered to be different enough to warrant a change of name, the Mk IV was powered by Hercules engines

# HURRICANE I

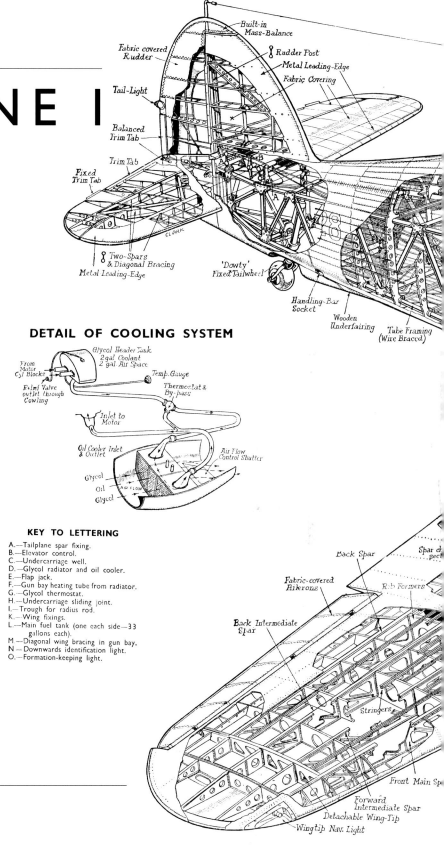

**DETAIL OF COOLING SYSTEM**

**KEY TO LETTERING**

A.—Tailplane spar fixing.
B.—Elevator control.
C.—Undercarriage well.
D.—Glycol radiator and oil cooler.
E.—Flap jack.
F.—Gun bay heating tube from radiator.
G.—Glycol thermostat.
H.—Undercarriage sliding joint.
I.—Trough for radius rod.
K.—Wing fixings.
L.—Main fuel tank (one each side—33 gallons each).
M.—Diagonal wing bracing in gun bay.
N.—Downwards identification light.
O.—Formation-keeping light.

This drawing was published in *The Aeroplane* at the height of the Battle of Britain (6 September 1940 issue), when Hurricanes were playing the principal role in defeating Hitler's previously victorious Luftwaffe. It was then reproduced in the second issue of *The Aeroplane Spotter*, and because this time it was only six inches across it was difficult to see the fine detail.

It is an excellent drawing, especially for such an early date. Clark was offered an aircraft to the latest standard, with metal-skinned wings and a constant-speed Rotol propeller with rounded spinner. In several of these texts I have criticised the British industry for being remarkably reluctant to learn how to make modern stressed-skin aircraft. Whereas the prototype Messerschmitt Bf 109 flew in May 1935 with stressed-skin wings, the prototype Hurricane flew six months later with outmoded Warren diagonal-truss wings with fabric covering held on by complicated screwed metal channels. If Britain had not been so backward, every Hurricane would have had a metal wing. The stressed-skin wing was appreciably stronger and much stiffer, though thanks to the method of attachment the fabric in the original wing did contribute significantly to strength. As it was, the all-metal wings did not appear until April 1939, being gradually introduced to production in the final weeks before the War. Other additions included the bullet-proof windscreen, rear-view mirror and cockpit armour. Clark even included the metal plate added to shield the pilot from exhaust flames at night, which was then a new addition.

Altogether Hawker Aircraft, at Kingston and Langley, built 10,030 Hurricanes, while Gloster Aircraft built 2750, and a further 1451 were made by Canadian Car & Foundry. Yet, towards the end of the war most had gone to India, Burma and other remote places, and the author never got his hands on one. The Hurricane had a reputation for being a steady gun-aiming platform, and if flown to the limits was probably a good match for a Bf 109E. At the same time, by the Battle of Britain Hurricanes were beginning to find life hard in Western Europe, and there are records of pilots being unable to catch Ju 88s that had dropped their bombs.

Except for Belgian Hurricanes, which had two 0.5 in and two 0.303 in (7.7 mm), all early aircraft had eight 0.303 in Brownings, as shown here. The Mk II introduced the Merlin XX, with a much better inlet system and new supercharger designed by Dr Stanley Hooker, which was just what the Hurricane needed to combat inevitable weight-growth. The IIA retained the eight-gun metal wing, while the IIB had four extra Brownings added beyond the landing lights, giving a rate of fire of 14,400 admittedly not terribly effec-

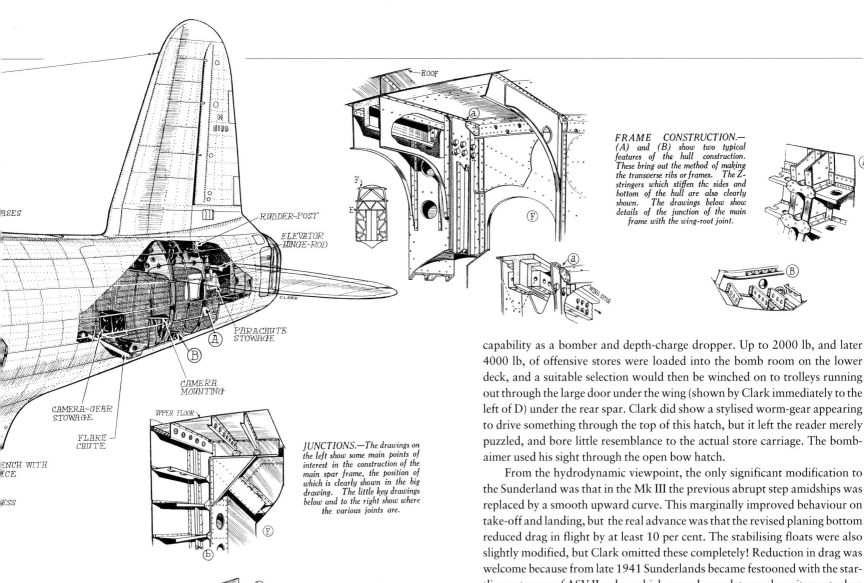

RUDDER-POST

ELEVATOR HINGE-ROD

CLARK

PARACHUTE STOWAGE

CAMERA MOUNTING

CAMERA-GEAR STOWAGE

FLARE CHUTE

UPPER FLOOR

ROOF

FRAME CONSTRUCTION.— (A) and (B) show two typical features of the hull construction. These bring out the method of making the transverse ribs or frames. The Z-stringers which stiffen the sides and bottom of the hull are also clearly shown. The drawings below show details of the junction of the main frame with the wing-root joint.

WING SPAR

JUNCTIONS.—The drawings on the left show some main points of interest in the construction of the main spar frame, the position of which is clearly shown in the big drawing. The little key drawings below and to the right show where the various joints are.

DOOR

capability as a bomber and depth-charge dropper. Up to 2000 lb, and later 4000 lb, of offensive stores were loaded into the bomb room on the lower deck, and a suitable selection would then be winched on to trolleys running out through the large door under the wing (shown by Clark immediately to the left of D) under the rear spar. Clark did show a stylised worm-gear appearing to drive something through the top of this hatch, but it left the reader merely puzzled, and bore little resemblance to the actual store carriage. The bomb-aimer used his sight through the open bow hatch.

From the hydrodynamic viewpoint, the only significant modification to the Sunderland was that in the Mk III the previous abrupt step amidships was replaced by a smooth upward curve. This marginally improved behaviour on take-off and landing, but the real advance was that the revised planing bottom reduced drag in flight by at least 10 per cent. The stabilising floats were also slightly modified, but Clark omitted these completely! Reduction in drag was welcome because from late 1941 Sunderlands became festooned with the startling antennas of ASV II radar, which caused us cadets much excitement when we got the relevant amendment list to Air Publication 1480A (the recognition manual). Later radar used civilised dishes in blisters under the wingtips.

I think this drawing gives the impression that cabin heating came from a tank of hot water at the very top of the hull. In fact it came from the exhaust of the No 2 (port inner) engine, which could be passed through a heat exchanger. The propellers, initially of two-position bracket-type, eventually became constant-speed DH Hydromatic units which could be feathered, an important requirement for aircraft able to operate 1000 miles from land. The serial N6133 on the rudder (the 22nd production aircraft) appears to have been inserted by a non-artist!

down on each side from the galley hatches. From September 1943 all new Sunderlands were in addition fitted with four fixed Brownings in the nose, bringing the number of guns to 18. This proved invaluable in attacking the heavily armed U-boats, which by then chose to fight it out on the surface.

Completely ignored by Clark was the Sunderland's extremely important

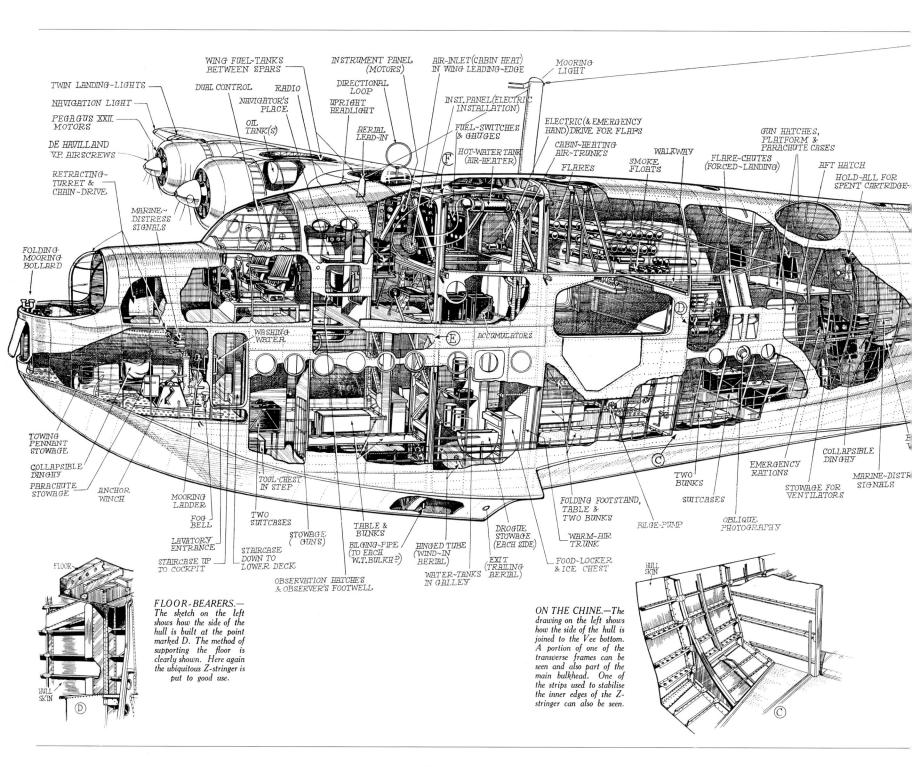

TWIN LANDING~LIGHTS

NAVIGATION LIGHT

PEGASUS XXII MOTORS

DE HAVILLAND V.P. AIRSCREWS

RETRACTING~ TURRET & CHAIN~DRIVE.

FOLDING MOORING BOLLARD

TOWING PENNANT STOWAGE.

COLLAPSIBLE DINGHY

PARACHUTE STOWAGE

ANCHOR WINCH

MOORING LADDER

FOG BELL

LAVATORY ENTRANCE

STAIRCASE UP TO COCKPIT

WING FUEL~TANKS BETWEEN SPARS

DUAL CONTROL

NAVIGATOR'S PLACE

OIL TANK(S)

RADIO

INSTRUMENT PANEL (MOTORS)

DIRECTIONAL LOOP

UPRIGHT HEADLIGHT

AERIAL LEAD~IN

MARINE~ DISTRESS SIGNALS

AIR-INLET(CABIN HEAT) IN WING LEADING~EDGE

INST. PANEL(ELECTRIC INSTALLATION)

FUEL~SWITCHES & GAUGES

HOT-WATER TANK (AIR-HEATER)

MOORING LIGHT

ELECTRIC(& EMERGENCY HAND)DRIVE FOR FLAPS

CABIN~HEATING AIR~TRUNKS

FLARES

SMOKE FLOATS

WALKWAY

GUN HATCHES, PLATFORM & PARACHUTE CASES

FLARE~CHUTES (FORCED~LANDING)

AFT HATCH

HOLD-ALL FOR SPENT CARTRIDGE~

ACCUMULATORS

WASHING WATER.

TWO SUITCASES

STOWAGE (GUNS)

TABLE & BUNKS

BILGING-PIPE (TO EACH W.T. BULKH'D)

HINGED TUBE (WIND~IN AERIAL)

DROGUE STOWAGE (EACH SIDE)

EXIT (TRAILING AERIAL)

WATER~TANKS IN GALLEY

FOOD-LOCKER & ICE CHEST

WARM~AIR TRUNK

FOLDING FOOTSTAND, TABLE & TWO BUNKS

BILGE-PUMP

TWO BUNKS

SUITCASES

EMERGENCY RATIONS

OBLIQUE PHOTOGRAPHY

STOWAGE FOR VENTILATORS

COLLAPSIBLE DINGHY

MARINE~DISTR SIGNALS

TOOL-CHEST IN STEP

STAIRCASE DOWN TO LOWER DECK

OBSERVATION HATCHES & OBSERVER'S FOOTWELL

FLOOR

HULL SKIN

D

**FLOOR-BEARERS.—**
*The sketch on the left shows how the side of the hull is built at the point marked D. The method of supporting the floor is clearly shown. Here again the ubiquitous Z-stringer is put to good use.*

HULL SKIN

C

**ON THE CHINE.—The**
*drawing on the left shows how the side of the hull is joined to the Vee bottom. A portion of one of the transverse frames can be seen and also part of the main bulkhead. One of the strips used to stabilise the inner edges of the Z-stringer can also be seen.*

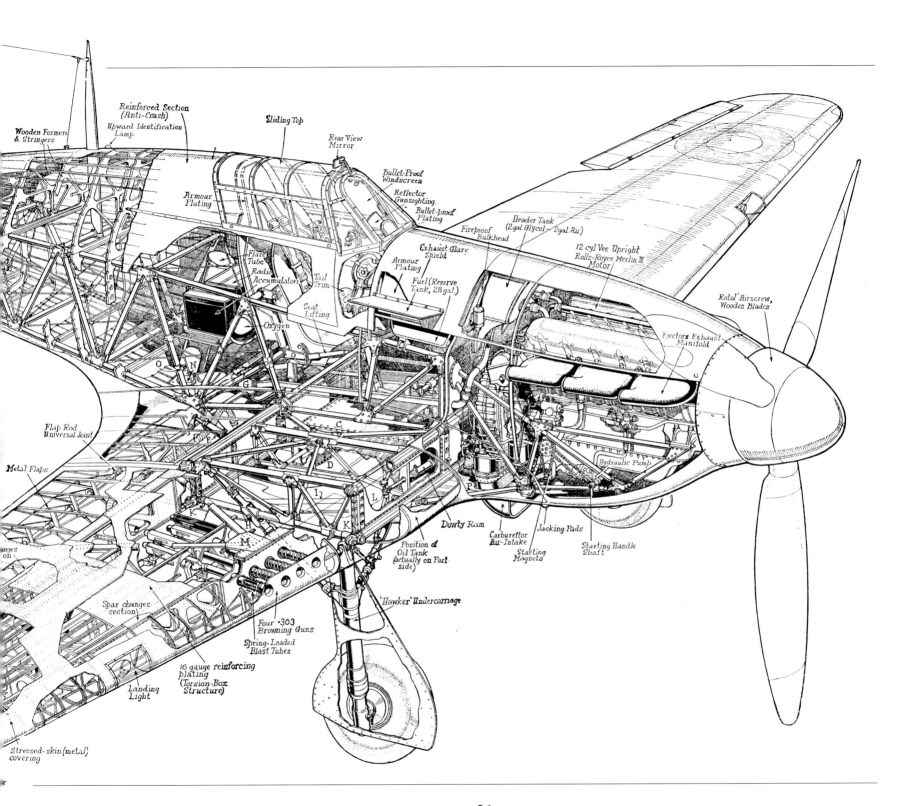

Wooden Formers & Stringers

Reinforced Section (Anti-Crash)
Upward Identification Lamp

Sliding Top

Rear View Mirror

Bullet-Proof Windscreen

Reflector Gunsighting.

Bullet-proof Plating

Armour Plating

Header Tank (2gal Glycol - 2gal Air)

Firebproof Bulkhead

12 cyl Vee Upright Rolls-Royce Merlin III Motor

Flare Tube Radio Accumulators

Exhaust Glare Shield

Armour Plating

Tail Trim

Fuel (Reserve Tank, 28 gal.)

Seat Lifting

Oxygen

Rotol 'Airscrew, Wooden Blades'

Ejectors Exhaust Manifold

O

N

G

Flap Rod Universal Joint

C

P E

Metal Flaps

D

Hydraulic Pump

I

L

K

H

K

M

Dowty Ram

Position of Oil Tank (actually on Port side)

Carburettor Air-Intake

Jacking Pads

Starting Handle Shaft

Starting Magneto

'Hawker' Undercarriage

Spar changes section

Four ·303 Browning Guns

Spring-Loaded Blast Tubes

16 gauge reinforcing plating (Torsion-Box Structure)

Landing Light

Stressed-skin (metal) covering

tive bullets per minute. The IIC, which was made in greater numbers (4711) than any other version, dramatically changed the picture with four 20 mm Hispano cannon, with 60-round drum feed. The IID had two 40 mm Vickers anti-tank guns, while the final model, the IV, had a 'universal' wing that could have any armament and could also handle the various underwing loads which were introduced from late 1940 onwards. These comprised bombs of 250 and later 500-lb, eight rockets (four under each wing), smoke apparatus or drop tanks of first 45 and then 90-gal size. Desert aircraft had a tropical filter ahead of the carburettor air inlet under the nose.

Sydney Camm's devoted design team numbered 98 when the prototype Hurricane flew, and had risen to 320 by the end of the war. Though the metal wing was new technology to them, the rest of the Hurricane was almost identical in principle to the biplanes of the 1920s. The fuselage, for example, was assembled from light-alloy tubes which were swaged to a square section to fit snugly to the plates at the joints. Everywhere were simple detail fittings, some of which could almost have been made with a hacksaw and file. One advantage of the primitive structure was that field repairs were easy. And the point could be made that, whereas fabric on the Wellington tended to rip off in dives at 350 mph, there is no record of any Hurricane fabric coming off even in a dive to beyond 400 mph, unless it had been damaged in battle first.

From this aspect the big radiator under the fuselage is hard to see, so Clark helpfully did an inset showing the cooling system. Also, having chosen his viewpoint, and drawn the right-hand side of the engine (not the same as the other side), he found he had to say that the oil tank was actually in the left wing. One feature that was on both sides of the engine was the hand turning gear, here called 'starting handle shaft'. Previous fighters had been started by swinging the propeller. Early Hurricanes were started by groundcrew cranking as hard as they could on both sides, and the hole low down on each side of the cowling was a feature of later Hurricanes even though they had electric starters. Clark forgot to add letter 'P' to his key; it referred to the SU updraught carburettor. Finally, I have no idea why he chose to use capitals and 'lower-case' (small) letters for his annotations, instead of the serifed capitals throughout which he usually employed.

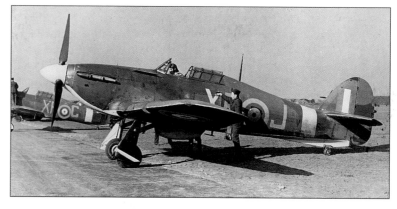

ABOVE Surveying his dials, a young American volunteer leans forward in the cockpit of his No 71 'Eagle' Sqn Hurricane I at Kirton-in-Lindsey in late 1940. A survivor of the Battle of Britain, this V-serialled machine was typical of the war-weary Hurricanes issued to the new squadron in place of their totally inadequate Brewster Buffalo fighters

LEFT No 111 Sqn proudly show off a pair of their new Hurricane Is up from Northolt in early 1938. A very small rendition of the unit crest can just be made out on the fins of both machines

# HENLEY

I doubt if many of today's aviation enthusiasts know much about the Hawker Henley. They might be surprised to learn that in the first two years of the War feelings ran quite high about it. This was because, while Hitler's Stukas were demolishing everything in their path, Britain's seemingly much better equivalent was in production as a target-tower. Both the aviation weeklies ran headlines 'A fine aeroplane wasted'.

The Henley was designed to specification P.4/34, calling for a high-speed close-support light bomber stressed for steep dive attacks. This would have been a valuable aircraft in the Battle for France, 50 mph faster than the Fairey Battle, much more agile and much better able to hit small targets. Instead, in 1936 the Air Ministry appeared to lose interest. The rival Fairey P.4/34 was turned into the Fulmar naval fighter, which was too slow to catch German bombers. The Henley was turned into a target tug. Gloster's contract for 350 was cut to 200, and all were delivered by May 1940, just when they were really needed in their original role.

To describe the original bomber first, its capacious fuselage was structurally like any other of Sydney Camm's designs, based on tubes with the ends swaged to a square section so that they could be easily joined by fishplates.

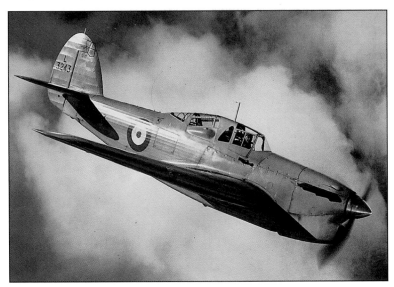

L3243 was the first of 200 production Henleys built, and was written off at Langham, on the Norfolk coast, in 1941 whilst serving with No I Anti-Aircraft Co-operation Unit

The wing, however, was a modern assembly from sheet, with machined spar booms and a stressed-skin covering. The outer wings were almost identical to those fitted to Hurricanes from mid-1939, though without the guns. The centre section was wider, increasing span to 47 ft $10^1/2$ in, to match the greater loaded weight of about 8400 lb.

The pilot sat above the wing spars under a rather clumsy canopy incorporating a small side door. A Vickers Mk V (the old belt-fed type, not the Type K gas-operated) was mounted in the right wing outside the propeller disc. The bomb-aimer looked after the radio, could use a free Lewis gun for defence, and in the level-bombing role could lie prone to aim bombs using a sight in the floor. The internal bay under the wing centre section housed two 250-lb bombs, and two more could be hung under the outer wings.

Whereas the Hurricane had the coolant radiator under the trailing edge, behind the retracted wheels, in the Henley it was directly under the engine, giving minimum weight of vulnerable piping and also saving weight. Putting the engine air inlet in the centre of the oil cooler, which itself was in the middle of the main radiator, was expected to avoid carburettor icing. In the article which accompanied Clark's drawing in *The Aeroplane* of 1 March 1939 'T J' (Thurstan James, later the magazine's Editor) wrote 'So far as can be found out, the thrust provided by the escaping cooling air offsets the drag'. I have no hesitation in describing this as a pious hope, though liquid cooling radiators with net positive thrust were indeed developed by the end of the War.

The engine was an early Merlin II. The same engine was fitted to Hurricanes at that time, but, instead of a two-blade fixed-pitch Watts wooden propeller, the Henley had a two-position Hamilton made under licence by de Havilland and fitted with a spinner. The secondary structure above and below the rear-fuselage longerons was made mainly of wood and fabric. As indicated, the rear bottom part was easily detachable. Clark indicated an upper main-structure fishplate with a B in a circle, but failed to produce the associated inset detail (the similarly indicated detail he did do related to the wing).

By February 1939, when Thurstan, Jimmy Clark and photographer Charles Sims descended on Hucclecote and the Brockworth airfield, the Henley was being produced as the Mk III target tug. Thurstan was given a ride by test pilot Maurice Summers, brother of the more famous 'Mutt' Summers of Vickers-Armstrongs, and eulogised about everything from the 'rocketing' climb (surely not that impressive, 10,000 ft in 8.5 minutes?) to the quietness and absence of draughts. He commented on the way, after a firing practice, the target and cable could be released, to be retrieved, brought back to the aircraft

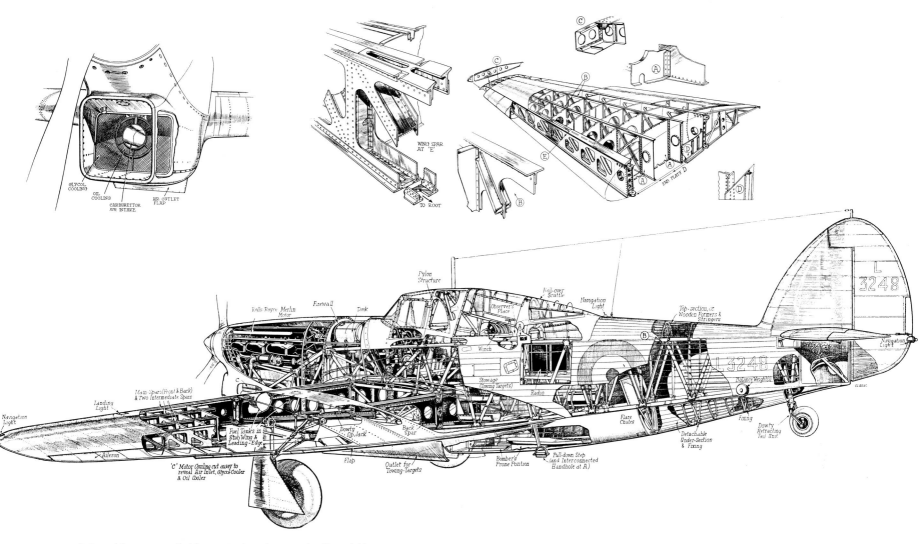

and the cable re-wound. Alternatively, a big windmill could be swung out on the left of the fuselage (not shown by Clark) to wind the cable back in the air. Pity Clark didn't illustrate a target drogue and show how the things were actually manhandled out and back (because I'd like to know).

Henleys entered service at many gunnery and bombing/gunnery schools from August 1939. Towing things was the quickest way of getting into trouble with the engines. I have a few things to say about this in connection with the Albemarle. With the poor Henley, trying to pull even the small Mk III sleeve at speeds that could be useful to a fighter caused rapid engine wear and unreliability. Limiting the speed to 220 mph, as was done, hardly gave fighter pilots a representative target. Accordingly, from October 1939 the 130 survivors were sent to AACU (Anti-Aircraft Co-operation Unit) squadrons, where the drogues were even bigger. One has only to read the Notes on Individual Aircraft in Frank Mason's Hawker volume in the Putnam series to see that Henleys were soon scattered all over Norfolk.

Two Henleys became testbeds for the Rolls-Royce Vulture, and one for the Griffon. The latter would have been ideal for the target-towing application. The aircraft Clark drew was the sixth production machine.

39

# HAMPDEN I

The Handley Page HP 52 Hampden was one of several important new bombers featured in the RAF expansion schemes of the late 1930s. Like the others, it was a modern cantilever monoplane, almost 100 mph faster than the fabric-covered biplanes, with engines in the 1000 hp class, twice the power the RAF was used to. It fell into a class of its own, between the Battle and Blenheim 'light bombers' and the Whitley and Wellington 'heavy bombers'. It was expected to be a formidable aircraft, able to look after itself in a close formation in daylight. Indeed, the pilot was given a fixed gun firing ahead, and the makers advertised it as 'a fighting bomber', suggesting that it could chase and shoot down other aircraft. Could they really have believed this?

What actually happened was quite different. Like all the others, the Hampden was a sitting duck for even a single Messerschmitt Bf 109E. For its size – the span was 69 ft 2 in, compared with 56 ft 4 in for a Blenheim and 84 ft for a Whitley – the Hampden was commendably manoeuvrable, but obviously its agility was not in the same class as a fighter. A Bf 109E could fly almost 100 mph faster, and was not in the least bothered by the defensive armament of a single hand-aimed Vickers K in the upper and lower rear positions, so it was very soon realised that the Hampden was not going anywhere near the Luftwaffe in daylight.

It had been designed to the same B.9/32 specification as the Wellington. On the drawing board it had seemed positively futuristic, and it still seemed pretty modern when the prototype appeared in June 1936. Its all-metal stressed-skin airframe was, like that of the later Halifax, designed in large sections which could be quickly bolted together, or unbolted. This facilitated assembly, transport by rail or road, and replacement of a part that had suffered major damage.

Except for the nose, the fuselage was made in left and right halves, each virtually completed with internal equipment and wiring before being joined together. This was more than just a good idea; like the Mosquito, the slim tail boom of the Hampden would have been virtually impossible to make in any other way.

Max did an old-style 'people and bombs' drawing. He ignored such things as the 'flap motion plates', which were compression links pivoted on parallel arms and serving both as hinges for the slotted flaps and as transmitters for the push of the operating jack. Other unusual features included slats on the outer wings (Max labelled them 'Slots', though the slot is the gap between the slat and the wing), and the retractable direction-finding antenna above the grotesquely narrow fuselage, which among other things isolated the navigator and pilot. The pilot's cockpit almost resembled that of a fighter. It gave the pilot an exceptional view ahead and down on both sides, and he was also high enough to see the upturned wingtips. What he couldn't see, except with some difficulty, were the compass and directional gyro. It would have been so easy to offset the massive control column, which carried an aileron wheel that almost filled the whole width of the cockpit. It was common to fly with the canopy slid back, which was very pleasant. Maximum bomb load was a useful 4000 lb (1814 kg).

Handley Page built 501 Hampdens, English Electric at Preston and Samlesbury built 770, and 160 were built by a group called Canadian Associated Aircraft. The Canadian contract was intended to give the firms involved experience preparatory to building Stirlings, but the Stirling plan was cancelled. Short & Harland in Belfast received contracts for 150 of a version designated the HP 53 Hereford, powered by Napier Dagger VIII engines. These proved so troublesome that the last 11 were delivered as Hampdens, the 150th and last becoming the prototype Hampden TB 1, carrying two 18-inch torpedoes, and if necessary two 500-lb bombs under the wings.

Devoid of unit markings, a trio of No 49 Sqn Hampdens sit idling at Scampton in late 1938. This unit was the first of 14 squadrons in Bomber Command to receive the type

Early daylight raids suffered heavy casualties. At No 44 Sqn a pilot short in stature but colossal in determination – Guy Gibson – dared to bypass official channels and got station workshops to fit each aircraft with twin guns in the rear positions. Armour was added, together with long flame-damped exhaust pipes. Thereafter Hampdens continued with Bomber Command until September 1942, by which time the D/F loop was inside a normal fixed 'acorn'. Hampdens pioneered the laying of sea mines, which was code-named 'gardening'. The last operational flights made by RAF Hampdens were meteorological sorties.

In at least two books it is stated in a photograph caption that the lower rear gun position had been reduced in height. On the contrary, the TB.1 torpedo bomber had a standard gunner station (it was cramped enough, any-way!) but the aft end of the weapon bay was made deeper. These aircraft saw much action, from 1942 with Coastal Command. Two squadrons, Nos 144 and 455, took their aircraft to the Murmansk/Vaenga region of the USSR, initially to protect convoy PQ.18.

When they returned to Britain they left their aircraft behind, because unlike many British aircraft the Russians thought the Hampden useful, and they continued in frontline service wearing Red Stars through to 1943. Unlike the British, the Russians take care not to destroy the last survivor of a famous type, and thanks to them a Hampden is today being restored to its former glory in Britain.

Millar's drawing appeared in *Flight* for 4 May 1939, the day after rival Clark's had been run in *The Aeroplane*!

# BOMBAY I

One could say the story of this 'bomber-transport' began in 1922, when the newly created Bristol (as distinct from British & Colonial) Aeroplane Company built a tiny Jupiter-engined racer. When the pilot tried to roll to the left, the wings twisted and the aircraft rolled to the right! This is disconcerting, and yet the same thing happened in 1927 with the Bagshot, a high-wing monoplane fighter with two Jupiter engines. The Air Ministry thereupon used the Bagshot for research into how to make monoplanes with torsionally stiff wings.

We must have been fairly incompetent. We could build fine wire-braced fabric-covered biplanes, but Bristol's chief designer, Frank Barnwell, came to the conclusion that the only way to make the Bagshot fly properly was to turn it into a biplane! The Air Ministry continued to believe the evidence of Dornier, Junkers, Northrop and many other foreign companies that cantilever monoplanes were possible, and to cut a long story short eventually got Bristol to build a monoplane to specification C.26/31, calling for an aircraft which could either drop bombs or carry 24 troops or other cargo.

Still known as the Bristol 130 when this shot was taken by Charles Brown in 1935, K3583 served as the prototype Bombay – this name was only adopted by the RAF in April 1937

The result was one of the biggest examples of overkill in the history of aircraft structures. As the cutaway shows, the wing had no fewer than seven spars, each of which was a strong plate girder, with the flanges made of high-tensile steel! Apart from the fabric-covered control surfaces, the entire aircraft was a massive all-metal structure mainly of Alclad (light alloy covered with aluminium to avoid corrosion). As a result, the Type 130 prototype weighed 13,000 lb empty, leaving only 5000 lb available for fuel, crew and payload.

The Bristol 130 was the largest aircraft built at Bristol until the Brabazon. First flown on 23 June 1935, it was at least a monoplane, powered by excellent Pegasus engines, but it had very timid narrow-chord split flaps, fixed landing gear with spatted main wheels, and fixed-pitch propellers, and could fairly be called pedestrian. Manually operated turrets at nose and tail were to have single Lewis guns, and the intention was to carry 'five 550-lb bombs' under the centre of gravity.

Considerable refinement led to the Bombay, 50 of which were ordered from a company called Short & Harland, which was formed at Belfast jointly by the aircraft firm and the Belfast shipbuilder. The Bombay was their first job, hotly followed by an even less-useful aircraft, the Hereford (see Hampden and Dagger entries). They built the 50 Bombays in 1939.

They had Pegasus XXII engines uprated to 1010 hp on 87-octane fuel housed in four aluminium tanks with a capacity of 412 gal. They still had simple short-chord cowlings, and had hand-turning gear stowed in the rear fuselage, as illustrated, but were usually started electrically. They drove Hele-Shaw constant-speed propellers which were the first products of another new firm formed by Rolls-Royce and Bristol, and thus called Rotol.

A hydraulic pump powered the flaps and the nose and tail turrets. The latter were the first power-driven turrets to be designed by Bristol, the B II and B III, which each had a Vickers K gas-operated gun. The gun lay on its side, which must have made it difficult to fit fresh drum magazines. Two more such guns could be fired from side windows. Primitive bombing gear could release 250-pounders, but a forest of 20-lb bombs had to be removed from internal racks by hand, the locking wire on the nose propeller snipped and then thrown out through the opened main door!

Of course, by the time war came these machines were used purely as transports, except for some hair-raising bombing in Abyssinia and Italian Somaliland, the Iraqi campaign and by night over Benghazi. In May/June 1940 hectic missions were flown to France, at first to bring supplies out and then to bring troops back. Aged 12, I lived in Eastcote, near Northolt airfield,

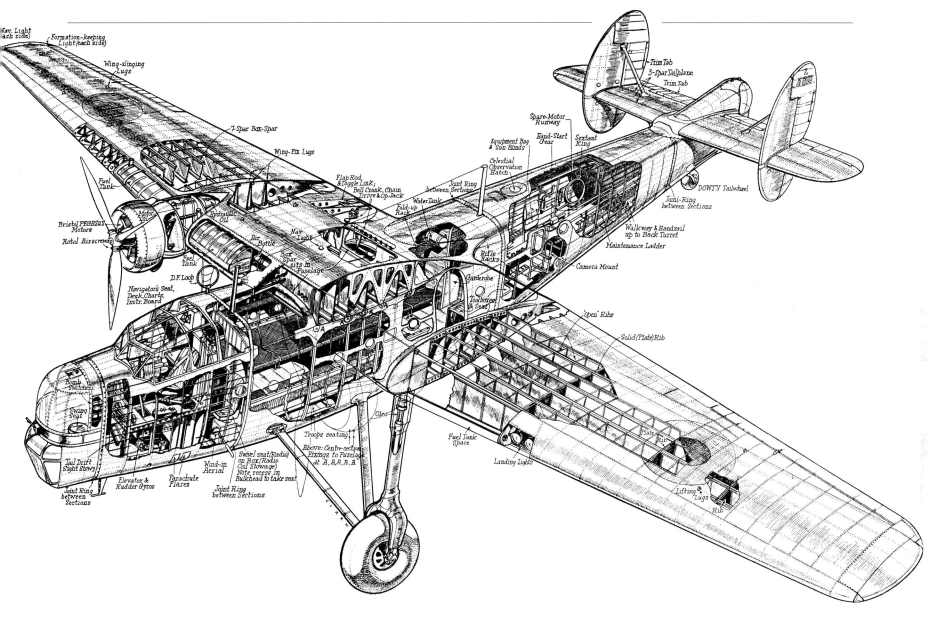

Nav. Light (each side)
Formation-keeping Light (each side)
Wing-slinging Lugs
7-Spar Box-Spar
Wing-Fix Lugs
Fuel Tank
Bristol PEGASUS Motors
Rotol Airscrews
Motor Oil
Hydraulic Oil
Air Bottle
Nav. Light
Fuel Tank
D.F. Loop
Flap Rod, & Toggle Link; Bell Crank, Chain Drive & Op. Jack
Box-Spar sits in Fuselage
Navigator's Seat, Desk, Charts, Instr. Board
Bomb Switches
Swing Seat
Tail Drift S'ight Stows
Joint Ring between Sections
Elevator & Rudder Gyros
Parachute Flares
Wind-in Aerial
Swivel seat (Radio) on Box (Radio Coil Stowage) Note recess in Bulkhead to take seat
Joint Ring between Sections
Above: Centre-section Fixings to Fuselage at A, A, A, A, A
Troops seating
Oleo
Water Tank
Fold-up Rack
Joint Ring between Sections
Equipment Bag & Sun Blinds
Celestial Observation Hatch
Rifle Racks
Garderobe
Toolboxes & Seat
Spare-Motor Runway
Hand-Start Gear
Sextant Ring
Walkway & Handrail up to Back Turret
Maintenance Ladder
Camera Mount
DOWTY Tailwheel
Joint-Ring between Sections
Trim Tab
3-Spar Tailplane
Trim Tab
'open' Ribs
Solid (Plate) Rib
Fuel Tank Space
Landing Lights
Plate Rib
Lifting Lugs
Rib
Rib

and was diverted one evening to find a Bombay on its belly just down the road. These aircraft worked hard to the end, their last duties being casualty evacuation from the Italian front, taking ten stretcher cases at a time. One crew alone brought out 6000 wounded.

Clark did a typically competent job. The 'gyros' under the floor near the rudder pedals formed part of a primitive autopilot. I couldn't help being amused by the 'celestial observation hatch' (most aircraft had astro domes instead of a hatch), and also by the French 'garderobe' instead of the more common word wardrobe, or even coat cupboard.

I doubt if any batch of 50 aircraft accomplished more hard work than the Bombays, but we British were wise to leave transport aircraft generally to the Americans. You could obviously accomplish more with 10,654 DC-3s.

# S K U A   I

I recently wrote a book about my own selection of aircraft which either failed to perform as advertised or were completely useless. Poor Blackburn Aircraft got in repeatedly, in some cases because they produced aircraft tailored exactly to an ill-advised official specification. For example, the Roc was a two-seat carrier-based fighter which entered service in 1940, even though its maximum speed was 168 kts! A seaplane version was significantly slower. Obviously useless, the Roc was a fighter version of the Skua 'fighter dive-bomber'. Absolutely flat out at 2750 rpm (a condition permitted for five minutes only), the Skua could reach a speed which varied from 176 kts at sea level to a dizzy 195 kts at 6500 ft, falling away thereafter. If you had to open the cooling gills to the position shown in the drawing you immediately lost about 20 kts!

Yet, in the context of its times, the Skua was positively futuristic. When it entered service with the Fleet Air Arm (FAA) in November 1938, every aircraft in FAA first-line squadrons was a fabric-covered biplane. Not only was the Skua a cantilever monoplane, of all-metal stressed-skin construction, but its outer wings housed four of the new Browning machine guns, firing ahead and aimed by the pilot with one of the new reflector sights. A hinged frame, normally recessed under the forward fuselage, could carry a 500-lb semi-armour-piercing bomb, and light series carriers for practice bombs could be attached under the wings.

Each wing could be folded manually around a skewed hinge to lie with its undersurface outwards against the rear fuselage. Blackburn were very proud of the way they managed to combine folding wings with a retractable undercarriage (an innovation for the FAA). Nevertheless, one wonders why, having introduced a hydraulic system energised by an engine-driven pump, they did not make the wings fold under power. Grabbing the handle on the wingtip and folding a wing of this size and weight would be no joke in an Arctic gale on a deck pitching and rolling in a stormy sea!

The hydraulic system was required for the landing gear and flaps. The former was unusually neat in comparison with the clumsy designs common in the 1930s, and each leg simply pivoted outwards to stow the wheel in the outer wing. The flaps were of modified Zap type (so-called from inventor Zaparka), which pivoted about mid-chord on strong arms at each end. Blackburn changed the geometry so that instead of the operating jack driving the leading edge, sliding on rails, the jack drove a lever attached to the flap's upper face, which at 90° depression became the rear face. Advantages of these flaps were a great reduction in the hinge moment (the operating force required) and the

fact that they could be locked hydraulically at any setting, with the drive system off-loaded. Of course, the flaps were used as dive brakes as well as for landing.

They held speed in a vertical dive to about 243 kts, though the propeller was still capable of overspeeding. The pilot sighted on the target and released the previously recessed bomb on its large hinged frame, which swung down to bring the bomb about five feet from the fuselage before final release. The extraordinary thing is, though the article which accompanied this drawing in *The Aeroplane* described the Skua's armament in some detail, Clark was obviously told not to show any of it! He gave no indication of any bombs. He drew four small rings in the leading edge, but was not allowed to draw in the Browning Mk II guns, nor the apertures in the spar nor the magazines or pneumatic firing system.

Of the observer's gun, not a word. It was a Lewis Mk IIIE (less often, a Vickers K) on a Fairey pillar mounting as on the Battle and several other types, with drum magazines nearby. Clark annotated 'THROTTLE', but this ought to have been unseen behind the more interesting Mk II reflector sight. Also omitted was the camera gun in the right wing root.

The Perseus XII engine had nine sleeve-valve cylinders, each identical with the 14 of the Hercules illustrated on another page. The engine power was given as 830 hp when this drawing was published, and amended to 905 hp

Sprayed up in wartime colours in place of its former silver overall, Skua I L2928 was part of the first order for 140 of the type placed with Blackburn by the Air Ministry in 1936

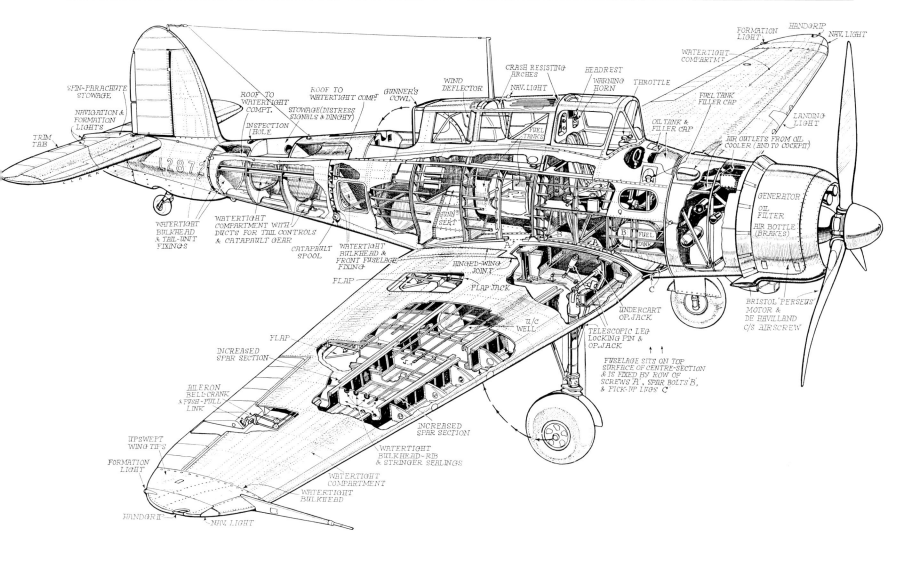

SPIN~PARACHUTE STOWAGE

NAVIGATION & FORMATION LIGHTS

TRIM TAB

ROOF TO WATERTIGHT COMPT.

ROOF TO WATERTIGHT COMP.ᵗ

STOWAGE (DISTRESS SIGNALS & DINGHY)

INSPECTION HOLE

GUNNER'S COWL

WIND DEFLECTOR

CRASH RESISTING ARCHES

NAV. LIGHT

HEADREST

WARNING HORN

THROTTLE

FORMATION LIGHT

HANDGRIP

NAV. LIGHT

WATERTIGHT COMPARTMT

FUEL TANK FILLER CAP

OIL TANK & FILLER CAP

LANDING LIGHT

AIR OUTLETS FROM OIL COOLER (AND TO COCKPIT)

FUEL TANKS

WATERTIGHT BULKHEAD & TAIL-UNIT FIXINGS

WATERTIGHT COMPARTMENT WITH DUCTS FOR TAIL CONTROLS & CATAPULT GEAR

CATAPULT SPOOL

WATERTIGHT BULKHEAD & FRONT FUSELAGE FIXING

GUNN.ᵣ SEAT

FLAP

FLAP JACK

HINGED-WING JOINT

GENERATOR

OIL FILTER

AIR BOTTLE (BRAKES)

B FUEL TANK

A

B

C

UNDERCART OP. JACK

U/C WELL

TELESCOPIC LEG LOCKING PIN & OP. JACK

BRISTOL 'PERSEUS' MOTOR & DE HAVILLAND C/S AIRSCREW

INCREASED SPAR SECTION

FLAP

AILERON BELL-CRANK & PUSH-PULL LINK

UPSWEPT WING TIPS

FORMATION LIGHT

HANDGRIP

NAV. LIGHT

INCREASED SPAR SECTION

WATERTIGHT BULKHEAD ~ RIB & STRINGER SEALINGS

WATERTIGHT COMPARTMENT

WATERTIGHT BULKHEAD

FUSELAGE SITS ON TOP SURFACE OF CENTRE-SECTION & IS FIXED BY ROW OF SCREWS 'A', SPAR BOLTS 'B', & PICK-UP LUGS 'C'

L2872

when it was republished two years later in *The Aeroplane Spotter*. Clark put a funny scimitar-like curve in one of the blades of his propeller, which was not of the C/S (constant-speed) variety but was a licensed Hamilton bracket type with a choice of only two pitch angles just 10° apart, which explains why it oversped in a vertical dive. Engine starting was by one of the first cartridge starters, drawn (but not annotated) as the smallest of the three horizontal drums behind the engine. The other drums were the compressed-air reservoir and the alcohol tank for deicing.

The main fuel tanks were identical (left and right mirror-image) 62-gal cells in the centre fuselage. This was not obvious from the drawing, which also did not indicate that the oval just above them was in fact the main fuel filler. The two circular inlets at the top of the engine cowl ducted air past the top cylinder to the oil cooler. What Clark called 'ducts for catapult gear' were actually the recesses for the A-frame arrester hook, and one cannot help but be amused by his failure to get in the whole of the word 'COMPARTMENT' behind the left wing!

# JU 86A-1

After 15 years pioneering the construction of aircraft with skins of corrugated light alloy, Junkers began in the early 1930s to switch to smooth stressed skin. Their first big twin-engined machine of this type was the prototype Ju 86, first flown on 4 November 1934. From it stemmed a useful succession of passenger airliners and bombers. In the mid-1930s the Ju 86 was modern and competitive. Five Ju 86D-1 bombers were sent to Spain and used with some success, but the Ju 86 bomber versions were never regarded by the Luftwaffe as anything other than interim types, due for quick replacement by the Do 17, He 111 and Ju 88. Thus, their impact on World War 2 was minimal, except by a handful operated by the air forces of Hungary and, ironically, South Africa. A handful of a later version served with the Luftwaffe in the Polish campaign, and even smaller numbers (perhaps 20) were operated as extended-span pressurized reconnaissance versions for use at altitudes considerably in excess of 40,000 ft. Service ceiling of the bomber illustrated would have been just under 20,000 ft.

Clark must have begun this drawing at the very start of the War. For that period it is quite detailed, but his employers would never have dreamed of sending him to Dessau! He must have based it on the wealth of published information available in German literature. I doubt if he had access to the manuals on the Kestrel-engined airliners supplied to South African Airways from 1936. One of the 18 aircraft sent to South Africa was a bomber, and all 18 were eventually re-engined with Pratt & Whitney Hornets and modified by the SAAF as reconnaissance-bombers. They played a big role in various

Down on its luck, this BMW-powered Ju 86E-2 has nosed over ever so gently in the thick snow at an unknown airfield in Germany in the winter of 1940

African campaigns, and I later encountered one abandoned at Waterkloof bearing numerous mission symbols.

This was a time when the British stuck a 'K' after almost every German military-aircraft designation. In the case of the Ju 86 this was quite correct, because export bomber versions were designated Ju 86K followed by a suffix number. Thus the most important export customer was Hungary, with the Ju 86K-2. Next in importance came Sweden with the K-4 and K-5, powered by the licence-built Bristol Pegasus.

What Clark actually drew was one of the handful (about 18) of the first production version, the Ju 86A-1. This was quickly supplanted in production by the Ju 86D-1, which had the fuselage extended behind the tail to improve stability. All versions had the same unusual main landing gear, with the wheels supporting the aircraft on vertical shock struts near the end of the very small centre section. Upon retraction the top of the leg was pulled inwards along a horizontal guide, the wheel ending up lying flat inside the outer wing. This was neat, and enabled a wing to be changed without having to put the aircraft on trestles, but it made the track much narrower than it appeared in the drawing. The prototypes had tailskids, but production versions had a castoring (artists never could spell) tailwheel which in Britain was self-centring, and in the USA self-centering.

Like the He 111, the usual method of carrying bombs was nose-up in vertical racks in the mid-fuselage. Here Clark went adrift in drawing two bombs in each cell and then labelling them as being 275 lb (125 kg) bombs. I have been unable to find such a bomb in any Luftwaffe handbook, or in the comprehensive Soviet guide to German bombs. There were four cells on each side, and each could house a single SC 100 (100-kg, 220.5-lb) bomb. As an alternative load the Ju 86 could carry 16 of the SC 50 size. On the other hand, the three hand-aimed MG 15 machine guns are quite accurate.

A small point is that Clark showed the initial version of this aircraft, powered like the first airline sub-type by the Junkers Jumo 205C-4 two-stroke diesel, rated at 600 hp (not 700 hp as stated by *The Aeroplane*). These engines had six long cylinders housing 12 opposed pistons. They burned fuel oil, so the drums immediately outboard of each engine ought to have been labelled "lubricating oil", to distinguish this oil from the fuel.

This drawing was published in *The Aeroplane* for 19 October 1939. It was republished in *The Aeroplane Spotter* for 22 May 1941, by which time there was no chance whatsoever of such an aircraft appearing on a bombing raid over the British Isles. At first glance the only thing to have been altered

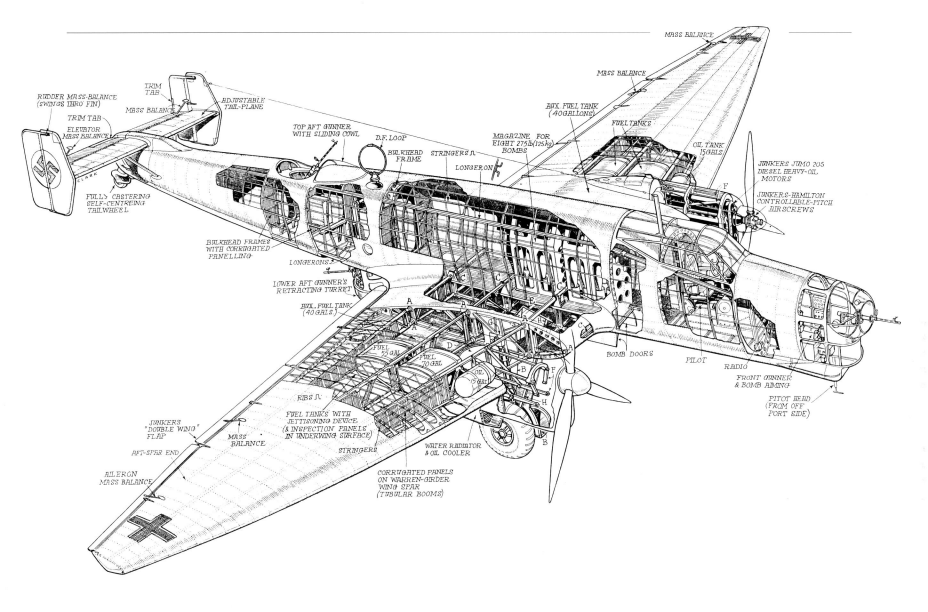

RUDDER MASS-BALANCE
(SWINGS THRO' FIN)

TRIM
TAB

MASS BALANCE

ADJUSTABLE
TAIL-PLANE

TRIM TAB
ELEVATOR
MASS BALANCE

CLARK

FULLY CASTERING
SELF-CENTREING
TAILWHEEL

BULKHEAD FRAMES
WITH CORRUGATED
PANELLING

LONGERONS

LOWER AFT GUNNER'S
RETRACTING TURRET

AUX. FUEL TANK
(40 GALS.)

TOP AFT GUNNER
WITH SLIDING COWL

D.F. LOOP

BULKHEAD
FRAME

STRINGERS

LONGERON

FUEL
55 GAL

FUEL
70 GAL

OIL
5 GAL

JUNKERS
"DOUBLE WING"
FLAP

AFT-SPAR END

AILERON
MASS BALANCE

MASS
BALANCE

RIBS

FUEL TANKS WITH
JETTISONING DEVICE
(& INSPECTION PANELS
IN UNDERWING SURFACE)

STRINGERS

CORRUGATED PANELS
ON WARREN-GIRDER
WING SPAR
(TUBULAR BOOMS)

WATER RADIATOR
& OIL COOLER

MASS BALANCE

MASS BALANCE

AUX. FUEL TANK
(40 GALLONS)

FUEL TANKS

MAGAZINE FOR
EIGHT 275lb (125kg)
BOMBS

OIL TANK
15 GALS.

JUNKERS JUMO 205
DIESEL HEAVY-OIL
MOTORS

JUNKERS-HAMILTON
CONTROLLABLE-PITCH
AIRSCREWS

F

BOMB DOORS

PILOT

RADIO

FRONT GUNNER
& BOMB AIMING

PITOT HEAD
(FROM OFF
PORT SIDE)

appeared to have been removal of the ring round the Swastika insignia on the tail (the original 1937 fins and rudders having been doped red, with the Swastika on a white disc in the centre). On closer inspection it could be seen that the entire drawing had been re-annotated with new labels in unseriffed capitals. Among other changes '55 GAL' had become '55 GALLS', and the same for the other capacities, and 'WING SPAR' had become the ungainly 'WINGSPAR'.

Less puzzling, but equally amusing, in the 1960s a rival publishing house that shall remain nameless copied this drawing exactly, but with a differently worded numbered key.

One obvious criticism of Clark's drawing is that he got the angles of the propeller blades completely wrong, especially the nearer (starboard) propeller whose lowest blade ought to have been rotated clockwise through about 30°. This poor shape was copied faithfully by his later imitators.

# Bf 109E

This drawing is an extraordinary mixture of good, bad and nonsense. The good part is Clark's unfailingly clean line work with a pen, the correct overall shape and the general impression given. The bad included the outdated tail insignia, the microscopic fuel tank (it actually held 88 gal and extended down the whole depth of the fuselage and then forward under the seat, in an L shape) and the time wasted on complicated shading. The nonsense included the armament, landing gear and radiators. Virtually all the errors had been put right by the time Clark came to draw the Bf 109F later in the War.

Most of the background is given in the text accompanying this later drawing, and it was decided to include this 1939 cutaway purely for comparative purposes. It appeared in *The Aeroplane* for 26 October 1939, by which time a great deal had been published about all versions of Bf 109, but no example had as yet fallen into Allied hands. I am not sure what was meant, in the text originally accompanying this drawing, by 'It has been compiled from information hitherto unavailable'.

Some of this information which clearly influenced the drawing was completely unreliable. For example, in the text the armament was given as 'one 23 mm (0.906 in) cannon fixed to fire through the hub of the VDM controllable-pitch airscrew, two 7.7 mm (0.312 in) machine guns in troughs on top of the cowling and two more in the wings outboard of the airscrew disc'. The writer added that British fighters had 'eight 7.6 mm (0.303 in) machine guns'.

For a start, 0.303 in is 7.7 mm, not 7.6, and the German calibre of 0.312 in is actually 7.92 mm, not 7.7. No 23 mm cannon was ever used by the Luftwaffe, and though a few E-3 fighters were originally built with a 20 mm MG FF firing through the spinner, these were as troublesome as the previous engine-mounted gun installations had been and almost all were quickly removed in service. The big hole in the spinner remained, however, to admit cooling air, but the belief that fire spat from it was to persist for ages. By far the most important part of the armament of the Bf 109E in the vast majority of its sub-types was two 20 mm MG FF cannon in the wings, in the positions shown by Clark as having machine guns. Each was fed by a 60-round drum, which required a broad curved bulge on the underside of the wing, together with a chute to eject empty cases. I am at a loss to explain the quite different blister drawn by Clark and labelled 'GUN DISCHARGE'.

As for the 'WATER RADIATORS', for a start the coolant was 50/50 water mixed with Glysantin (ethylene glycol), which was a stronger glycol mix than used by the British Merlin for most of the War. This was cooled by the two radiators under the rear part of the wings immediately outboard of the

Flying one of the last Emils still in frontline service by the spring of 1942, Leutnant Steindl brings his appropriately marked Bf 109E-4/B in close for the camera, en route to Stalingrad. The chevron marking on his elaborately camouflaged aircraft denotes his position as *Geschwader* adjutant for JG 54

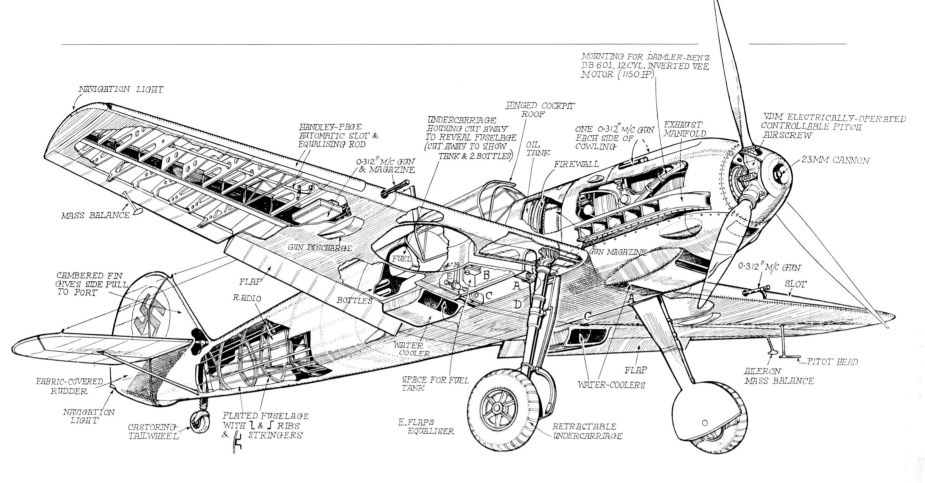

NAVIGATION LIGHT

HANDLEY-PAGE AUTOMATIC SLOT & EQUALISING ROD

MASS BALANCE

0·312" M/C GUN & MAGAZINE

UNDERCARRIAGE HOUSING CUT AWAY TO REVEAL FUSELAGE (CUT AWAY TO SHOW TANK & 2 BOTTLES)

HINGED COCKPIT ROOF

OIL TANK

FIREWALL

MOUNTING FOR DAIMLER-BENZ DB 601, 12 CYL. INVERTED VEE MOTOR (1150 HP)

ONE 0·312" M/C GUN EACH SIDE OF COWLING

EXHAUST MANIFOLD

VDM ELECTRICALLY-OPERATED CONTROLLABLE PITCH AIRSCREW

23MM CANNON

GUN DISCHARGE

CAMBERED FIN GIVES SIDE PULL TO PORT

FLAP

RADIO

FUEL

GUN MAGAZINE

0·312" M/C GUN

SLOT

BOTTLES

E B A

C D

WATER COOLER

SPACE FOR FUEL TANK

C

FABRIC-COVERED RUDDER

NAVIGATION LIGHT

CASTORING TAILWHEEL

PLATED FUSELAGE WITH Ⱡ & ſ RIBS & ⱶ STRINGERS

E. FLAPS EQUALISER

RETRACTABLE UNDERCARRIAGE

FLAP

WATER-COOLERS

AILERON MASS BALANCE

PITOT HEAD

roots. The flaps actually came closer together and were made integral with the outlets from the radiators, as explained in the Bf 109F text. Clark clearly never saw the actual aircraft. As for the radiator under the engine, this cooled lubricating oil, not water. The blisters that can be seen near it were needed to let the coolant pipes go from the front of the engine to the wing radiators.

The text that accompanied this drawing went on to say 'The cantilever undercarriage retracts outwards into the wings in which the wheels fill the whole space between the spar and leading edge. In the latest version the operation is believed to be by an electric motor through worm and segment gearing with auxiliary hand gear'. Clark overdid the size of the apparently huge hole needed to house the retracted wheel, and invented a wonderfully simplistic worm-gear drive. The wheel bay was in fact behind the front spar, and as in all other versions the leg was retracted by a hydraulic jack.

One thing the text got right, but which was not told to the artist, is that in the Bf 109E the tailplane was pivoted as well as being strut-braced, and its incidence could be adjusted from the cockpit by an irreversible screwjack, the limits being +3°/-8°. In the later Bf 109 versions the tailplane was without a bracing strut and was fixed to the fin.

The author would challenge the 1939 text when it proclaimed 'The aileron control in particular is brilliant'. The truth is that it was indeed brilliant in the airfield circuit, but in wartime fighter pilots tend to go a bit faster, and at anything over 500 km/h (311 mph) the ailerons got really heavy. In a dive they felt locked solid, but then early Spitfires weren't very good trying to roll at high airspeeds either.

And, of course, until late 1941 the 'Messerschmitt' had one big advantage over its opponents in that under negative-g the engine didn't splutter and cut out. The DB 601 had direct injection, which was a really good feature. The intake to its sideways-on supercharger was on the port (left) side, and thus could not be shown by Clark's drawing.

Finally, the specification published with this cutaway gave most of the figures quite accurately, but for some reason thought the overall length was '9.8 m (32 ft 0 in)'. The actual length was 8.64 m (28 ft 4 in)

# Bf 109F

When it came to captured aircraft, the artist was often up against problems. He could not expect the co-operation of the manufacturer, nor the loan of the detailed engineering manuals! If the aircraft was complete, even if damaged, and perhaps in flying condition, then he virtually had to draw what he could see from the outside, and possibly have to do so after making notes and sketches for a single afternoon. To produce this drawing Clark took his earlier artwork for the Bf 109E (not that featured on page 49) and modified it. As mentioned earlier, this original was not one of his better efforts, and consequently neither is this – this rendition is drawn around the aircraft's Daimler-Benz engine, a captured example of which he was able to study for some time, separated from the Bf 109 and displayed in a Farnborough hangar.

Of course the Bf 109 was dominated by its engine. The DB 601N, though no more powerful (1200 hp for take-off) than a contemporary Merlin, had a capacity of almost 34 litres, and the DB 605 of the far more numerous Bf 109G hit 35.7, compared with only 27 litres for the Merlin. Conversely, the Bf 109 was significantly smaller than a Hurricane or Spitfire, a factor which really showed if one watched a mock combat from a distance as some airshow crowds can do today. Not only that, but the German fighter had a remarkable structural simplicity.

For example, the fuselage, made in left and right halves, had just a few light stringers covered by strips of skin wrapped right round and overlapped at their flanged edges (Willy Messerschmitt's original sketch of this still exists). Like the Spitfire, the wing had almost all its strength in a single spar,

but not only was this totally different in form (comprising a conventional vertical sheet web with flanged booms) but it was much further back at almost 50 per cent chord. The drawing shows the simple three-pin attachment of the wing to the root rib, the forward attachment also locating the rear of the main-leg pivot.

Bayerische Flugzeugwerke (as it was when the Bf 109 was designed) pivoted the main legs to the root rib so that it could be changed without the need for a jack or trestles. At first there was nothing inside the wing except the operating linkages to the slotted flaps and ailerons. The leading-edge slats were automatic, and in combat manoeuvres could disconcertingly open on one wing only. Whether or not this also caused snatching of the ailerons (which it often did), it randomly yawed the aircraft, and made gun aiming very difficult. All wartime Bf 109s had the two engine coolant radiators recessed under the rear part of each inboard wing. Behind the wide, but shallow, radiator matrix (Z in the drawing) were upper and lower flaps which could be opened or closed to adjust the cooling airflow (Y). The turbulent boundary layer was ducted above the radiator and out through the upper flap (X). For take-off both flaps were lowered to 15° or 20°, and for landing to about 45°.

Every Bf 109 had a canopy which hinged open to the right. The author's abiding impressions of the cockpit were that it was cramped, especially in width, that with the hood shut you felt you were never going to get out, and that the sliding side window was flimsy and prone to jam. Rear view was poor, and you held your arm far out in front to reach the stick. This was fine fore and

A quartet of unmarked Bf 109F-2s run up their engines at dispersal somewhere in western Russia in the autumn of 1941

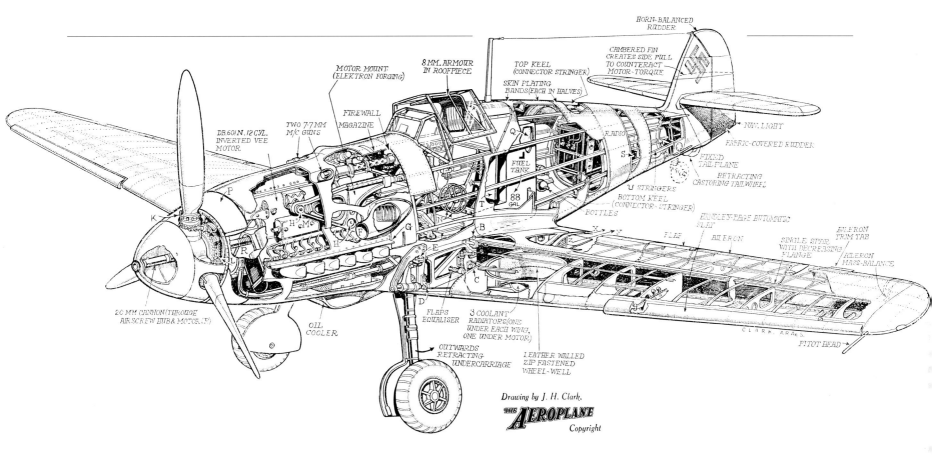

Drawing by J. H. Clark.
THE AEROPLANE
Copyright

aft, enabling the pilot to overcome the heavy elevators, but it was difficult to apply lateral force, and in a fast dive the ailerons felt locked solid! Lack of rudder trim was another annoying fault, which made one's leg get quickly tired. Clark showed the camber on the vertical tail which was intended to ease torque problems on take-off, but the swing to the left as the throttle was opened could still catch people out.

Only one of the handwheels labelled N was the laborious landing-gear drive; the other worked longitudinal trim. The 'BOTTLES' were of course oxygen. The Bf 109F was reputed to be the best version to fly, though it had weak armament. Often the cannon was the high-velocity MG 151/15 in place of the old MG/FF or the MG 151/20. The preceding Bf 109E usually had a 20 mm MG/FF in each wing, and cutting the spar to accommodate these guns caused endemic weakness which, despite thicker skins, made pilots bear in mind the need never to overstress the wings. There could hardly have be a worse fault in a fighter!

With the later Bf 109G the cannon were again mounted in or under the wings. On the Bf 109F the guns above the engine were two MG 17s of 7.92 mm calibre (not 7.7 as indicated by Clark), whilst on the G these were usually replaced by the 13 mm MG 131, causing a bulge on each side of the forward fuselage.

Like most German wartime aircraft the big engine was mounted on one-piece bearers forged in Elektron, a low-density alloy of magnesium. Almost all the liquid-cooled vee-12 engines, by Junkers as well as DB, were inverted and had the supercharger on one side (the left side in the case of the DB engines), fed by a prominent side inlet. Clark suggested the '3 COOLANT RADIATORS' were the same, but in fact the oil cooler under the engine was totally unlike the engine radiators. The retractable tailwheel was found on only a few versions of the Bf 109. On the G it could be locked to reduce swing at the start of the take-off run.

Altogether, this was a rather simple drawing of a simple aircraft. One is left feeling respect for the pilots who racked up scores of 200 or 300 using an aircraft that bristled with severe shortcomings.

# He 111

In 1932 the brothers Siegfried and Walter Günter put the name Heinkel 'on the map' with the 234-mph He 70 passenger/mail carrier for Luft Hansa. They then scaled this up to produce the twin-engined He 111, first flown on 25 February 1935. Like the He 70, there were also to be bomber versions. Despite being vulnerable, the He 111 was one of the great aircraft of World War 2. Like the Bf 109, Bf 110 and Ju 88, all the marvellous replacements for it failed to enter service, and the old Heinkel had to soldier on to the end of the War, by which time over 7300 had been delivered. They dropped more bombs, throughout Europe and North Africa, than any other Luftwaffe aircraft.

Like the He 70, all the numerous He 111 versions prior to the He 111F of late 1937 had a graceful wing of near-elliptical planform. On 2 November 1939 *The Aeroplane* published a Clark cutaway of what it called the 'He 111K Mk V', showing this wing mated with a new short all-glazed nose with no separate pilot windscreen. The pilot normally looked through the distant front panels, but for landing he could raise his seat and stick his head up behind an upward-hinged windscreen. There was indeed such a nose, though it was asymmetric, the gunner's hemisphere being offset to the right to give the pilot a better view. The trouble was, only a single prototype (with civil registration D-AQUO) had both the new nose and the original wing (the structure of which our James had invented).

An He 111H-11 has its Jumo 211 engines run up to ensure that both are operating correctly prior to the pilot waving the chocks away and the mission commencing

From 1938 all production aircraft had a straight-tapered wing which was easier to make. By the spring of 1939 production was concentrated on the He 111H, powered by the Jumo 211, and the otherwise basically identical He 111P, powered by the Daimler-Benz DB 601, both engines being rated at 1100 hp. Though *The Aeroplane* surmised that 'the DB has probably been standardised, because the Jumo 211 is needed for . . . the Ju 88, four-engined Ju 89 and small Ju 87 . . .', in fact the Jumo-powered He 111H was to be the standard version to the end of the war, made in 23 sub-variants, and ending with the more powerful Jumo 213.

Of course the He 111 was a clean and smooth stressed-skin machine, with a fuselage of remarkably streamlined shape. As a boy I had a cigarette card with a coloured picture of an earlier version, giving the speed as 313 mph, but when I actually flew in a late-war example, and flew it for a while, the maximum speed at low level seemed to be about 350 km/h, or 217 mph. It was a nice and sedate aeroplane, which didn't want to hurry. Conversely, when you throttled back, unless the wheels were extended, it didn't want to slow down. The Luftwaffe called it der Spaten (the spade), because of the amazing wing chord. Look at the Heinkel in the RAF Museum and you will agree the wing was much broader than it looks in Clark's drawing. Wing area was 942 ft$^2$, compared with 840 ft$^2$ for the Wellington, which had a span 12 ft greater.

The usual internal bomb load was eight SG 250 bombs of 551 lb each, carried nose-upwards in vertical cells, with a narrow passage between the four on each side. Many other loads were possible, and the external loads in most P or H versions could include a bomb weighing 4410 lb. The He 111H-6 was an important version equipped to launch two torpedoes. It was one of the few variants sometimes seen with the 'stinger' gun in the tail. Another last-ditch attempt to discourage fighters was a device for launching grenades.

Like unreliable authors, confused artists are likely to be repeatedly copied by others. One can make excuses for the November 1939 He 111 drawing, but this second bite at the same cherry ought to have got it right. Above the engine we have F, described merely as an 'air intake'. We also have an odd 'oil cooler' in the inboard leading edge. After the War *Pilot Press* did a more considered drawing, which correctly labelled the big inlet in the top of the cowling 'oil cooler air intake', but then copied Clark and put the oil cooler in the inboard leading edge. Later still, the same publisher did a detailed drawing of the DB-engined He 111P-2. Here, the inlet above the cowl was called the 'carburettor intake' (overlooking the fact that the engine had no carburettor) and the big oil cooler was labelled 'filter assembly'. On the left of the engine was the

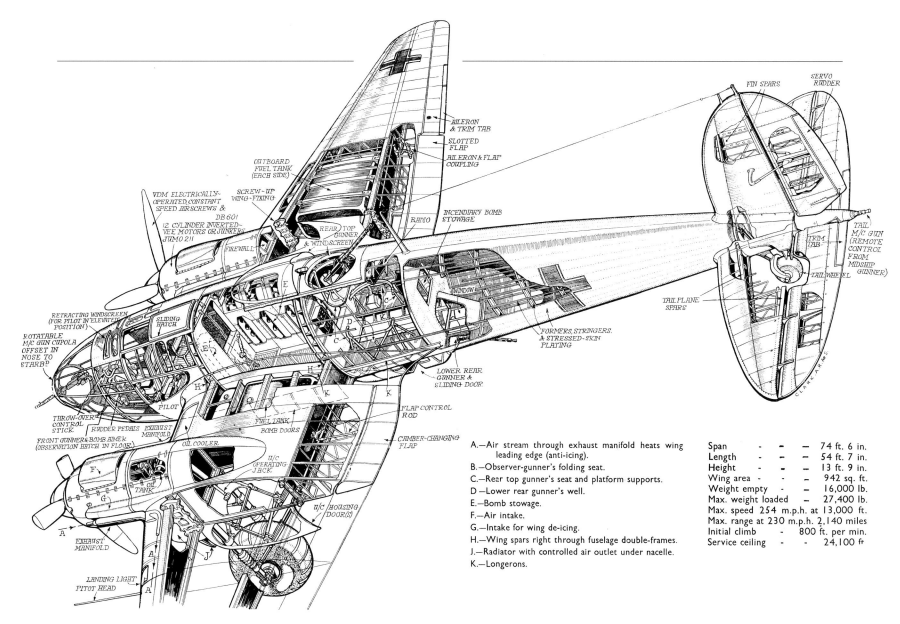

A.—Air stream through exhaust manifold heats wing leading edge (anti-icing).
B.—Observer-gunner's folding seat.
C.—Rear top gunner's seat and platform supports.
D—Lower rear gunner's well.
E.—Bomb stowage.
F.—Air intake.
G.—Intake for wing de-icing.
H.—Wing spars right through fuselage double-frames.
J.—Radiator with controlled air outlet under nacelle.
K.—Longerons.

| | | |
|---|---|---|
| Span | — — — | 74 ft. 6 in. |
| Length | — — — | 54 ft. 7 in. |
| Height | — — — | 13 ft. 9 in. |
| Wing area | — — | 942 sq. ft. |
| Weight empty | — — | 16,000 lb. |
| Max. weight loaded | — | 27,400 lb. |
| Max. speed 254 m.p.h. at 13,000 ft. | | |
| Max. range at 230 m.p.h. 2,140 miles | | |
| Initial climb | — | 800 ft. per min. |
| Service ceiling | — — | 24,100 fr |

'supercharger intake'. One wonders how the engine decided which lot of air it was going to use!

Clark correctly described the 'control stick' as being of the throw-over type, so that a co-pilot on the right could take over, but I never saw a Heinkel that had a copilot station, as it would have prevented access for the front gunner/bomb-aimer. The massive control pillar was roughly on the centreline, from the top of which a horizontal arm pointing to the left like a signpost carried the aileron wheel. I think the throw-over feature must have been so that

someone else could quickly take over should the pilot be killed. Another strange label is 'sliding door' in the ventral gondola for crew entry. I never saw an entry door that didn't hinge inwards from the top. According to later cutaways, Clark's 'incendiary bomb stowage' actually showed the location of the flares and markers. The tiny (too tiny) cylinder immediately in front of the dorsal gunner was the direction-finding antenna, and the pitot head was actually further out on the left wing – Clark had to bring it in next to the landing light to fit the space available on the page, which cut off most of that wing.

# STIRLING I

Today, most aviation enthusiasts have either never heard of the Stirling or they know that it was an unpopular death-trap because it couldn't climb above about 12,000 ft and got shot down in droves. They might be astonished to learn that, though Stirling crews would have liked a lot more altitude performance (service ceiling was actually said to be 17,000 ft), they loved this huge aircraft for its majesty, beautiful handling and general air of refinement. Those crews that survived tended to convert to Lancasters, which at first appeared crude, noisy and cramped, besides lacking dual control.

Short Brothers at Rochester, in Kent, won the contract to supply the first four-engined heavy bomber to the RAF since the V/1500 of 1918. The official view was that, whatever other heavy bombers might follow, the Stirling would be the supreme aircraft that would win any future war. The firm were in the process of opening a subsidiary, Short & Harland, at Belfast (later the parent firm moved there), and both factories tooled up to build Stirlings. First, Rochester built a half-scale test aircraft, before flying the full-size machine on

14 May 1939. Belfast flew their first Stirling in October 1940. Later a huge Shadow Factory, run by Austin Car Co. at Longbridge, Birmingham, outproduced either, but yet another Shadow plant, run by the Rootes car group, were transferred on to Blenheims and Beaufighters.

One often pays a penalty for being first. With remarkable shortsightedness, the 1936 Air Ministry specification demanded that the new heavy bomber should fit into existing hangars, and this meant that the wing span was restricted to only 99 ft 1 in. This was the principal reason for the poor altitude performance. The other really serious drawback to this early design was that in 1936 bombs came in 250 or 500-lb sizes, with talk of a slim armour-piercing bomb of 2000 lb. The Stirling was accordingly given six wing bomb cells and a gigantic internal bomb bay over 42 ft long, but divided up into three narrow full-length sections which later proved to be incapable of carrying any of the 'blockbuster' bombs which had been developed from 1940 onwards.

A further shortcoming (like all other British heavy bombers) was that

Ready to receive its load of bombs, a No 7 Sqn Stirling I sits at the edge of the peri track at Oakington in 1941, surrounded by bustle and activity in the hours before its next night raid. This unit were the initial recipients of the RAF's first 'big four' of World War 2 when they re-equipped with Stirlings in August 1940. They continued to fly the Short bomber until its replacement with Lancasters in May 1943

# HALIFAX I

In a few hundred years' time people interested in World War 2 aircraft will all be familiar with the Lancaster and B-17, because books by the truckload have been written about them. Hardly anyone will know that the B-17 was far outnumbered by the B-24 Liberator, or that there were over 11,000 Wellingtons or Pe-2s, and the Halifax will be virtually forgotten. This is, of course, outrageous. The Halifax was one of the great aircraft of the war. Tens of thousands – including almost all the Canadians in No 6 Group and the Free French in Nos 346 and 347 Sqns – went to war in it, and not a few thousand died in it. Unlike the Lancaster, Halifaxes were used for duties other than bombing. Also unlike the Lancaster, the many versions were visibly different.

The original requirement was to be met by a 26,000-lb HP 56 with two Vulture engines, but by the time the prototype flew on 25 October 1939, it was the 40,000-lb HP 57 with four Merlins. It looked very much like Clark's drawing, except that it had slats, and beam guns instead of a mid-upper turret. To facilitate production, transport and repair, the airframe was made as 24 separate parts, which when virtually complete with internal equipment were rapidly bolted together at the joints Clark indicated.

The drawing is fine, though 'CARBURETTER' is a mid-Atlantic spelling,

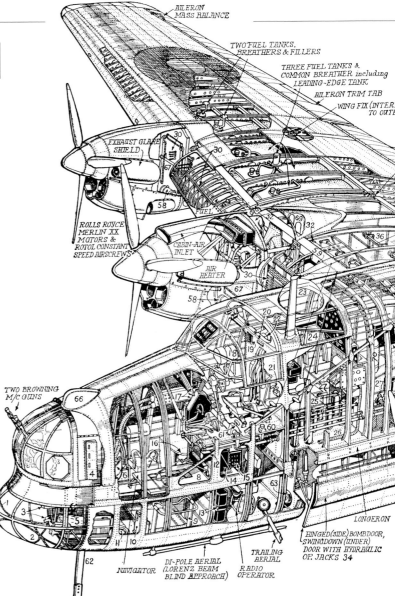

1—Navigation light
2—Bomb aimer's flat window
3—Bomb sight and arm rests
4—Turret balance flap
5—Bomb aimer's cushion
6—Hot-air hoses in spent cartridge tray
7—Navigator's folding seat
8—Navigator's table, lamp and chart
9—Camera stand
10—Parachute stowage
11—Gyro azimuth stand
12—Repeater compass
13—HT and LT units (radio)
14—Transmitting and receiving sets (radio)
15—Main electrical panel
16—Step-up to pilot's cockpit (parachute stowage underneath
17—Main instrument panel, engine controls
18—Folding seats (second pilot and engineer)
19—Fuel cock controls
20—Motor starter buttons
21—Emergency flare releases
22—Sextant rest
23—Astro-dome
24—Engineer's instrument panel
25—Engineer's platform
26—Hot air to wireless operator (oxygen bottles nearby)
27—Boxed-in engine control runs
28—Accumulators
29—Rudder and elevator controls
30—Motor controls (out of 27)
31—Emergency hydraulic hand pumps and hydraulic accumulators
32—Hot air trunks from heater on inboard motors
33—Lower spar boom

34—Bomb door hinges and op. jacks
34a—Rear hinge, no jack
35—Doors to wing bomb cells
36—Wing bomb door operating rods and jack
37—Leading edge section
38—Rest bunk each side
39—Jointing frames
40—Step up to turret
41—Flame floats and sea markers
42—Ammunition tracks
43—Flare chutes
44—Emergency axe stowage
45—Elsan lavatory
46—D/R compass
47—Bulkhead and door to tail gunner
48—Tailplane fixings
49—Elevator hinge lever
50—Elevator control lever
51—Rudder trim controls
52—Rudder control rods
53—Flap controls and op. jack
53a—Interconnecting wires (port to starboard flap)
54—Aileron controls
55—U/C doors and op. jack
56—Fuel tank supports
56a—Undercarriage bungee device
57—Carburetter air intake
58—Glycol tank (airscrew de-icing)
59—Oil tank for inboard motor
60—Rudder trim
61—Aileron trim
62—Pressure head
63—Trailing aerial reel stowage
64—Glycol header tank
65—Inspection door along wing leading edge

66—Cover for turret connections
67—Motor firewall
68—U/C op. jacks
69—U/C and U/C doors accumulators
70—Radiator and landing lamp jack accumulator
71—Radiator jack
72—Landing-Light op. jack
73—Quadrant distributor on engineer's panel 24
74—Distributor
75—Tank          (alongside
76—Pump accumulators  Glycol tank 58)
77—Engine driven pump
78—Junior distributor

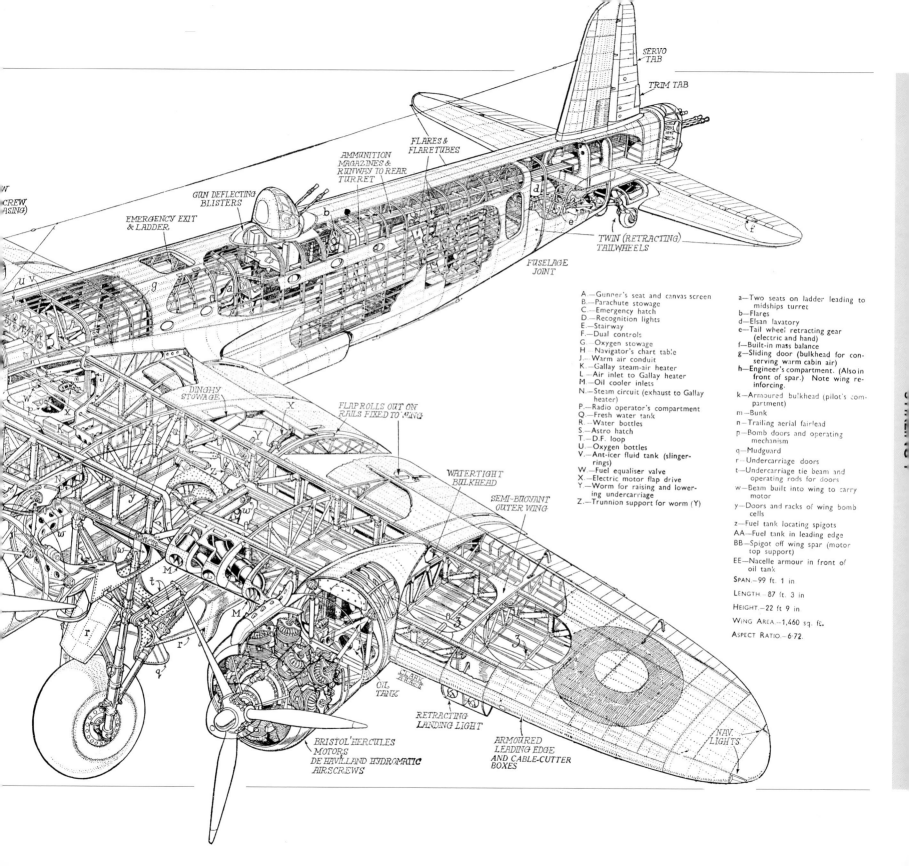

SERVO
TAB

TRIM TAB

FLARES &
FLARETUBES

AMMUNITION
MAGAZINES &
RUNWAY TO REAR
TURRET

GUN DEFLECTING
BLISTERS

TWIN (RETRACTING)
TAILWHEELS

EMERGENCY EXIT
& LADDER.

FUSELAGE
JOINT

CREW
ASING)

DINGHY
STOWAGE

FLAP ROLLS OUT ON
RAILS FIXED TO WING

WATERTIGHT
BULKHEAD

SEMI-BUOYANT
OUTER WING

BRISTOL HERCULES
MOTORS
DE HAVILLAND HYDROMATIC
AIRSCREWS

OIL
TANK

RETRACTING
LANDING LIGHT

ARMOURED
LEADING EDGE
AND CABLE-CUTTER
BOXES

NAV.
LIGHTS

A.—Gunner's seat and canvas screen
B.—Parachute stowage
C.—Emergency hatch
D.—Recognition lights
E.—Stairway
F.—Dual controls
G.—Oxygen stowage
H.—Navigator's chart table
J.—Warm air conduit
K.—Gallay steam-air heater
L.—Air inlet to Gallay heater
M.—Oil cooler inlets
N.—Steam circuit (exhaust to Gallay
    heater)
P.—Radio operator's compartment
Q.—Fresh water tank
R.—Water bottles
S.—Astro hatch
T.—D.F. loop
U.—Oxygen bottles
V.—Ant-icer fluid tank (slinger-
    rings)
W.—Fuel equaliser valve
X.—Electric motor flap drive
Y.—Worm for raising and lower-
    ing undercarriage
Z.—Trunnion support for worm (Y)

a—Two seats on ladder leading to
   midships turret
b—Flares
d—Elsan lavatory
e—Tail wheel retracting gear
   (electric and hand)
f—Built-in mass balance
g—Sliding door (bulkhead for con-
   serving warm cabin air)
h—Engineer's compartment. (Also in
   front of spar.)  Note wing reinforcing.
k—Armoured bulkhead (pilot's compartment)
m—Bunk
n—Trailing aerial fairlead
p—Bomb doors and operating
   mechanism
q—Mudguard
r—Undercarriage doors
t—Undercarriage tie beam and
   operating rods for doors
w—Beam built into wing to carry
   motor
y—Doors and racks of wing bomb
   cells
z—Fuel tank locating spigots
AA—Fuel tank in leading edge
BB—Spigot off wing spar (motor
    top support)
EE—Nacelle armour in front of
    oil tank

SPAN.—99 ft. 1 in
LENGTH.—87 ft. 3 in
HEIGHT.—22 ft 9 in
WING AREA.—1,460 sq. ft.
ASPECT RATIO.—6·72

whereas before the war there was much interest in ventral turrets – indeed the Stirling was to have had a Boulton Paul Type O ventral turret with twin 20 mm cannon, which would have been really useful – interest in defence against belly attack withered, and no such turret was ever fitted. Accordingly, when it was a matter of life and death, there was no defence against the Luftwaffe's upward-firing nightfighters.

Yet another design problem was the requirement that the huge airframe should be capable of being quickly dismantled to fit in packing cases matched to small British rail wagons. Clark showed most of the joints in his drawing. He also clearly showed the huge Gouge-type flaps, which rolled out on curved tracks. Lacking span, Arthur Gouge made these enormous in chord, extending across 48 per cent of the chord of the wing. Like the mighty main landing gears and twin tailwheels, the flaps were operated by electrically driven screwjacks. The main legs were modified in 1939 to carry the doors halfway down, which looked very strange but actually made each unit simpler and stronger. On retraction the gear hinged at a gatefold, the lower part swinging aft while the upper part pivoted forwards to raise everything below, including the doors, into the nacelle. The gear was supposed to have a reputation for trouble, but I never met a Stirling crewmember with a word to say against it.

As well as being one of the biggest aircraft of its day – the overall length was 87 ft 3 in, rising to over 90 ft in the Mk V – the Stirling was complicated throughout. One has only to look at the fuel tanks to sympathise with the flight engineers, especially as all the tanks in each wing had different capacities. A less-obvious problem is that, ignoring the success achieved in the USA with simple mechanical linkages, the Air Ministry insisted that for aircraft of this size the connections between the cockpit and other parts of the aircraft (notably the engine throttles) had to be effected by some clever new mechanism. On my one (dual) trip in a Stirling I was carefully briefed not to be abrupt with the four long and slender throttle levers, which operated via patented Exactor controls using supposedly incompressible hydraulic fluid to transmit the pilot's or engineer's often very small movements precisely along very long pipelines.

The RAF received 1771 Mk I and Mk III bombers, 450 Stirling IV transport/glider tugs and 160 of the unarmed Mk V transports. Throughout, the standard engine was the 1650-hp sleeve-valve Hercules XVI, bombers having flame-damped exhausts as shown by Clark. He also was permitted to mention the leading-edge cable cutters, but of course not H$_2$S radar, of which Stirlings were the first carriers to go into operation. Finally, I can understand his wish not to use 'i', 'l' and 'o' as small key letters, but I wonder why he omitted 'c', 's' and 'u'? It may have been due to objections on the grounds of security.

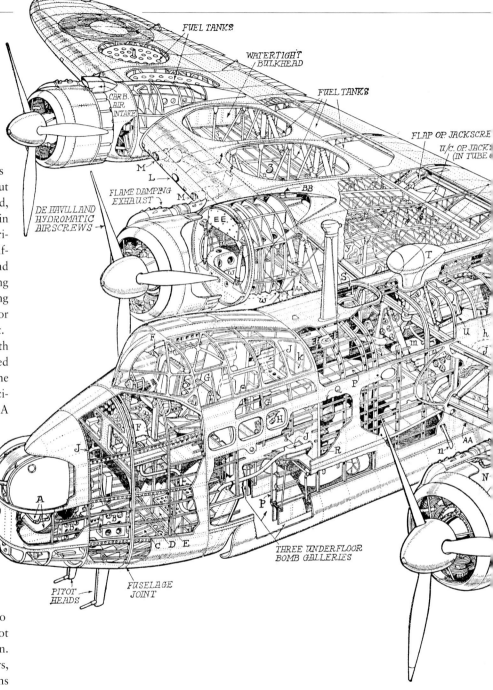

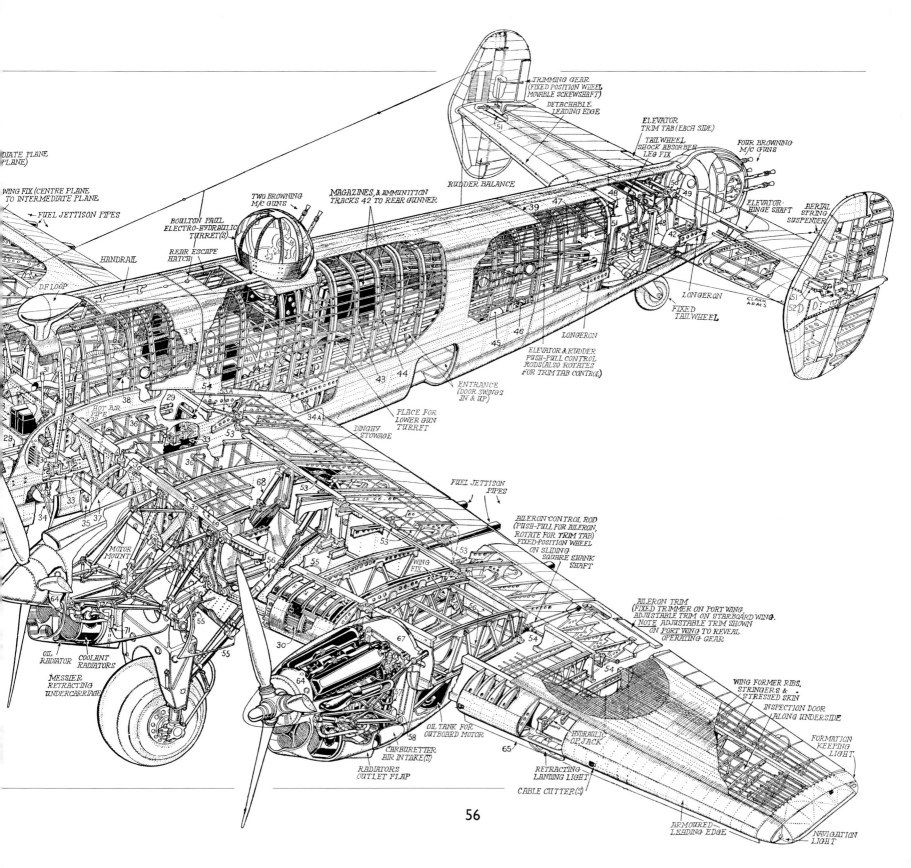

TRIMMING GEAR
(FIXED POSITION WHEEL,
MOVABLE SCREWSHAFT)

DETACHABLE
LEADING EDGE

ELEVATOR
TRIM TAB (EACH SIDE)

TAILWHEEL
SHOCK ABSORBER
LEG FIX

FOUR BROWNING
M/C GUNS

RUDDER BALANCE

ELEVATOR
HINGE SHAFT

AERIAL
SPRING
SUSPENDER

DIATE PLANE
PLANE)

WING FIX (CENTRE PLANE
TO INTERMEDIATE PLANE

FUEL JETTISON PIPES

TWO BROWNING
M/C GUNS

MAGAZINES, & AMMUNITION
TRACKS 42 TO REAR GUNNER

BOULTON PAUL
ELECTRO-HYDRAULIC
TURRET(S)

REAR ESCAPE
HATCH

HANDRAIL

CLARK
A.R.A.E.S

DF LOOP

LONGERON

FIXED
TAILWHEEL

ELEVATOR & RUDDER
PUSH-PULL CONTROL
RODS (ALSO ROTATES
FOR TRIM TAB CONTROL)

LONGERON

ENTRANCE
(DOOR SWINGS
IN & UP)

HOT AIR
PIPE

PLACE FOR
LOWER GUN
TURRET

DINGHY
STOWAGE

FUEL JETTISON
PIPES

AILERON CONTROL ROD
(PUSH-PULL FOR AILERON,
ROTATE FOR TRIM TAB)
FIXED-POSITION WHEEL
ON SLIDING
SQUARE SHANK
SHAFT

WING
FIX

AILERON TRIM
(FIXED TRIMMER ON PORT WING,
ADJUSTABLE TRIM ON STARBOARD WING.
NOTE ADJUSTABLE TRIM SHOWN
ON PORT WING TO REVEAL
OPERATING GEAR

MOTOR
MOUNT

WING FORMER RIBS,
STRINGERS &
STRESSED SKIN

INSPECTION DOOR
ALONG UNDERSIDE

OIL
RADIATOR

COOLANT
RADIATORS

MESSIER
RETRACTING
UNDERCARRIAGE

FORMATION
KEEPING
LIGHT

OIL TANK FOR
OUTBOARD MOTOR

CARBURETTER
AIR INTAKE(S)

HYDRAULIC
OP JACK

RADIATORS
OUTLET FLAP

RETRACTING
LANDING LIGHT

CABLE CUTTER(S)

ARMOURED
LEADING EDGE

NAVIGATION
LIGHT

56

between English carburettor and American carbureter. Clark drew but didn't indicate the big flexible connectors in the prominent fuel-jettison pipes which allowed the flaps to be lowered. Though next to 'hydraulic accumulators', misspelt item 28 was electric batteries, and 46 was the sensing unit of the distant-reading compass, placed for minimum magnetic interference and driving a dial on the cockpit panel.

A nationwide production programme was quickly organised. Handley Page built 1592 Halifaxes at Cricklewood and bolted them together at the Park Street and Colney Street plants at Radlett. English Electric made 2145 in Lancashire, with assembly at Samlesbury. Fairey made 661 at Stockport, Rootes Group 1070 at Speke (Liverpool) and the LAPG (London Aircraft Production Group) 710. LAPG comprised motor body-builders in north-west London, plus London Transport's Aldenham bus depot, with assembly at Leavesden. Total production was 6178.

As an ATC cadet in 1942 I was excited to watch the Mk II, as drawn by Clark, on the line at Radlett. The pristine camouflage, absolute newness of every component and brilliant reflections from the many areas of Perspex left a deep impression. By 1944, when I was flying in Leavesden's Mosquitoes, one could study the very much better Mk III aircraft which also came out of that factory. These had a Perspex nose, extended wingtips, 1615 hp Bristol Hercules engines, rectangular fins and four-gun Boulton Paul electrically driven turrets in the dorsal and tail positions. A few squadrons realised that the danger came from below, and fitted a ventral turret with a 0.5 in Browning.

A different (FN 64, twin 0.303 in) ventral turret had flown on two early Halifaxes, but ventral turrets went out of fashion just when they should have been top priority. In their place often came the $H_2S$ mapping radar. This big installation was first flown on 27 March 1942 on Halifax V9977 (the second Mk II from English Electric). Two months later this aircraft was flown into a Welsh hill, killing the five top men in the HMV (EMI) radar development team led by the brilliant Dr Alan Blumlein.

Abiding impressions of the Halifax are overshadowed by the contrast between the early and later marks. All had a nice pilot position with a control wheel like a flat X joined by side handgrips, all eight fingers working the brakes. The long tubular throttle levers were connected to the engines by Bloctubes, which were low-friction tubes filled with cables on which were threaded 'olives' and connecting bits, like beads on a necklace, so that one could push as well as pull. Behind the pilot was the aft-facing flight engineer while, unlike a Lanc, the signaller and navigator were in front of or below the cockpit, though the astro dome was behind it.

The entry door was unlike that of a Lanc, and on the opposite side. On average, 2.45 crewmembers escaped from stricken 'Hallis', whereas the figure for Lancasters was only 1.7 (in each case out of seven, or eight for special Pathfinders). Again, unlike a Lanc, there were three large bomb cells in the centre section of the wing on each side of the fuselage. Most 'Hallis' had the British Messier main landing gear, based on a giant magnesium casting, but the Mk V had a conventional Dowty unit built up from steel and dural tubing. The tailwheel was retractable in the Mk I, fixed in IIs and most IIIs and retractable in late marks.

There were many versions. Even standard bombers were often packed with high-power electronic countermeasures for No 100 Gp, or used for towing the Hamilcar, but of course Stirling IVs could also. Other Halifaxes were meteorological sensors.Several variants were painted white and did a great job with Coastal Command. Altogether the story of the Halifax is a magnificent one, deserving to be shouted from the roof-tops.

Devoid of any distinguishing fuselage codes, this Halifax I boasts unpainted exhaust glare shields on each of its four engine cowlings. This photograph was taken in January 1943

# HALIFAX III

There could hardly be a greater contrast between two cutaway drawings of the same aircraft as the Clark and Millar drawings of the Halifax. The styles of drawing are as utterly different as are the two versions of the aircraft depicted.

Though a bit of Halifax history is given with Clark's drawing, it is worth

running through the various marks here. The prototype established the span of the square-tipped wings as 98 ft 10 in, and had Handley Page's patented slats on the outer wings. Though power-driven turrets were fitted at the nose and tail, there was no mid-upper or ventral turret, hand-aimed beam guns being installed instead. The production Halifax I differed only in details, the most obvious being removal of the slats.

In the Mk II, the first major production version, the engines were 1280 hp Merlin XXs, incorporating the more efficient inlet and supercharger which were the first contribution to Rolls-Royce by Dr Stanley Hooker. The beam guns were replaced by a Boulton Paul two-gun dorsal turret similar to that used on the Lockheed Hudson and Ventura I. This high-drag feature was wisely removed from the Mk II Series I, along with the nose turret, which was replaced by a bluff aluminium fairing. Also, during Mk II production the radiators were replaced by a more efficient Morris block type, generally similar to those used on the Beaufighter II and Lancaster.

Quite early in production British Messier found themselves hard-pressed to keep pace with output of the main landing gears, based on a huge Elektron casting, so Dowty designed a more conventional steel-tube levered-suspension alternative. This was fitted to the Mk V, made by Fairey and Rootes, with the same variations and Series suffixes as the Mk II. The GR II and GR V were ultra-long-range versions for Coastal Command, painted sea grey and white and often fitted with an FN64 ventral turret, a 0.5 in Browning in a reinforced nose and four-blade propellers.

Where the bombers were concerned, most changes were made in order to increase flight performance, and this objective continued to be dominant. Accordingly, the Mk II Series IA introduced a completely new streamlined nose moulded in Perspex, with a single Vickers K gun pivoted in the centre. The six prominent fuel-jettison pipes were removed, a four-gun Boulton Paul dorsal turret was fitted, the tailwheel was made retractable, the astrodome (Max calls it an 'astral dome') was reduced in height, the radio antenna mast was replaced by attaching the wire to the direction-finding loop fairing, and smooth-finish paint was used on external surfaces. Several manufacturers also paid great attention to improving the fit of the bomb and landing-gear doors and other joints, and adding sealing tape where possible.

Most Mk II Series IA bombers had the Merlin XXII (unchanged ratings), and one aircraft was tested with the inner nacelles extended beyond the trailing edge. Another, designated Mk II Series II, was powered by two-stage Merlin 61s mounted lower down, with extended inner nacelles, driving four-

Framed by the port Hercules XVI engines, whose flame dampers are clearly visible, a factory-fresh Halifax III undergoes power checks prior to departing on its delivery flight

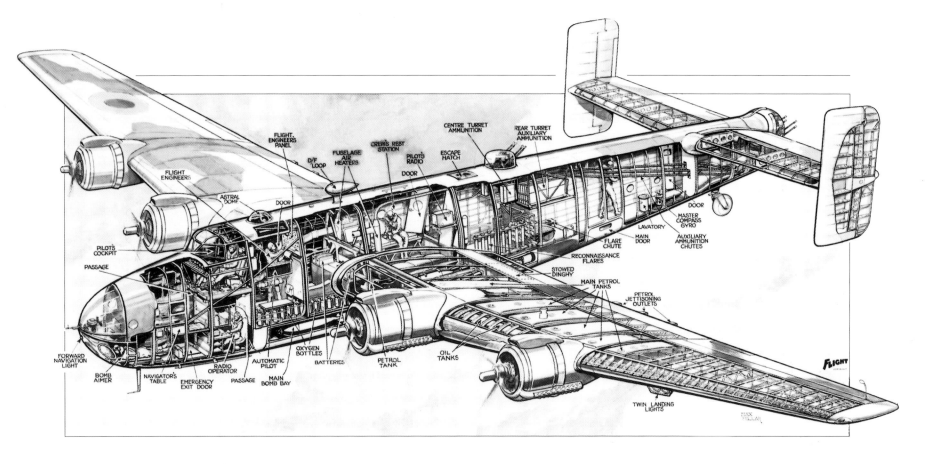

blade propellers. This was intended to lead to the high-altitude B IV, which was never built. On the other hand, several aircraft tested larger fins of rectangular form. These cured fin/rudder stalling and improved bombing accuracy, and became standard on all future versions.

First flown on 12 October 1942, the Mk III, illustrated here, switched to the 1615 hp Bristol Hercules XVI sleeve-valve radial. This enabled production Mk III aircraft, from summer 1943, to be cleared to 65,000 lb, 10,000 lb heavier than the Mk I. Some squadrons, suddenly learning about night fighters attacking from below, replaced the H$_2$S radar by a hand-aimed 0.5 in gun, and a few aircraft even had the FN 64 turret.

By 1944 the B III had the wings extended to rounded tips with a span of 104 ft, and this excellent version was the most numerous of all. All late-production aircraft had the vastly improved Rose tail turret, with two 0.5 in guns. Some IIIs, like Vs and VIIs (very like the later III) were equipped for paratroops and glider towing.

The ultimate bomber was the 320-mph B VI, with 1800 hp Hercules 100 engines and full tropicalization. The C VIII was a transport with armament removed, 11 passenger seats and the weapon bay fitted to take a giant projecting pannier pre-loaded with four tons of cargo. The A IX was an airborne forces transport with special navaids and equipped for paratroops and glider towing. There were many sub-versions, including civilianised Halifaxes and, postwar, extensively modified civil Haltons.

Max's drawing of an early B III was almost a throwback to earlier times, with cloudy background and crew at work. He concentrated on equipment rather than the basic aircraft, not bothering to annotate the Rotol constant-speed propellers, carburettor inlet ducts above the cowlings and long flame-damping exhaust pipes.

I do not know why he called the rear-turret magazines 'auxiliary ammuniton', and I think he must have been mistaken in showing fuel-jettison pipes.

# Hs 126

Ihave to say at the outset that I do not know whether this drawing is accurate or not. In the pre-War years Clark was not averse to inventing what went on inside German aircraft. In the 1960s this drawing was copied exactly by another British publisher, the only changes being to omit the 'wireless generator' and the spat from the tailwheel, but that doesn't mean a thing. It looks pretty authentic, especially as he took the trouble to do a couple of inset details, so I'll give our James the benefit of the doubt and assume it was done from published magazine articles, which is highly probable.

As is obvious, this aircraft was an exact German counterpart of the British Lysander, as a two-seat tactical observation machine, though it had no slats and never tried to equal the 'Lizzie's' short-field performance. The prototype, powered by a Jumo 210 inverted-vee engine, flew in late 1936. Oddly, the Hs 126 was planned as a derivative of the earlier Hs 122 with a Bramo Fafnir radial engine, and this ultimately became the standard engine, but the initial Hs 126A series were built in 1938 with the engine shown by Clark.

Many of the initial batches of Hs 126As served with the Condor Legion in Spain, and survivors went on to equip units of Franco's air force until the 1950s. A batch of 16 were ordered by the Royal Hellenic Air Force, and in 1940 these played a significant part in harassing the Italian army as it ineffectually tried to invade Greece. Thus, when Hitler came to the rescue of his ally, the Hs 126 found itself fighting both for and against the *Wehrmacht*.

By this time Clark was setting himself a high standard, and this drawing lays bare almost everything. Apart from the fabric-covered control surfaces, the airframe was all-metal stressed-skin, and the result was an extremely pleasant aircraft. Like so many wartime machines, early in its life in 1938 it seemed very modern and fast and by 1942 it was regarded as a mere hack with which to harass partisans and tow DFS 230 gliders. A South African told me these aircraft were much prized as captures in the Libyan desert, because they were handy utility transports, but that very few were available. Indeed, though total production was something over 780, the type made only a minor impact on the conflict and was soon replaced in frontline units by the Fw 189.

Clark may have based his drawing on an A-0 pre-production aircraft, especially as he indicated a red stripe on the tail with the swastika on a white disc. Most of this batch had the windmill-driven generator and spatted tailwheel. The fuel tank held 119 gal, so I am at a loss to explain why endurance was just two hours, giving a range of 400 miles. In the frontline the mainwheel spats were junked, as happened to spats everywhere in World War 2.

Clark clearly showed the fixed MG 17 firing ahead, with a 500-round belt, and the observer's MG 15 on an Arado swing-over mount, loaded with no fewer than 13 saddle magazines each feeding 75 rounds alternately from left and right spools. The observer also managed the big Zeiss Rb vertical topographic camera, as well as a hand-held camera normally clipped to the

The pilot keeps the engine running as the observer climbs out of the Hs 126 with a message for ground troops involved in hand-to-hand combat in the Crimea during the Soviet summer offensive of 1943

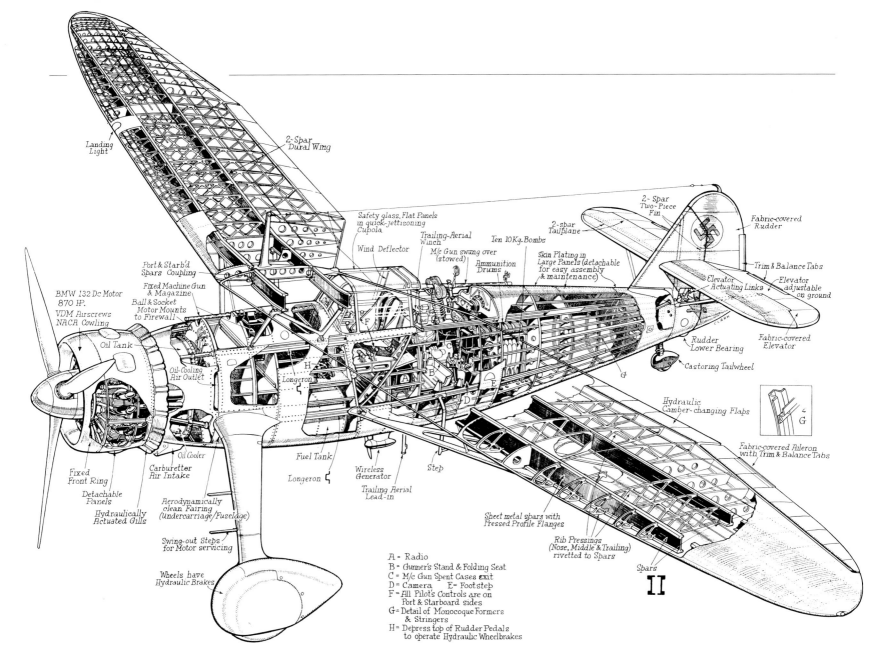

Landing Light

2-Spar Dural Wing

BMW 132 Dc Motor 870 H.P.
VDM Airscrews
NACA Cowling

Oil Tank

Port & Starb'd Spars Coupling

Fixed Machine Gun & Magazine

Ball & Socket Motor Mounts to Firewall

Oil-Cooling Air Outlet

Longeron

Safety glass, Flat Panels in quick-jettisoning Cupola

Wind Deflector

Trailing-Aerial Winch

M/c Gun swing over (stowed)

Ten 10 Kg. Bombs

Ammunition Drums

Skin Plating in Large Panels (detachable for easy assembly & maintenance)

2-Spar Two-Piece Fin

2-spar Tailplane

Elevator Actuating Links

Fabric-covered Rudder

Trim & Balance Tabs

Elevator adjustable on ground

Rudder Lower Bearing

Castoring Tailwheel

Fabric-covered Elevator

Fixed Front Ring

Detachable Panels

Hydraulically Actuated Gills

Oil Cooler

Carburetter Air Intake

Aerodynamically clean Fairing (undercarriage/Fuselage)

Swing-out Steps for Motor servicing

Wheels have Hydraulic Brakes

Fuel Tank

Longeron

Wireless Generator

Trailing Aerial Lead-in

Step

Sheet metal spars with Pressed Profile Flanges

Rib Pressings (Nose, Middle & Trailing) rivetted to Spars

Hydraulic Camber-changing Flaps

Fabric-covered Aileron with Trim & Balance Tabs

Spars

A = Radio
B = Gunner's Stand & Folding Seat
C = M/c Gun Spent Cases exit
D = Camera    E = Footstep
F = All Pilot's Controls are on Port & Starboard sides
G = Detail of Monocoque Formers & Stringers
H = Depress top of Rudder Pedals to operate Hydraulic Wheelbrakes

II

left side of the cockpit. I do not believe there was any sighting system for the ten SC10 bombs, whose location must have had an influence on the centre of gravity. Clark did not indicate that immediately below the wing strut on the left side it was possible to attach a rack for a single SC100 (220.5-lb) bomb.

In the first year of the War the Luftwaffe had it all its own way in Poland and the French campaign, and the Hs 126A, with the BMW engine, flew hun-dreds of missions on observation, strafing and bombing. By this time the pro-duction version was the Hs 126B, with the more powerful 900-hp Bramo Fafnir, but times were getting harder. In the desert a single *Staffel* suffered severe attrition, while on the vast Eastern Front these aircraft, like their Henschel predecessors, the Hs 123 dive-bombers, soon found themselves rel-egated to nocturnal harassing raids and training.

# Do 17/215

At the start of World War 2 the Luftwaffe's frontline bombing strength included important contributions made by Dornier aircraft roughly in the class of the Blenheim, with engines of around 1000 hp. Even the British general public knew that they had such slim fuselages they were called 'flying pencils'. The latest version was thought to be the Do 215, though when this drawing was published a second time, in *The Aeroplane Spotter* for 17 April 1941, the caption commented 'The Do 17Z is structurally the same as the Do 215 except that the DB 601 12-cyl inverted-vee liquid-cooled motors are replaced by two 1000 hp Bramo Fafnir 9-cyl radial air-cooled motors'. So the author and his friends made models of the Do 215. We had no idea that this was an unimportant version for export customers.

Another universal belief was that the cunning Germans, having started to rearm in defiance of the Versailles Treaty, cloaked their deadly new bombers in the guise of airliners, with false civil registrations. In the case of the Do 17 the reverse was true. The first of three prototypes was flown in autumn 1934 as a six-seat high-speed airliner. It had a modern stressed-skin airframe, because nobody had longer experience of such structures than Dornier Metallbauten. Powered by two 660 hp BMW engines, it had a high wing which merged at the roots into a body only 1.4-m (55 in) from floor to ceiling, so the passengers had no chance of standing up inside! Other features included slotted flaps and fully retractable landing gear.

This DB 601-engined Do 215B-0 was one of 18 ordered by the Swedish Air Force but then embargoed upon completion in Germany. They all later served with the Luftwaffe

Though fast and attractive, the Do 17 was an almost obvious non-starter as a passenger transport, and after being evaluated by Deutsche Luft Hansa the prototypes languished unwanted. By sheer chance a Luft Hansa captain who had been a Dornier test pilot decided to try one of them out. When he had done so he immediately told the air ministry in Berlin that in his opinion the design ought to be developed as a bomber. The result was a succession of Do 17 bomber versions, with a new twin-finned tail and powered by various BMW, Bramo and Daimler-Benz vee, inverted-vee or air-cooled radial engines. The version drawn by Clark as an inset was probably meant to be the Do 17P, powered by 865 hp BMW 132N (not 132Dc) engines. They usually had only two cameras, but always had a third MG 15 firing down to the rear from a hatch in the floor. In the Condor Legion in Spain they were quite modern aircraft, though defence downward and to the rear proved almost non-existent because the belly gun had such a small field of fire. In 1940 some had two additional MG 15s installed, but by 1941 the P was found only in the Balkans. I am puzzled by Clark's extraordinary location of the direction-finding loop, which was actually above the wing just to the left of the aircraft centreline.

Like so many late-1930s bombers, the Do 17 began with three individually aimed machine guns and then tried to do better. In 1938 Dornier designed a completely new forward fuselage making provision for a crew of four (five in one version). The key factor was an increase in depth so that a prone gunner could aim a ventral MG 15 with a much wider field of fire than the unsatisfactory hatch. The nose was redesigned with numerous flat glazed panels, and the entire crew compartment was covered by a glazed canopy. The new family were designated as various sub-types of Do 17Z.

Four men in close proximity was thought to improve morale, and it was repeated in several other Luftwaffe bombers. Defensive armament at first remained just three small guns, the front MG 15 being either fixed and fired by the pilot or gimbal-mounted and aimed by the navigator/bomb-aimer. In the Battle of Britain two extra MG 15 guns were added to fire to either side through beam windows, and a few aircraft had locally contrived twin-gun lash-ups firing to the rear. Bomb load was one tonne (2205 lb). Like some of the slim-body versions, the slotted flaps were replaced by the split type.

Standard engine of the Do 17Z was the Bramo (BMW) Fafnir radial, rated at 1000 hp. This was only marginally adequate for an aircraft whose weight had been appreciably increased, but the 17Z proved a reliable and popular aircraft whose only drawback was vulnerability to modern fighters.

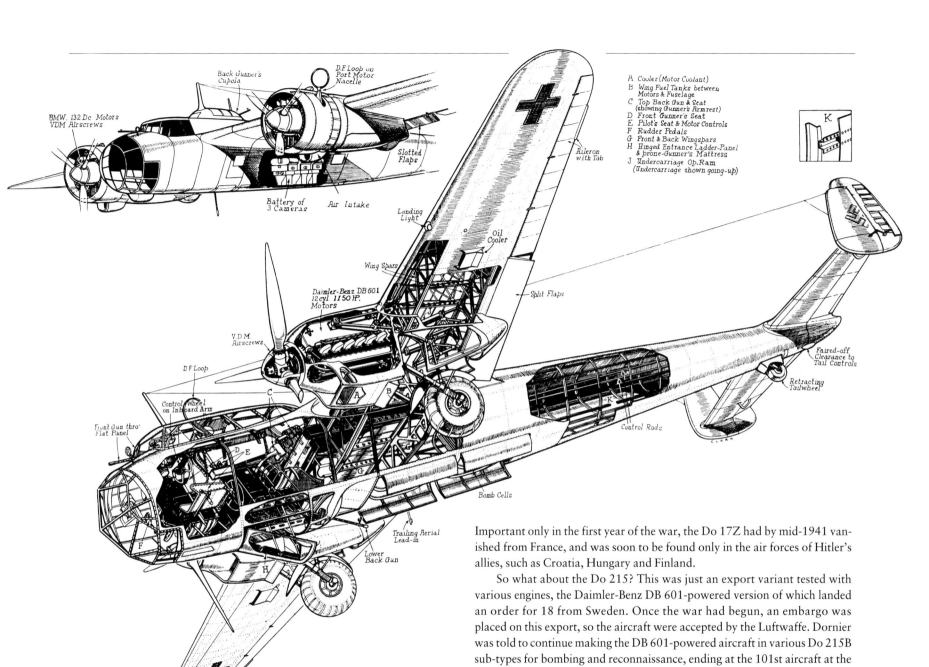

Back Gunner's Cupola

D.F.Loop on Port Motor Nacelle

BMW. 132 Dc Motors VDM Airscrews

Slotted Flaps

Battery of 3 Cameras

Air Intake

A  Cooler (Motor Coolant)
B  Wing Fuel Tanks between Motors & Fuselage
C  Top Back Gun & Seat (showing Gunner's Armrest)
D  Front Gunner's Seat
E  Pilot's Seat & Motor Controls
F  Rudder Pedals
G  Front & Back Wingspars
H  Hinged Entrance Ladder-Panel & prone-Gunner's Mattress
J  Undercarriage Op.Ram (Undercarriage shown going-up)

K

Aileron with Tab

Landing Light

Oil Cooler

Wing Spars

Daimler-Benz DB 601 12 cyl 1150 H.P. Motors

Split Flaps

V.D.M. Airscrews

Faired-off Clearance to Tail Controls

Retracting Tailwheel

D.F. Loop

Control Wheel on Inboard Arm

Control Rods

Front Gun thro' Flat Panel

Bomb Cells

Trailing Aerial Lead-in

Lower Back Gun

Important only in the first year of the war, the Do 17Z had by mid-1941 vanished from France, and was soon to be found only in the air forces of Hitler's allies, such as Croatia, Hungary and Finland.

So what about the Do 215? This was just an export variant tested with various engines, the Daimler-Benz DB 601-powered version of which landed an order for 18 from Sweden. Once the war had begun, an embargo was placed on this export, so the aircraft were accepted by the Luftwaffe. Dornier was told to continue making the DB 601-powered aircraft in various Do 215B sub-types for bombing and reconnaissance, ending at the 101st aircraft at the beginning of 1941. In mid-1941 one was modified into a nightfighter with the first version of Lichtenstein airborne radar. A succession of victories with this aircraft scored by Oblt Ludwig Becker overcame aircrew scepticism of new technology, and opened the way to the Luftwaffe's formidable force of radar-equipped nightfighters, almost all of which were Bf 110s or Ju 88s.

# Bf 110

When one considers the wealth of material on Luftwaffe aircraft published in open literature in Germany in 1936-40, and the fact that virtually all these aircraft could be studied from public highways until after the outbreak of war, the apparent British ignorance of them passes understanding. In 1937, as a ten-year-old, I was taken by an uncle to the Bayerische Flugzeugwerke factory and design offices outside Augsburg. There, among a feast of Bf 109s (and at that time nobody in Britain had ever thought of calling them Me 109s), was an impressive twin-engined fighter called, not surprisingly, the Bf 110. We walked around it, and I touched parts of it. Willy Messerschmitt told me it was 'just as fast as the Bf 109'.

Came the war, and we British appeared to forget everything we must have learned about German aircraft. By 12 January 1940 we even had the odd crashed Bf 110 in France to study, but on that date a drawing appeared in *The Aeroplane* that I am amazed Clark was prepared to put his name to. By this time called (only by us) the Me 110, both the text and cutaway were a collection of ignorant supposition and incorrect guesses. Enough of that!

A little over a year later this ignorance could no longer be sustained. Though he took the same viewpoint, Clark prepared a completely fresh drawing, basing it mainly on a Bf 110C-4, though by this time we had various subtypes to choose from. The contrast between the two drawings is total. It is, of course, the second drawing that is reproduced here. By this time it was realised that the coolant radiators in the Bf 110s we were meeting were like those of the DB-engined 109, snuggled into the underside of the wing out-board of the rear part of the nacelle. We also discovered that there were four MG 17s in the top of the nose, that (except in recce versions) there were two cannon under the cockpit instead of under the nose and that the main under-carriage had a single leg inboard of the wheel – in his original effort Clark had invented a totally different arrangement and drawn it most convincingly; can't trust nobody! This time, instead of drawing ovals, Clark got the fins and rudders right, and he also realised that the tailplane was pivoted, which in those days was unusual. Its incidence was automatically reduced when the flaps were lowered, this action also causing the ailerons to droop.

I think he got his main spar too far aft – having correctly said that it was at 39 per cent chord, he drew it at least half-way back. Surprisingly, having identified the fixed machine guns, he might have said the cannon were MG FFs and that the rear gun was an MG 15. I am intrigued by his label saying that the 'glasshouse' could be jettisoned. Bill Green, who ought to know, said that in the DB 605-engined nightfighters the extra crewman (radar operator) in the middle would have been trapped if the gunner had been killed, blocking his way out. I remember the roof of the Bf 110G hinging open not only above the pilot but also behind the radio mast (the rear canopy was hinged to the right), quite apart from the aft end where, in many G-versions, there was an upward-firing pair of cannon which blocked the exit in that direction.

In all the wartime versions prior to the G, the engines were Daimler-Benz DB 601s rated at 1100 or 1350 hp. To get the centre of gravity in the right place they were deeply recessed into the wing, so the air inlet to the super-

Surrounded by empty fuel drums, these derelict Bf 110s have been abandoned where they sat during the German retreat northwards through Italy in late 1943. They have already been stripped of their nose cannon, engines and tail units

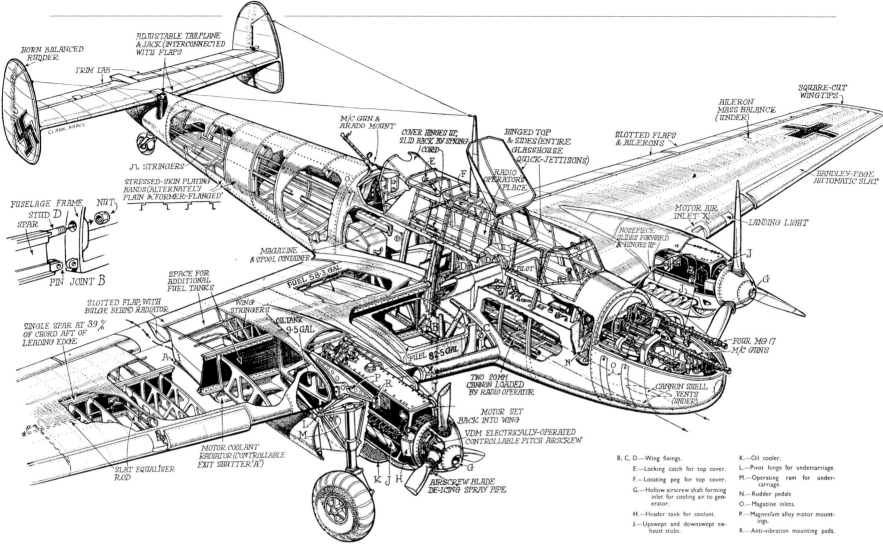

HORN BALANCED RUDDER

TRIM TAB

ADJUSTABLE TAILPLANE & JACK (INTERCONNECTED WITH FLAPS)

CLARK. ARAeS

⊓ STRINGERS

STRESSED-SKIN PLATING BANDS (ALTERNATELY PLAIN & 'FORMER-FLANGED')

FUSELAGE FRAME STUD D NUT SPAR

PIN JOINT B

SPACE FOR ADDITIONAL FUEL TANKS

SLOTTED FLAP, WITH BULGE BEHIND RADIATOR

SINGLE SPAR AT 39% OF CHORD AFT OF LEADING EDGE

SLAT EQUALISER ROD

MAGAZINE & SPOOL CONTAINER

M/C GUN & ARADO MOUNT

COVER HINGES UP, SLID BACK BY SPRING CORD

FUEL 58·3 GAL

WING STRINGERS

OIL TANK 9·5 GAL

FUEL 82·5 GAL

MOTOR COOLANT RADIATOR (CONTROLLABLE EXIT SHUTTER 'A')

HINGED TOP & SIDES (ENTIRE GLASSHOUSE QUICK-JETTISONS)

RADIO OPERATOR'S PLACE

NOSEPIECE SLIDES FORWARD & HINGES UP

PILOT

TWO 20MM CANNON LOADED BY RADIO OPERATOR

MOTOR SET BACK INTO WING

VDM ELECTRICALLY-OPERATED CONTROLLABLE PITCH AIRSCREW

KJH

AIRSCREW BLADE DE-ICING SPRAY PIPE

SLOTTED FLAPS & AILERONS

AILERON MASS BALANCE (UNDER)

SQUARE-CUT WINGTIPS

HANDLEY-PAGE AUTOMATIC SLAT

MOTOR AIR INLET 'X'

LANDING LIGHT

FOUR MG 17 M/C GUNS

CANNON SHELL VENTS (UNDER)

B, C, D.—Wing fixings.
   E.—Locking catch for top cover.
   F.—Locating peg for top cover.
   G.—Hollow airscrew shaft forming inlet for cooling air to generator.
   H.—Header tank for coolant.
   J.—Upswept and downswept exhaust stubs.

K.—Oil cooler.
L.—Pivot hinge for undercarriage.
M.—Operating ram for undercarriage.
N.—Rudder pedals.
O.—Magazine inlets.
P.—Magnesium alloy motor mountings.
R.—Anti-vibration mounting pads.

charger on the left side was in the leading edge instead of being on the cowling. Clark drew a detail showing the simple construction of the rear fuselage, almost exactly as on the Bf 109 (whereas the Me 210/410 were split down the centreline). The label 'MAGAZINE & SPOOL CONTAINER' may need some explaining. The radio operator not only manned the MG 15 rear gun, which he reloaded by taking 75-round saddle magazines (looking like a letter B on its side) and clipping them on top, but he also had to reload the MG FF cannon by heaving the 60-round drums out of the large box, each drum weighing 63 lb, and clipping them on the cannon in the floor. Presumably it was these drums which Clark called spools.

As noted elsewhere in the Me 210 story, the Bf 110 had to soldier on to the end of the war. A total of about 6050 were delivered, and in 1943-44 they shot down more RAF heavy bombers than all other nightfighters combined – a total of thousands rather than hundreds. Few aircraft have been made to carry so many extra items of equipment, including extra guns, radar and a host of stores beneath the wings. I was fortunate to fly a late G-model, devoid of all the paraphernalia, and thought I had seldom encountered a nicer aircraft. Only many years later did I read that it was supposed to have a disconcerting tendency to swing on take-off and landing. What a pity that not one is airworthy today!

# Ju 87B

Three of the most important aircraft of the War were the Fairey Battle, Junkers Ju 87 and Ilyushin Il-2. All were single-engined frontline attack machines, and all were easy meat for fighters, but there the similarity ended. The Il-2, the famous *Shturmovik*, was heavily armoured and had such devastating firepower it knocked out half the heavy tanks on the Eastern Front. The Ju 87 Stuka was designed to dive vertically and thus place heavy bombs on bridges, crossroads or ships, and in 1937-40 it caused devastation and terror from Spain to the English Channel, via Poland. In contrast, the Battle was designed for level bombing and was important merely because of the fact that, with the Blenheim, it almost wiped out an entire generation of gallant, fully-operational aircrew, a crippling loss to a still-small RAF.

Today, the best-known of this trio is probably the Stuka. This word is merely the abbreviated form of the long German word meaning a dive-bomber, but today whenever it is used everyone knows the Ju 87 is meant. In 1928-31 Junkers had produced quite a number of radial-engined K 47s for several air forces, and in Germany these were specifically used to research the

StG 3 *Geschwaderkommodore* Oberstleutnant Walter Siegel flew this Ju 87D-1/Trop until it was abandoned near Derna, in Libya, in mid-1942. It was assigned to 8./StG 3 at the time

accuracy possible in steep dive attacks. Results were encouraging, dives at 90° giving hits almost always within 30 m (100 ft) of the aiming point. As a result, from 1933 Dipl-Ing Hermann Pohlmann led the design of the Ju 87, and the first prototype (using a Kestrel engine which Rolls-Royce thought was going direct to Warnemünde to be installed in their Heinkel He 70) made its first flight in April 1935.

From the outset it had a structure of almost unbreakable strength, with a stressed skin which Junkers no longer stiffened by corrugations. Features included a sharply cranked wing (the reason for which was far from obvious), fixed 'trousered' landing gear, patented 'double wing' trailing-edge surfaces which served progressively as ailerons outboard and flaps inboard, a twin-finned tail, and tandem cockpits for the pilot and radio-operator/gunner with upward-hinged canopies.

By the time the production Ju 87A went to war in Spain in late 1937 it had a single fin, dive brakes under the outer wings, an MG 17 7.92 mm gun in the right wing, an MG 15 in the rear cockpit, a crutch for a 500-kg (1102-lb) bomb, and lines painted on the window beside the pilot which, when aligned with the horizon, denoted dive angles of up to 90°.

In Spain the Luftwaffe's Condor Legion perfected the technique. When *The Aeroplane* published Clark's drawing on 23 February 1940 it repeated an account of these operations which had been published in June 1939 by the Junkers Nachrichten. It explained how the Ju 87s attacked in a *Kette* (chain), rolling over into the vertical dive one after the other. What the lavishly produced company magazine did not report was that on one occasion a complete *Kette* flew, one after the other, into the ground.

The result was that, with the Askania instrument firm, an automatic system was devised. When a red light appeared on the panel, triggered by a sensitive contact altimeter, the pilot pressed a button on the stick to initiate a pull-out at 6g which guaranteed that the Stuka would avoid terra firma!

The Luftwaffe started World War 2 at 04.26 on 1 September 1939 with an attack on a Polish bridge by three Ju 87Bs. This was the version drawn by Clark, with a 1200-hp Junkers Jumo 211Da engine with direct injection, redesigned fuselage, sliding canopies, MG 17s in both wings and, to strike terror, air-driven sirens on the modified landing gear with spats instead of trousers. Of course, it was able to play its central role in Hitler's Blitzkrieg (lightning war) solely because the Luftwaffe had command of the sky.

I never got aboard a Ju 87, but Capt Eric M 'Winkle' Brown, RN, included the later Ju 87D among his 487 types (487 counting, for example, all

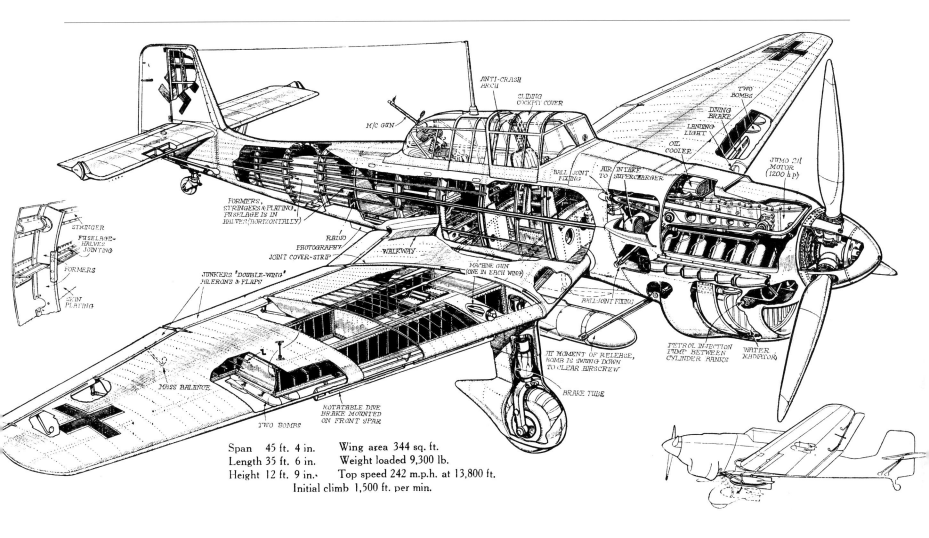

STRINGER

FUSELAGE-
HALVES
JOINTING

FORMERS

SKIN
PLATING

ANTI-CRASH
ARCH

SLIDING
COCKPIT COVER

M/C GUN

TWO
BOMBS

DIVING
BRAKE

LANDING
LIGHT

OIL
COOLER

JUMO 211
MOTOR
(1200 h.p.)

FORMERS,
STRINGERS & PLATING.
FUSELAGE IS IN
HALVES (HORIZONTALLY)

BALL JOINT
FIXING

AIR INTAKE
TO SUPERCHARGER

RADIO

PHOTOGRAPHY

JOINT COVER-STRIP

WALKWAY

JUNKERS 'DOUBLE-WING'
AILERONS & FLAPS

MACHINE GUN
(ONE IN EACH WING)

BALL-JOINT FIXING

MASS BALANCE

AT MOMENT OF RELEASE,
BOMB IS SWUNG DOWN
TO CLEAR AIRSCREW

PETROL INJECTION
PUMP BETWEEN
CYLINDER RANKS

WATER
RADIATOR

BRAKE TUBE

ROTATABLE DIVE
BRAKE MOUNTED
ON FRONT SPAR

TWO BOMBS

Span     45 ft. 4 in.
Length  35 ft. 6 in.
Height   12 ft. 9 in.

Wing area 344 sq. ft.
Weight loaded 9,300 lb.
Top speed 242 m.p.h. at 13,800 ft.
Initial climb 1,500 ft. per min.

the Spitfires and Seafires as one). Among the improvements in the D version were a more powerful Jumo 211J, with the oil cooler under it instead of above, coolant radiators under the wings and a new canopy.

Writing in *Air International*, he recalled 'From its broad-blade Junkers VS 11 propeller to the trim tabs on its big square-cut rudder it gave an impression of being a lot of aeroplane for one engine to pull . . . Once settled down to the cruise the feeling of vulnerability became almost oppressive, accentuated by the high position of the pilot's seat and the good visibility through the large glasshouse canopy . . . A dive angle of 90° is a pretty palpitating experience, for it feels as if the aircraft is over the vertical . . . but the Ju 87 was a genuine 90° screamer! For some indefinable reason it felt right, standing on its nose.'

Clark's drawing was of the intermediate quality appropriate to the 'Phoney War' period. It was done long before he had even a crashed example to study 'in the flesh', and he gave it pre-war markings. The main radiator in the Ju 87B was under the engine, and did not use water but Glysantin (ethylene glycol). Much of the detail must have come from the Junkers magazine mentioned earlier. The drawing was reproduced in *The Aeroplane Spotter* for 20 March 1941.

By this time Clark could have added the prominent siren at the top of the landing-gear leg, but the only change he made was to replace his 'Junkers-Hamilton' bracket-type propeller by the VDM constant-speed type actually fitted.

# Do 217E-2

This aircraft was yet another example of Britain's seemingly non-existent intelligence prior to the War. The prototype flew in August 1938, and six had flown from the Dornier factory at Friedrichshafen before the War. Any kid could have taken pictures. Even after the conflict had begun, the later versions could be seen on flight test from neutral Switzerland, yet we somehow managed to avoid learning of the Do 217's existence. At last, in January 1942 *The Aeroplane Spotter* published a fuzzy picture of the Do 217, showing that it had grotesquely swollen engine nacelles, crowing that it did not bear the German censor's stamp and thus was 'a real cat out of the bag'. Unfortunately, by this time downed examples could be examined, and their nacelles were quite normal.

On the face of it, the Do 217 ought to have been formidable, even though it perpetuated the classic Luftwaffe formula for bombers. This was to use two engines, giving maximum speed around 500 km/h (311 mph) and service ceiling not much over 20,000 ft, making it a nice easy target for an intercepting fighter. What made the Do 217 a bit better was that it could carry no less than four tonnes (8818 lb) of bombs, or a torpedo internally, and the upper and lower rear guns were the excellent 13 mm MG 131, the dorsal gun being in an EDL131 electrically driven turret. At the front were a fixed MG 151/15, and in the E3 version, as drawn by Max Millar, a hand-aimed 20 mm MG FF for attacks on shipping. There were usually two beam-firing MG 15s, though Max drew four. Some aircraft had twin MG 81s firing aft from the tailcone.

This tailcone had originally incorporated a large petal-type airbrake for dive bombing, but after prolonged troubles the idea of dive bombing was abandoned. The auto-pullout tabs on the elevators were retained but never used, as was the very long torsion tube which had extended from the cockpit to the tail to drive the dive brake! Henceforth, the E-series, as used by KG 2 from French bases, skulked over Britain by night at over 20,000 ft – and still considered themselves lucky to get back. It was 1942 before the Do 217 became operational in quantity, and by this time Beaufighter and Mosquito nightfighter crews had learned how to interpret flickering green blips, so it was a totally different ball-game from the Blitz of 1940.

Moreover, whereas everyone in the Luftwaffe liked the Do 17Z, the Do 217 was from the start a reluctant beast to tame. It tried to swing on take-off, and in cruising flight tended to oscillate about all axes, especially in yaw, even after the slats had been added along the inner edges of the fins. The E-series Do 217 had only one thing going for it and that was the BMW 801, which is featured in cutaway form later in this book. Coming up astern, an intercepting nightfighter crew saw tiny red pinpoints of light from the numerous fishtails. In contrast, the exhausts from the He 219A nightfighter of 1944 were brilliant golden beacons visible from many miles away!

As Max showed, the ailerons drooped with the flaps on take-off and landing. Every little helped, because the Do 217 had an exceptionally high wing loading, and a full-load take-off was a real challenge. Today, we would probably replace the split flaps by Fowlers, extend them to the tips and use spoilers for lateral control. The flaps, like the landing gear and almost everything else on the Do 217, were driven electrically. Their maximum angle was 55°, and selecting flaps down automatically screwed on negative tailplane

Although perhaps not as fast or nimble as other Luftwaffe nightfighters, the Do 217N-2/R22 *Rustsätze* was nevertheless a formidable weapon, packed with a deadly mix of 7.92 mm MG 17 machine guns and 20 mm MG 151 cannon, firing both horizontally and at 70° angles

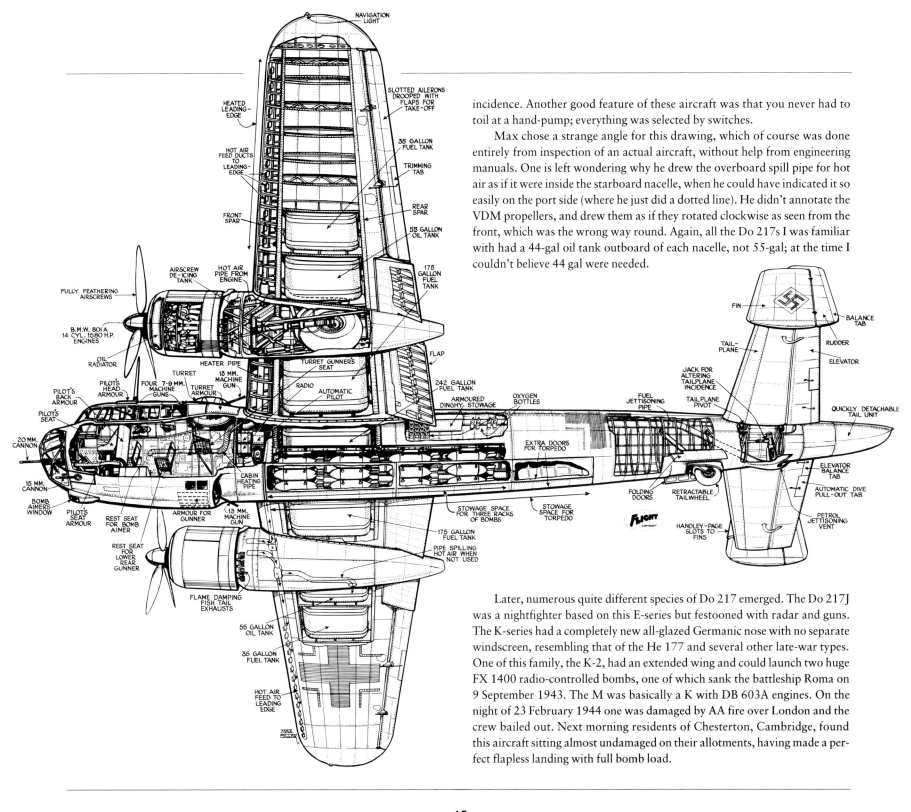

incidence. Another good feature of these aircraft was that you never had to toil at a hand-pump; everything was selected by switches.

Max chose a strange angle for this drawing, which of course was done entirely from inspection of an actual aircraft, without help from engineering manuals. One is left wondering why he drew the overboard spill pipe for hot air as if it were inside the starboard nacelle, when he could have indicated it so easily on the port side (where he just did a dotted line). He didn't annotate the VDM propellers, and drew them as if they rotated clockwise as seen from the front, which was the wrong way round. Again, all the Do 217s I was familiar with had a 44-gal oil tank outboard of each nacelle, not 55-gal; at the time I couldn't believe 44 gal were needed.

Later, numerous quite different species of Do 217 emerged. The Do 217J was a nightfighter based on this E-series but festooned with radar and guns. The K-series had a completely new all-glazed Germanic nose with no separate windscreen, resembling that of the He 177 and several other late-war types. One of this family, the K-2, had an extended wing and could launch two huge FX 1400 radio-controlled bombs, one of which sank the battleship Roma on 9 September 1943. The M was basically a K with DB 603A engines. On the night of 23 February 1944 one was damaged by AA fire over London and the crew bailed out. Next morning residents of Chesterton, Cambridge, found this aircraft sitting almost undamaged on their allotments, having made a perfect flapless landing with full bomb load.

# Fw 190

In the autumn of 1941 RAF fighter pilots engaged in offensive sweeps over northern France began to encounter disconcertingly agile fighters with a radial engine. The first engagement resulted in a 3-0 win by four of the enemy over a much larger force of Spitfire Mk Vs. In London the official view was that these unknown fighters might be 'captured French Curtiss Hawks'. This the RAF pilots found hard to believe, because these new enemies could out-perform the Mk VB on every count except possibly turning circle. Gradually our intelligence machine noticed in German magazines advertisements claiming that the Focke-Wulf Fw 190 was the fastest fighter in the world. Had they spoken to any small boys around Bremen airport in the last three months of peace they might have learned about this fighter two years earlier, because the prototype was taxiing there in May 1939, and was on flight test from 1 June.

No information appeared even in *The Aeroplane Spotter* until 26 March 1942, when readers were told about 'the Fw 190H'. This was another of the pointless designations invented by someone in London. The report stated 'The Fw 190H has not appeared to be very formidable. The Spitfire appears to have the whip hand in combat'. Wars are not won by wishful thinking, and even when, by an amazing bit of luck, we captured an intact example on 23 June 1942, the redoubtable *Spotter* scorned 'its short range . . . the supply of only 115 gallons . . .', omitting to note that Spitfires had only 85 gallons.

Gradually we admitted that the Fw 190 was an absolutely outstanding fighter, with no deficiencies whatsoever. It was a shock to hear on the one o'clock news at the time Peter (now Sir Peter) Masefield reveal that the armament was four cannon and two machine guns, and moreover that two of the cannon were of the formidable Mauser 151/20 type with high muzzle velocity and high rate of fire, as well as electrically fired ammunition. Aircraft designers in the Allied camp studied the installation of the engine in order to see how an air-cooled radial could power such an impressive fighter. Not least, they were astonished at the all-electric complexity of the Fw 190, which had small and large electric actuators all over it, as well as an unprecedented electro-mechanical computer to give total control of the engine.

Jimmy Clark was the first artist let loose on the captured fighter at Farnborough, and he did an outstanding drawing, bearing in mind that nothing could actually be cut open to show him what was inside. He worked at such pressure that he found he had used letter 'A' for two quite different things, and also used 'J' for the rods that retained the beautiful clear-view canopy and the pivoted anchors that slid along them. When he got to 'Z' he began again using small letters, jumping from 'b' to 'd'. He got in a muddle over 'U' and 'j', and in an inset made 'U' look like 'u'. I was puzzled by 'FUEL 51' under the cockpit, until I realised he didn't have room to add 'GAL'.

ABOVE Oberleutnant Armin Faber's 'gift' to the RAF took the form of this Fw 190A-3, formerly of III./JG 2
LEFT An anonymous Fw 190 cruises at height over German farmland in late 1942

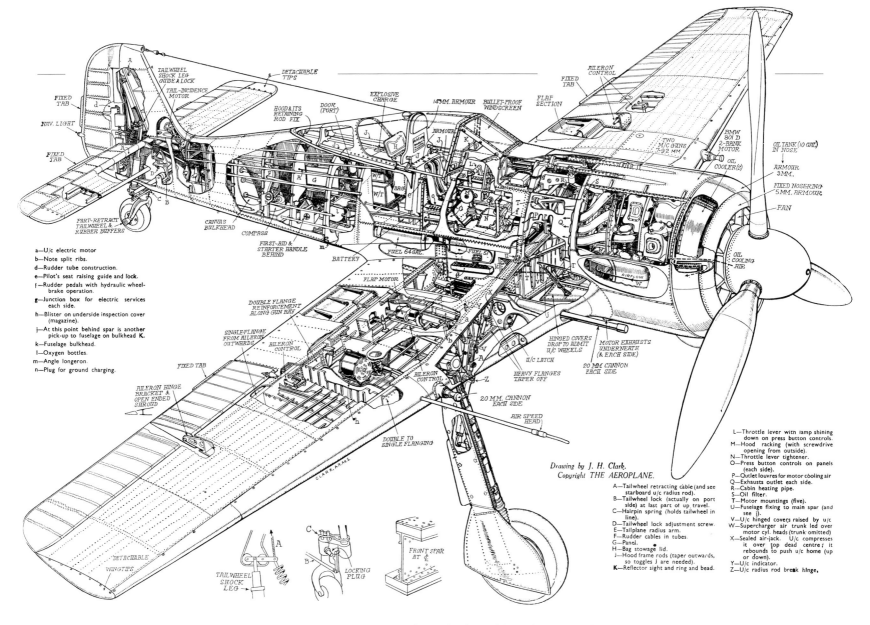

FIXED TAB
NAV. LIGHT
FIXED TAB
TAILWHEEL SHOCK LEG GUIDE & LOCK
TAIL-INCIDENCE MOTOR
DETACHABLE TIPS
EXPLOSIVE CHARGE
HOOD & ITS RETAINING ROD FIX
DOOR (PORT)
14MM. ARMOUR
BULLET-PROOF WINDSCREEN
ARMOUR
AILERON CONTROL
FIXED TAB
FLAP SECTION
BMW 801 D 2-BANK MOTOR
TWO M/C GUNS 7·92 MM
OIL COOLER(S)
OIL TANK (10 GAL) IN NOSE
ARMOUR 3MM.
FIXED NOSERING 5MM. ARMOUR
FAN
PART-RETRACT TAILWHEEL & RUBBER BUFFERS

a—U/c electric motor
b—Note split ribs.
d—Rudder tube construction.
e—Pilot's seat raising guide and lock.
f—Rudder pedals with hydraulic wheel-brake operation.
g—Junction box for electric services each side.
h—Blister on underside inspection cover (magazine).
j—At this point behind spar is another pick-up to fuselage on bulkhead K.
k—Fuselage bulkhead.
l—Oxygen bottles.
m—Angle longeron.
n—Plug for ground charging.

CANVAS BULKHEAD
COMPASS
FIRST-AID & STARTER HANDLE BEHIND
BATTERY
FUEL 64 GAL.
FUEL 51
FLAP MOTOR
OIL COOLING AIR

FIXED TAB
DOUBLE FLANGE REINFORCEMENT ALONG GUN BAY
SINGLE-FLANGE FROM AILERON OUTWARDS
AILERON CONTROL
HINGED COVERS DROP TO ADMIT U/C WHEELS
MOTOR EXHAUSTS UNDERNEATH (& EACH SIDE)
U/C LATCH
AILERON CONTROL
HEAVY FLANGES TAPER OFF
20 MM. CANNON EACH SIDE
U/C INDICATOR

AILERON HINGE BRACKET & OPEN ENDED SHROUD
20 MM. CANNON EACH SIDE.
AIR SPEED HEAD

DETACHABLE WINGTIPS
DOUBLE TO SINGLE FLANGING

Drawing by J. H. Clark.
Copyright THE AEROPLANE.

A—Tailwheel retracting cable (and see starboard u/c radius rod).
B—Tailwheel lock (actually on port side) at last part of up travel.
C—Hairpin spring (holds tailwheel in line).
D—Tailwheel lock adjustment screw.
E—Tailplane radius arm.
F—Rudder cables in tubes.
G—Panel.
H—Bag stowage lid.
J—Hood frame rods (taper outwards, so toggles J are needed).
K—Reflector sight and ring and bead.

L—Throttle lever with lamp shining down on press button controls.
M—Hood racking (with screwdrive opening from outside).
N—Throttle lever tightener.
O—Press button controls on panels (each side).
P—Outlet louvres for motor cooling air
Q—Exhausts outlet each side.
R—Cabin heating pipe.
S—Oil filter.
T—Motor mountings (five).
U—Fuselage fixing to main spar (and see j).
V—U/c hinged covers raised by u/c
W—Supercharger air trunk led over motor cyl. heads (trunk omitted)
X—Sealed air-jack. U/c compresses it over top dead centre; it rebounds to push u/c home (up or down).
Y—U/c indicator.
Z—U/c radius rod break hinge.

FRONT SPAR AT ₵
TAILWHEEL SHOCK LEG
LOCKING PLUG

Long after the war *Macdonald* published Bill Green's masterwork *Warplanes of the Third Reich*, in which appeared an exact copy of Clark's drawing with occasional trivial changes (such as the fuel-tank shading) and errors (such as all the stringer rivets being continued to the wingtips), and with numbered annotations. Later still John Weal did a completely fresh drawing from the same viewpoint, and later still Mike Badrocke did the best drawing of all, but of an Fw 190A-8 from a completely different aspect.

I doubt if any aircraft cutaway has been studied with such avid interest as this valuable effort by Clark in the summer of 1942. It was a matter of life and

death, and though learning about the enemy doesn't necessarily make him easier to shoot down, at least it removes the fear one feels for the unknown.

This was far from the case with the Fw 190. The more one studied it, the greater one respected the airframe, systems, armament, pilot view and, not least, its superb combat agility, with a rate of roll that hardly any Allied aircraft could match. Something like 19,500 were built, though as with all German wartime mass-production aircraft no exact total is possible. Dozens of sub-types carried an incredible diversity of armament fits, including a torpedo or a 1.8-tonne (3968-lb) bomb!

# GERMAN 'TWINS' IN DETAIL

Instead of presenting a whole aircraft, these detail drawings are reproduced complete with their captions as they appeared in *The Aeroplane* for 18 October 1940. They give a flavour of the time.

At that date the Battle of Britain was fast being replaced by the 'night Blitz', which was far less costly to the Luftwaffe, but did almost nothing to bring about a speedy German victory. The official end of the great daylight battle was 31 October. By this time the Luftwaffe had lost 1733 aircraft, the majority of which were brought down over the British Isles. It was therefore much harder to sustain the previous ignorance of German aircraft.

Nevertheless, we still persisted in refusing to give some of the most important types their correct designations. The classic cases, of course, were the Messerschmitt 109 and 110. To this day many of the fighter pilots who fought these aircraft find it hard to believe that they were actually the Bf 109 and Bf 110. Indeed, a letter published in the (US) Air Force Magazine for May 1995 actually states 'It never was called the Bf 109'! To muddy the waters further, today's successors to the BFW (Bayerische Flugzeugwerke) company always refer to the 109 and 110 with the prefix Me. What triggered the mistake in the first place was that the world speed record gained by the Me 209

(designed after the company had become Messerschmitt AG on 11 July 1938) was considered by the Nazi propaganda machine to be an obvious way of extolling the virtues of the Luftwaffe's most important fighter, so it was presented to the Fédération Aéronautique Internationale as the 'Me 109R'. This made everyone think it was some kind of version of the fighter.

As for the 'He 111K Mk VA', this was pure invention. For some reason, the original elliptical-winged versions were called He 111 Mk IIA, while the wartime bombers were called the Mk VA, or, in the case of the torpedo-bomber, the HaE – why HaE, with a small a and small capital E for Heaven's sake?. At last, on 21 October 1943, *The Aeroplane Spotter* announced 'Recently a German magazine published an article on the He 111 which has thrown new light on the system of numbering. The old designations similar to 'He 111K Mk VA were merely concoctions produced in this country because the correct system was not known'.

It's all very well to talk about 'the fog of war', but the fact remains that every Luftwaffe aircraft was immediately identifiable by several metal nameplates, permanently riveted on. These gave the true and complete type designation, as well as construction number, a contract number and, usually, two

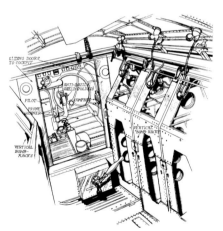

THE BUSINESS PART.—The bomb compartment of the Heinkel He 111K bomber, looking forward. On the right are three of the eight vertical bomb racks arranged in fours on each side of the central gangway. Each rack can accommodate a 250 kg. (550 lb.) bomb stowed nose uppermost. The electrical release gear is above each rack. Forward can be seen the pilot's seat and swing-over control column on the left and the nose gunner's position on the right.

A RADIO COMPASS.—The dial of the "homing" device attached to the loop aerial of the Heinkel He 111K. The handle at the bottom rotates the face to pick up the indicated track. The radio compass is attached to the starboard side of the nose cockpit, where it is operated by the front gunner-bomb aimer beside the pilot as shown in the drawing on the left.

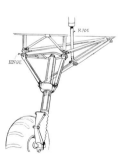

A NEAT LAYOUT.—The starboard undercarriage leg of the Messerschmitt Me 110 two-motor fighter. When retracted backwards the wheel is completely enclosed behind hinged doors. A curious point is that although emergency pneumatic operation is provided, there is no hand gear. Also, the wheel is not locked up or down but held in position by hydraulic pressure.

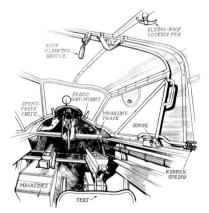

AN UNENVIABLE POSITION.—Looking aft into the radio operator's and aft gunner's position in the narrow fuselage of the Messerschmitt Me 110. The hinged back portion of the cockpit cover can be raised to an angle of about 30 degrees to afford a better field of fire for the single aft gun on the Arado mounting. It can be elevated to about 60 degrees and traversed to about the same angle sideways in the rear hemisphere. Ten spool containers hold a total of 750 rounds o ammunition.

dates. With a fair proportion of those 1733 aircraft able to be inspected, it is difficult to see why we waited a further three years until a German magazine could tell us about Heinkels. What kind of person could read off a nameplate, for example, 'He 111H-6' and say, 'Ah, this is an He 111K Mark VA'?

Strangely, though at the start of the War we did invent the 'Ju 88K', quite early in the Battle of Britain someone actually believed a nameplate and said we had shot down a Ju 88A-1. Yet on the same occasion, a nameplate clearly giving the designation of a twin-engined fighter as a Bf 110C-5 was published in *The Aeroplane* as 'an Me 110C-5'.

Enough of this nitpicking. These drawings are like a breath of fresh air, because at least we can know they were genuine, and drawn direct from the shot-down hardware.

The nose-up stowage of the bombs in the He 111 was held by the Allies to reduce bombing accuracy, but this was seldom important. In any case, if precision had been demanded, the tumbling trajectory could have been allowed for in the design of the Lotfe bombsight. In the lower left view the inlet to the 'flexible pipe' was clipped underneath the MG 15 gun. The radio compass dial was not part of the Knickebein radio-beam navigational guidance, which proved such an unpleasant shock when, in the teeth of opposition from the ignorant, it was unravelled by the brilliant Dr R V Jones four months before these drawings appeared. This pioneer high-precision navaid was especially cunning, because it needed no special cockpit display, the steering information being presented on the Lorenz blind-approach landing system.

In the fourth drawing on page 72 Clark drew in the MG 15 gun end-on, so it wasn't too obvious. He also appeared to connect the flexible spent-case pipe on the left instead of underneath. One of the saddle magazines can be seen above the gun, but he didn't make it clear how fresh magazines were fed round the track.

In the drawing immediately below I believe the aft-bay tank was 680 litres, or 149.6 gal. Of course, the Ju 88's underwing racks were not just for dive bombing, and this initial Service version was highly suspect structurally and had to be handled with kid gloves, all aerobatics being forbidden. Clark would have been surprised to see what was inside the 'gigantic affair' main leg. The Ringfeder shock-absorber is described in the Ju 88 section.

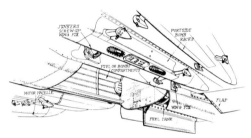

JUNKERS BOMB GEAR.—Underneath the centre section of the port wing and the fuselage of the Junkers Ju 88-A1 bomber. The two external bomb racks for dive-bombing are on the right beneath the port wing root. Each can hold a 250 kg. (550 lb.) bomb. In the centre section of the fuselage is a compartment for sixteen 50 kg. (110 lb.) bombs or for a fuel tank of 1,200 litres (264 gals.). Behind that is another compartment which normally contains a 690-litre (151 gal.) tank, though it can take bombs instead.

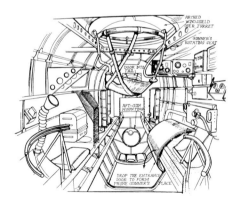

AFT VIEW.—Looking aft from the centre section of the Heinkel He 111K. In the floor is the underslung cupola for the under gunner protecting the tail. The entrance door is open, providing easy ingress or escape by parachute. The top gunner's seat is slung from the gun ring in the roof and is surprisingly comfortable when not under fire. The radio apparatus is on the right and incendiary bomb containers beyond. The flexible pipe on the left is for empty cartridge cases.

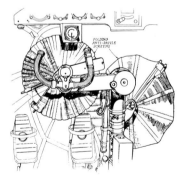

PROTECTION FROM GLARE.—These fans attached to the control column of the Heinkel He 111K can be opened in a circular manner to protect the pilot from being blinded by the glare of searchlights at night. The transparent nose of the Heinkel makes this particularly necessary. The control column itself can be swung over to the right for emergency use. The dashboard is slung from the roof.

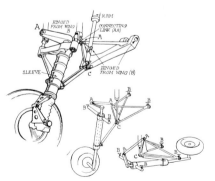

A GIGANTIC AFFAIR.—The starboard undercarriage leg of the Junkers Ju 88-A1 bomber. The leg is about 7½ ft. long. As shown diagrammatically, the wheel turns through 90 degrees as it is raised and lies flat in the wing. This is done by a series of links turning the oleo leg through an external fixed sleeve.

# CATALINA I

Founded in 1918 by Maj Reuben H Fleet, one of the great pioneers of the US aviation industry, Consolidated Aircraft went through many vicissitudes before in 1929 becoming firmly established in a giant factory at Buffalo, NY. Here, new hire Isaac M 'Mac' Laddon quickly showed himself to be a master of the new technology of all-metal stressed-skin construction, creating mailplanes, fast monoplane fighters and big flying boats (in US parlance, boat seaplanes). A typical 1930 product was the US Navy P2Y, a flying boat with two 750-hp engines and a forest of struts and wires.

Laddon told the Navy he could make flying boats as streamlined as the new cantilever landplanes, and on 28 October 1933 an order arrived for the prototype XP3Y. To Consolidated it was the Model 28, and the prototype was flown at Buffalo on 28 March 1935. The timing was just right for World War 2. Without ever changing the engines, the Model 28 proved capable of considerable development, including amphibian versions, and by 1945 more had been made than of any other flying boat or seaplane in history.

When the prototype made its maiden flight the company was in the throes of reorganisation. Among other things it moved from freezing Buffalo to sunny San Diego, where test flying would be not only less hazardous but also possible all year round. The move was made possible by receipt of a

Serving the troops in one of World War 2's forgotten combat zones, a US Navy PBY-5A is relieved of mail sacks at Amchitka, in the Aleutians, in June 1943

gigantic order (for 1935) for 60 of the new Model 28s, with the Navy designation PBY (patrol, bomber, Consolidated). In October 1935 the San Diego plant was starting to make PBYs, with 800 employees, 411 of whom had come from Buffalo. The Model 28 prototype came too, via the Canal Zone, setting records. More orders came, and by 1942 the San Diego works alone had 46,000 on the payroll.

Laddon made good on his promise of a clean exterior. The wing, 104 ft across, was made in three parts, the centre section being carried on a big streamlined pylon which housed the flight engineer. An innovation was the way the tip floats retracted outwards, under electric power, to form the tips of the wings. Though the PBY typically cruised at a mere 99 kts, on a 30-hour mission the small drag saving was probably significant. Another innovation was deicing by exhaust gas heat-exchangers, though many aircraft (including that drawn by Clark) had the Goodrich type. These were black strips of rubber bonded to the leading edges, containing internal tubes which were alternately inflated pneumatically and deflated to make ice crack and blow away.

One of the first foreign operators of the Catalina was the Dutch Air Force, who ordered 48 PBY-5s for use in the East Indies. All but nine of these were lost to Japanese attacks

# LANCASTER I

In the author's opinion this was one of the best cutaways drawn during World War 2. Jimmy Clark chose the right viewpoint, got his perspectives right (apart from the starboard inner – even the propellers were acceptable) and clearly had sufficient time to do the job with absolute thoroughness. And it had to be thorough, because by this time were getting really complicated. When we study this drawing we begin to appreciate the effort involved in building 7377 of these aircraft, each with many hundreds of hydraulic pumps, jacks and valves, and an even greater number of electric motors, relays and switches.

The basic design of the 'Lanc' dated from 1936, and first flew as the Manchester, with two engines and a span of 80 ft 2 in. Even when the span was increased to 90 ft 1 in, and the tail redesigned, this remained flawed by its unreliable engines. The answer was to increase span yet again to 102 ft exactly, and fit four 1260 hp (later 1640 hp) Rolls-Royce Merlins. The famous engine firm had no available design capacity, but by sheer luck the Beaufighter II installation had been designed as a quick-change 'power egg' by Rolls-Royce at Hucknall. Likewise, Bristol had developed an ecu (engine change unit) for the more powerful Hercules. This sleeve-valve radial was fitted to the Lancaster II, with long flame-damping exhausts. Despite the greater power, the Mk II had a slightly lower ceiling, as well as reduced range, but 300 were nevertheless built to guard against a shortage of Merlins.

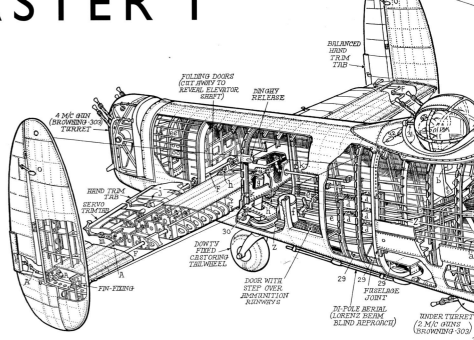

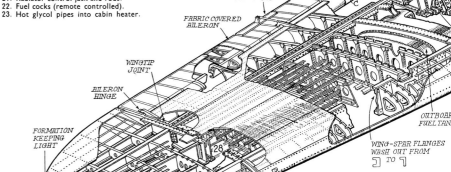

A. Rudder and elevator trim.
B. Control column stops and seat raising cam.
C. Aileron control.
D. Throttle controls.
E. Rudder bars.
F. Rudder and elevator control rods.
G. Aileron trim cables to screw rod.
H. Service piping along bomb bay.
J. Parachute stowage (end of Nav. Table).
K. Oxygen bottle stowages.
L. Observer's window blister.
M. Bomb lock units in floor.
N. Longeron joint flanges and holes.
P. Spar flange reinforcement.
Q. Hydraulic reservoir.
R. Signal pistol.
S. Armoured doors.
T. Rest bunk and 15 oxygen bottles underneath.
U. Spar webs extended into former frames.
V. Spar flanges.
W. Flap op. cylinder and op. rods.
X. Reconnaissance flares.
Y. Flare chute shown stowed and in position.
Z. Tail gun ammunition magazine and runways.
a. Under-turret magazines.
b. Top turret magazines.
d. Vacuum flasks stowages.
e. Dead-man's handle (puts rear turret fore and aft to extricate gunner through sliding door).
f. Elsan lavatory.

g. Tailwheel leg spigoted into tailplane.
h. Tailplane halves joints.
j. Elevator trim screw rod and cables.
k. Tailplane fix to fuselage.
m. Elevator hinge bracket.
n. Bomb door op., jack and mud brushes (and at front end).
p. Hinged leading edge.
q. Starboard fuel tank (580 gal.) space.
r. Glycol tank.
t. Undercarriage and motor bracket.
w. U/c radius rod and jack anchorages.
x. Fuel tank structure (swash-plate former plates, stringers, plating and bullet-proof skinning).
y. Fuel tank support strap.
z. Wing trailing section spar (bolted to wing rear spar).
1. Navigation light.
2. Bomb aiming sight.
3. Flat window (no distortion) and glycol anti-icing spray pipe.
4. Air-speed pressure head.
5. Glycol pump for "3."
6. Bomb aimer's body rest.
7. Emergency exit.
8. Ventilator.
9. Camera (through floor).
10. Pump.
11. Glycol tank (window spray) and step.
12. Bomb aimer's squint into bomb bay.

13. Detail of front turret mounting ring.
14. Compressed air bottle.
15. Pilot's glycol pump (cockpit window spray).
16. D.F. loop.
17. Astro-dome.
18. Rubber headroom buffer (cut away to show half-framed jointing). Note bullet-proof glass panel above.
19. Curtain.
20. Dinghy stowage (starboard wing).
21. Radiator control jack and rods.
22. Fuel cocks (remote controlled).
23. Hot glycol pipes into cabin heater.

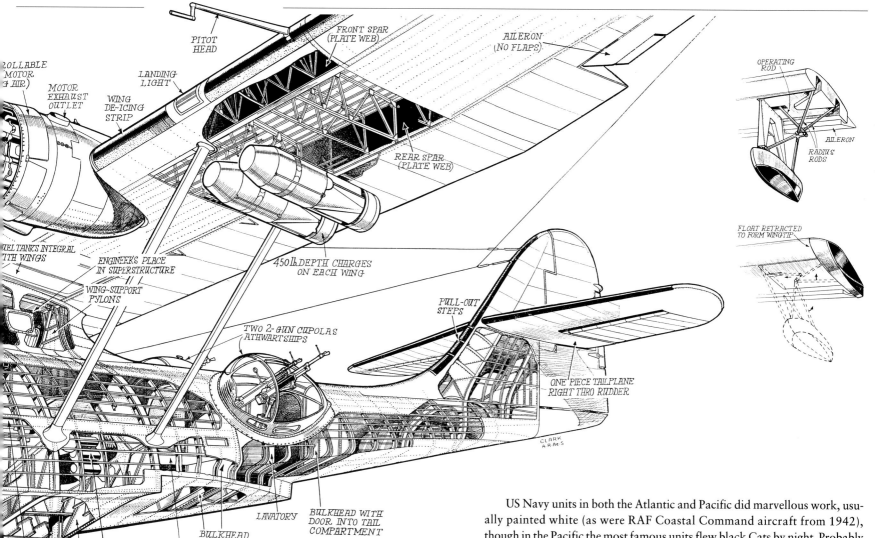

PITOT
HEAD

FRONT SPAR
(PLATE WEB)

AILERON
(NO FLAPS)

LANDING
LIGHT

OPERATING
ROD

2OLLABLE
MOTOR
G AIR)

MOTOR
EXHAUST
OUTLET

WING
DE-ICING
STRIP

AILERON

REAR SPAR
(PLATE WEB)

RADIUS
RODS

FLOAT RETRACTED
TO FORM WINGTIP

EL TANKS INTEGRAL
TH WINGS

ENGINEER'S PLACE
IN SUPERSTRUCTURE

450 lb DEPTH CHARGES
ON EACH WING

WING-SUPPORT
PYLONS

PULL-OUT
STEPS

TWO 2-GUN CUPOLAS
ATHWARTSHIPS

ONE PIECE TAILPLANE
RIGHT THRO RUDDER

CLARK
A.R.Ae.S

LAVATORY

BULKHEAD WITH
DOOR INTO TAIL
COMPARTMENT

BULKHEAD

FLAME FLOAT
STOWAGE

REST COMPARTMENT
(BUNKS EACH SIDE)

WATER
TANK

BULKHEAD
AT STEP

HEAD

CATALINA I

GST in the Soviet Union. Total production in North America was 3290, plus an as-yet unverified number in the Soviet Union (including the KM-2 version with 1650 hp ASh-82 engines). The 'Cat' served with every Allied air force or naval air force. An increasing proportion were fitted with radar, at first with external dipole antennas and finally with a gimballed-dish scanner in a streamlined nacelle carried on a pylon above the cockpit.

US Navy units in both the Atlantic and Pacific did marvellous work, usually painted white (as were RAF Coastal Command aircraft from 1942), though in the Pacific the most famous units flew black Cats by night. Probably the RAF remembers the 'Cat' chiefly because on 26 May 1941 a Catalina of No 209 Sqn found the Bismarck after the Royal Navy had lost contact, and Cats shadowed this formidable enemy until she could be brought to battle.

My abiding memory of these fine aircraft was their glider-like quality, the wing being too big to need flaps and the engines seldom needing high powers, which made for modest noise levels (so unlike a Shackleton). My only disconcerting moment was in a US Army OA-10 amphibian version at Northolt. Looking back from a blister, with engines idling, the tail was vibrating and rocking so wildly I was sure something would break. We took off, and from then on the tail was steady as a rock!

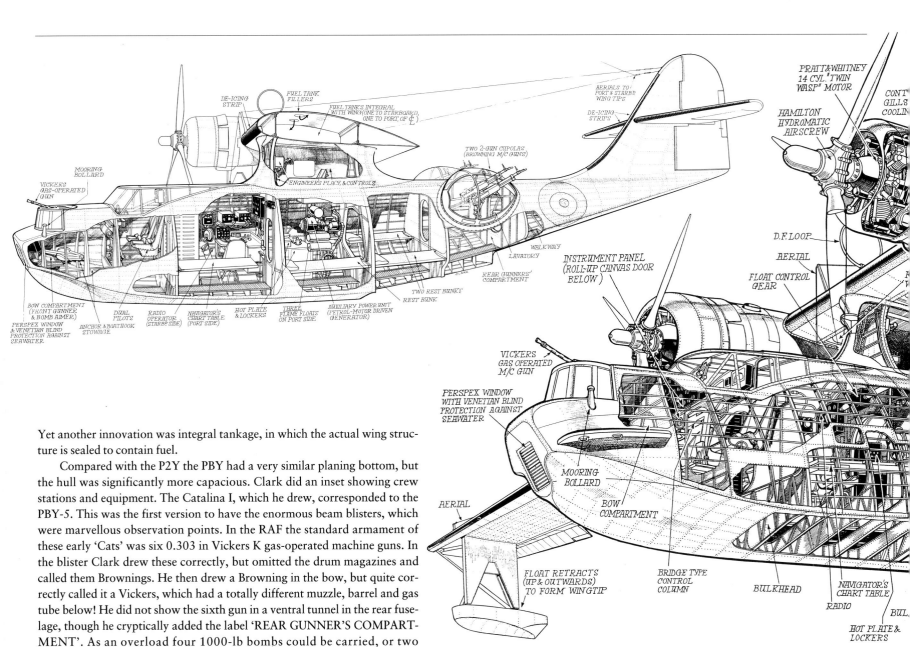

DE-ICING
STRIP

FUEL TANK
FILLERS

FUEL TANKS INTEGRAL
WITH WING (ONE TO STARBOARD,
ONE TO PORT, OF Ç)

AERIALS TO
PORT & STARB?
WING TIPS

PRATT & WHITNEY
14 CYL. "TWIN
WASP" MOTOR

CONT?
GILLS
COOLIN?

DE-ICING
STRIP

HAMILTON
HYDROMATIC
AIRSCREW

TWO 2-GUN CUPOLAS
(BROWNING M/C GUNS)

MOORING
BOLLARD

ENGINEER'S PLACE & CONTROLS

VICKERS
GAS-OPERATED
GUN

CLARK

D.F. LOOP
AERIAL

WALKWAY
LAVATORY

INSTRUMENT PANEL
(ROLL-UP CANVAS DOOR
BELOW )

FLOAT CONTROL
GEAR

REAR GUNNERS'
COMPARTMENT

TWO REST BUNKS
REST BUNK

BOW COMPARTMENT
(FRONT GUNNER
& BOMB AIMER)

DUAL
PILOTS

RADIO
OPERATOR
(STARB? SIDE)

NAVIGATOR'S
CHART TABLE
(PORT SIDE)

HOT PLATE
& LOCKERS

THREE
FLAME FLOATS
ON PORT SIDE)

AUXILIARY POWER UNIT
(PETROL-MOTOR DRIVEN
GENERATOR)

PERSPEX WINDOW
& VENETIAN BLIND
PROTECTION AGAINST
SEAWATER.

ANCHOR & BOATHOOK
STOWAGE

VICKERS
GAS OPERATED
M/C GUN

PERSPEX WINDOW
WITH VENETIAN BLIND
PROTECTION AGAINST
SEAWATER

MOORING
BOLLARD

BOW
COMPARTMENT

AERIAL

FLOAT RETRACTS
(UP & OUTWARDS)
TO FORM WINGTIP

BRIDGE TYPE
CONTROL
COLUMN

BULKHEAD

NAVIGATOR'S
CHART TABLE

RADIO

BUL?

BUL?

HOT PLATE &
LOCKERS

Yet another innovation was integral tankage, in which the actual wing structure is sealed to contain fuel.

Compared with the P2Y the PBY had a very similar planing bottom, but the hull was significantly more capacious. Clark did an inset showing crew stations and equipment. The Catalina I, which he drew, corresponded to the PBY-5. This was the first version to have the enormous beam blisters, which were marvellous observation points. In the RAF the standard armament of these early 'Cats' was six 0.303 in Vickers K gas-operated machine guns. In the blister Clark drew these correctly, but omitted the drum magazines and called them Brownings. He then drew a Browning in the bow, but quite correctly called it a Vickers, which had a totally different muzzle, barrel and gas tube below! He did not show the sixth gun in a ventral tunnel in the rear fuselage, though he cryptically added the label 'REAR GUNNER'S COMPARTMENT'. As an overload four 1000-lb bombs could be carried, or two torpedoes.

Rather unusually, the US Navy adopted the British name. By 1942 several versions were coming into production, not only at San Diego but also by Consolidated's New Orleans division, and at the Naval Aircraft Factory, Boeing Aircraft of Canada, Canadian Vickers and also under licence as the

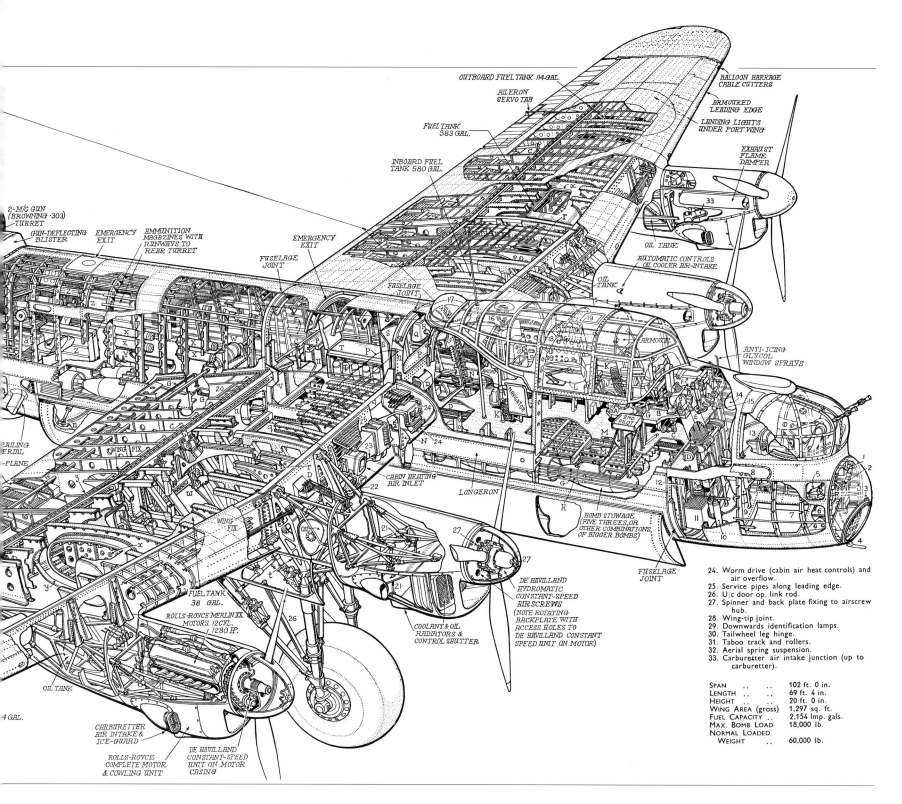

OUTBOARD FUEL TANK 114 GAL.

AILERON SERVO TAB

FUEL TANK 383 GAL.

INBOARD FUEL TANK 580 GAL.

BALLOON BARRAGE CABLE CUTTERS

ARMOURED LEADING EDGE

LANDING LIGHTS UNDER PORT WING

EXHAUST FLAME DAMPER

2~M/G GUN (BROWNING ·303) TURRET

GUN-DEFLECTING BLISTER

EMERGENCY EXIT

AMMUNITION MAGAZINES WITH RUNWAYS TO REAR TURRET

FUSELAGE JOINT

EMERGENCY EXIT

FUSELAGE JOINT

OIL TANK

AUTOMATIC CONTROLS OIL COOLER AIR-INTAKE

OIL TANK

ANTI-ICING GLYCOL WINDOW SPRAYS

ARMOUR

RADIO

NAVIGATOR

2ND. PILOT

TRAILING AERIAL -PLANE

WING FIX

CABIN HEATING AIR INLET

LONGERON

BOMB STOWAGE (FIVE THREES, OR OTHER COMBINATIONS OF BIGGER BOMBS)

FUSELAGE JOINT

WING FIX

FUEL TANK 38 GAL.

ROLLS-ROYCE MERLIN XX MOTORS. 12 CYL. 1280 H.P.

DE HAVILLAND HYDROMATIC CONSTANT-SPEED AIR SCREWS (NOTE ROTATING BACKPLATE WITH ACCESS HOLES TO DE HAVILLAND CONSTANT SPEED UNIT ON MOTOR)

COOLANT & OIL RADIATORS & CONTROL SHUTTER

OIL TANK

4 GAL.

CARBURETTER AIR INTAKE & ICE-GUARD

ROLLS-ROYCE COMPLETE MOTOR & COWLING UNIT

DE HAVILLAND CONSTANT-SPEED UNIT ON MOTOR CASING

24. Worm drive (cabin air heat controls) and air overflow.
25. Service pipes along leading edge.
26. U/c door op. link rod.
27. Spinner and back plate fixing to airscrew hub.
28. Wing-tip joint.
29. Downwards identification lamps.
30. Tailwheel leg hinge.
31. Taboo track and rollers.
32. Aerial spring suspension.
33. Carburetter air intake junction (up to carburetter).

| SPAN | .. | .. | 102 ft. 0 in. |
| LENGTH | .. | .. | 69 ft. 4 in. |
| HEIGHT | .. | .. | 20 ft. 0 in. |
| WING AREA (gross) | | | 1,297 sq. ft. |
| FUEL CAPACITY | .. | | 2,154 lmp. gals. |
| MAX. BOMB LOAD | | | 18,000 lb. |
| NORMAL LOADED WEIGHT | | .. | 60,000 lb. |

RIGHT This brilliant Charles E Brown shot shows the Lancaster I in all its graceful glory. Note that the nose gunner has depressed the twin 0.303s in his turret so as to gain a better view of Brown's camera-ship

BELOW No 50 Sqn Lancaster I R5689 was flown specially for the press from its Swinderby base in August 1942

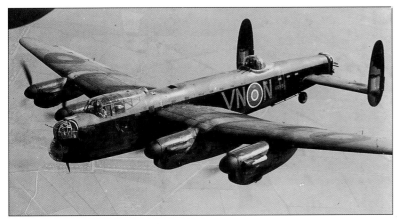

Like most of the big wartime programmes. making Lancasters was a nationwide job. For example, the Mk II's wings were made by Armstrong Whitworth Aircraft (AWA) at Bitteswell and Baginton, near Coventry, whereas the fuselage sections were constructed by five Midlands firms and assembled at the tram sheds of the Northampton Corporation. Tails were made by Pearce's shoe factory, and final assembly was by AWA, first at Sywell, and later at Baginton.

Likewise, the standard Mk I was made by hundreds of firms and assembled by A V Roe at Chaddington and Woodford, near Manchester, and at Yeadon, near Leeds, and by Metropolitan-Vickers, AWA, Austin Motors and Vickers-Armstrongs at Castle Bromwich (Birmingham) and Chester. Almost as many were made of the Mk III, with Packard Merlin engines and, later, broad 'paddle-blade' propellers.

Performance of the Lancaster was so much better than predicted that chief designer Roy Chadwick was at a loss to account for it. Pressed, he wondered if it had something to do with the neat nacelles whose top met the wing at the leading edge, instead of extending back above the wing. In times of crisis many Lancasters were dived by their pilots to indicated speeds nudging 400 mph, despite the high-drag (and seldom needed) mid-upper turret and fixed tailwheel. Only at the end of the war did the tailwheel get the Marstrand anti-shimmy tyre with twin treads. A more obvious change was that from the Mk III the bulged Perspex nose was extended $7^{1}/_{2}$ in further forward to reduce the inclination of the $20^{13}/_{16}$-in-diameter bomb-aiming window.

One of the few real criticisms of the Lancaster was that it was exceedingly difficult for the crew to get out of in dire emergencies, primarily due to the large obstruction of the wing spar intersecting the fuselage – this is clearly visible in this drawing.

Clark showed the FN64 ventral turret, which was to prove the only one really needed. Tragically, it was absent from almost every Lancaster sent over Germany except for those built as Mk IIs, so many hundreds of crews were killed by upward-firing nightfighters which they never saw. He also drew the cavernous bomb bay filled with 15 GP bombs of 1000 lb, whereas perhaps 80 per cent of Lancaster missions – over Germany at least – were flown with a 4000-lb 'cookie' and anything up to 16 containers of 4-lb incendiaries. Oddly, he drew in some of the small cartridge-operated balloon-cable cutters along the leading edge, but perhaps did not know what they were. Of course, he could not show the $H_2S$ radar, because when he did the drawing in September 1942 this was highly secret and only just coming into use. Another item that may have been secret was the quantity of ammunition for the FN20 tail turret – for each of the four guns, 1900 rounds in the box and 600 in the feed track, which he called a 'runway'.

Altogether, this was a splendid drawing of a splendid aircraft. Many hundreds of Bomber Command veterans will enjoy fingering their way through the places that once brought so much fear, excitement and enduring comradeship.

# Me 210

Early in World War 2 we British were rather schizophrenic. Whilst on the one hand we rubbished the German aircraft actually encountered, we went out of our way to publicise new and formidable types we thought the enemy was preparing for us. Among the latter were the Do 29, Fw 187 and 198, He 113, Ju 89 and Me Jaguar and 210. Of these only the Me 210 actually existed as a production type. It seemed to have everything: speed, power, agility, devastating armament and, for the first time, quite effective rear defence with an MG 131 13-mm heavy machine gun in a remotely controlled barbette on each side behind the wing. On 6 September 1942 some visited Yorkshire, where two were shot down by Typhoons (I believe these were the 'Tiffy's' third and fourth combat victories). As a result Clark was able to produce this drawing.

What we apparently had no knowledge of is that this seemingly formidable aircraft was the greatest failure and scandal in the entire history of Luftwaffe procurement. Long after the war, when we were better informed, Bill Green wrote (in *Warplanes of the Third Reich*) 'The Me 210 V1 made its maiden flight on September 5, 1939, with Dr-Ing Hermann Wurster at the controls. This initial flight was considered to be successful only as much as its pilot succeeded in landing the V1 in the condition in which it left the ground'.

There followed years of anguish and torment trying to make this truly malevolent flying machine behave itself. Throughout this time the mighty political weight of the Luftwaffe, from Goering down, was forcing through massive production programmes, to replace the Bf 110 which the Me 210 was supposed to have made obsolete. Eventually, in February 1942 the three

factories building the Me 210 were brought to a halt, and the old Bf 110 was put back into production. About 200 Me 210s had been completed, and 370 were on the assembly lines. Among other things this was reckoned to have cost Germany about 600 aircraft, and it cost Willy Messerschmitt his job.

Aviation is an ironic business, and as soon as production was halted solutions began to be found. The rear fuselage was made longer and deeper, the leading-edge taper on the outer wings was reduced, and finally (changing the designation to Me 410) the engines were changed to the big DB 603A rated at 1850 hp. Of course, by this time word of the 210 had spread throughout the Luftwaffe, so crews were at first suspicious of the 410. In fact, by 1943 the Me 410 was a reasonable counterpart to the Mosquito, a fact played upon by German publicity in dubbing it the Hornisse (Hornet).

Of course, unlike the Mosquito, the Messerschmitt 210 and 410 were conventional all-metal stressed-skin machines. Studying Clark's drawing it is not difficult to see which bits of structure he could inspect in the shot-down specimen(s) he saw. He made the point that not only the fuselage but also the tailplane was made in two halves. In the case of the tailplane the halves were the top and bottom, and they could even 'unfold' at the leading edge. The dive brakes operated in a way often seen on modern sailplanes, the arms carrying the angle-sections swinging out above and below the wing on common pivots. Unlike the Bf 109 and 110, the wing centre section was in one piece, the spars being continuous across the fuselage. A detail showed the machined forging that located the outer main spar just outboard of the nacelle.

It is easy to criticise with hindsight. I feel sure that Clark never saw one

This pre-production Me 210A-0, seen at Regensburg in late 1941, has been fitted with a pair of non-standard four-bladed props. Notice the large number of yet to be delivered Bf 109s and 110s parked in the background

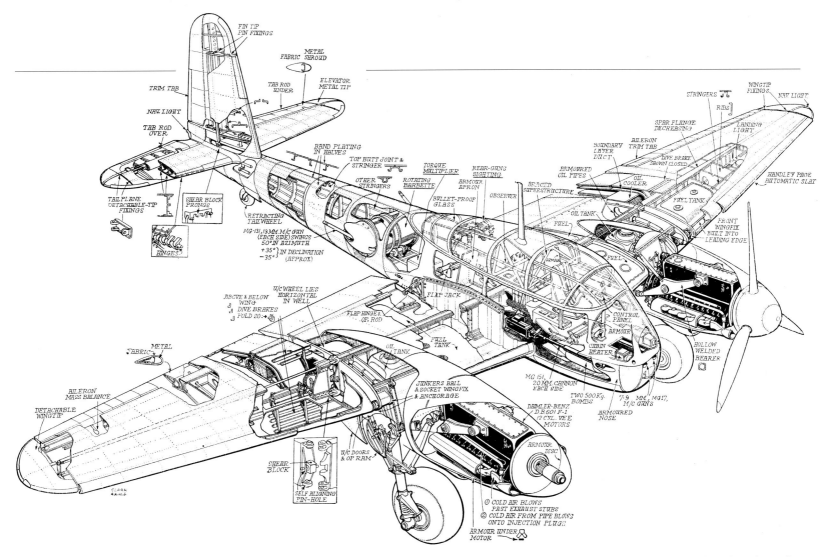

of the MG 131 guns (though surely he was familiar with it by this time?), because he drew them like boomsticks instead of having fat perforated air-cooling jackets and muzzle flash-eliminators. He also cannot have seen the workings of the barbette drum, which he rendered in a totally stylised form bearing little resemblance to the actual hardware, nor did he show how the 13 mm ammunition was fed round the outside of the drum.

More astonishingly, he drew the engine coolant radiators, which were wide but shallow boxes mounted in ducts under the wing outboard of the nacelles as in the Bf 110. He then had a brainstorm and labelled the port (left) radiator 'OIL COOLER', and even showed it as being fed by armoured oil pipes. Of course, these pipes (one out, the other return) carried engine coolant, which was usually a 50/50 mix of Glysantin (glycol) and water with a trace of anti-corrosive additive. The oil coolers were directly under the

engines, as in the Bf 109 and Bf 110. He hinted at the oil cooler inlet under the left engine, but did not label it (he must have wondered what it was for). After the war a rival publisher copied this drawing exactly, and thus copied the same mistake, in this case labelling both radiators as the oil coolers!

Having elected to draw the aircraft from this aspect Clark found he could not show the engine supercharger and its circular ram inlet, which in Daimler-Benz engines was on the left (the opposite of the petrol-fuelled Jumo 211 and 213). Another gaff is his label (2) under the right engine. The cooling air was not blown on to 'injection plugs' but on to the sparking plugs. The fuel injectors were on the opposite side of each block, underneath the engine, and did not need cooling. At least he drew attention to the fact that the engines were mounted on hollow welded [steel] bearers, which was a reversal of the normal practice of using solid forged Elektron (magnesium alloy).

# Ju 88

Far more than any other aircraft, the Junkers Ju 88 was Germany's equivalent of the Mosquito in that it served in every role imaginable and was a truly great aircraft. For so large and heavy a machine its performance and manoeuvrability were truly astonishing. I wrote somewhere that the later versions with Jumo 213 or BMW 801 engines made one feel you could win the war with one propeller feathered. Yet at the beginning of the conflict, not only were we British almost totally ignorant of an aircraft that had been flying in increasing numbers since 1936, and been described in detail in open German literature, but we also had to delude ourselves that everything the enemy had was rubbish. For example, *Flight* for 5 December 1940 told us 'The whole Ju 88 is a collection of numerous "brainwaves", but it is not a good aeroplane, since it has failed in its function'. Nothing could have been further from the truth.

Clark's artwork depicted a Ju 88A-1 drawn from a damaged captured example. He chose an unusual viewpoint, but at least that helped him to

Devoid of both its starboard Jumo 211 engine and underfuselage gondola, a battered I./KG 51 *Edelweiss* Ju 88A-4 is inspected by men from the Air Ministry in October 1940

show the racks for heavy bombs under the inner wing, the remarkable landing gear and not least the exceedingly powerful dive brakes. I wonder if anyone who saw this drawing wondered if the propellers were really that size? It wouldn't have done any harm to make one or two blades their actual length.

By the time Junkers designed the Ju 88 they had long since moved on from corrugated skin to become masters of smooth stressed-skin construction which, in the case of this aircraft, was flush-riveted and always of high quality. In all early versions the engines were various sub-types of the company's own Jumo 211, typically rated at 1340 hp.

The installation was most unusual in that this inverted-vee engine was cooled by a circular engine and oil radiator group mounted on the front, with airflow controlled by gills as in a radial. In contrast to the Bf 110, the cowlings were extremely long, so the Luftwaffe called it der drei-finger 88 ('the three-finger 88').

As in Britain, the engines were assembled into self-contained power units complete with some accessories, the rest being left behind on an airframe-mounted gearbox, so that not only could engines be quickly changed, but they could even be changed for engines of a different type. Thus, by January 1940 the Ju 88B was flying with the BMW 801 radial, in the 1600 hp class.

The early Ju 88A-1 drawn by Clark had a span of 60 ft 3$^{1}/_{2}$ in, with hydraulically operated flaps and drooping ailerons extending to the tips. By 1940 the standard wing had been extended to 20 metres (65 ft 7$^{1}/_{2}$ in), leaving the ailerons unchanged and thus ending well inboard of the new tips. As the war continued, new sub-types appeared without the dive brakes, until by the end of the war dive brakes were a rarity. This was partly because, thanks to RAF Bomber Command, the dominant production versions from 1943 onwards were nightfighters.

Most A-series Ju 88s had two fuselage bays for anything up to 28 SC50 bombs of 110 lb each. With reduced internal load the four big underwing racks could each carry an SC250 of 551 lb, while the A-4 and subsequent versions could carry four SC500 bombs of 1102 lb each. With such a load dive attacks were not attempted, and in fact the A-1 was highly suspect structurally, to such a degree that all aerobatics were forbidden. This was emphatically not the case with later versions!

The main undercarriage was exceedingly tall, notable for having a single cantilever strut, and for retracting backwards while the wheel axle rotated through 90°. Less obvious was the unusual (probably unique) method of

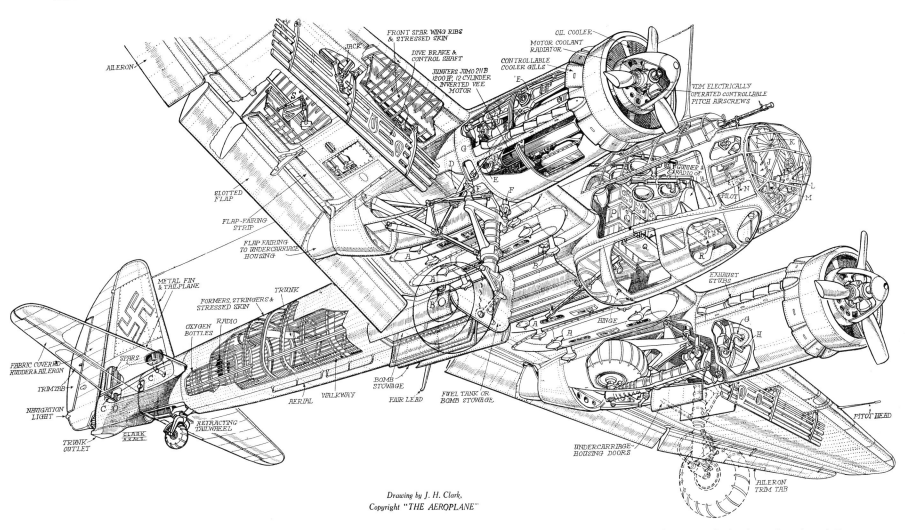

Labels on drawing:

AILERON

FRONT SPAR WING RIBS & STRESSED SKIN

JACK

DIVE BRAKE & CONTROL SHAFT

JUNKERS JUMO 211B 1200 HP, 12 CYLINDER INVERTED VEE MOTOR

OIL COOLER

MOTOR COOLANT RADIATOR

CONTROLLABLE COOLER GILLS

VDM ELECTRICALLY OPERATED CONTROLLABLE PITCH AIRSCREWS

GUNNER & RADIO OP

PILOT

SLOTTED FLAP

FLAP-FAIRING STRIP

FLAP FAIRING TO UNDERCARRIAGE HOUSING

METAL FIN & TAILPLANE

FORMERS, STRINGERS & STRESSED SKIN

TRUNK

EXHAUST STUBS

OXYGEN BOTTLES

RADIO

HINGE

FABRIC COVERED RUDDER & AILERON

SPARS

TRIM TAB

NAVIGATION LIGHT

AERIAL

WALKWAY

BOMB STOWAGE

FAIR LEAD

FUEL TANK OR BOMB STOWAGE

TRUNK OUTLET

CLARK A.R.A.E.S

RETRACTING TAILWHEEL

UNDERCARRIAGE HOUSING DOORS

PITOT HEAD

AILERON TRIM TAB

Drawing by J. H. Clark,
Copyright "THE AEROPLANE"

shock absorption. Called Ringfeder, the leg housed a long stack of spring-steel rings with chamfered (bevelled) edges which fitted together. Landing shocks pushed the rings slightly into each other, the bounce being cushioned by friction as the rings separated again.

The aircraft drawn by Clark was one that had been hastily modified during the Battle of Britain to have four MG 15 machine guns, two fired from the aft dorsal position and the other two from beam windows, all having to be independently aimed, fired and their magazines changed by one man! Some details, such as the ball-and-socket spar attachments and aileron mass-balance, had previously been drawn by Clark after viewing crashed Ju 88s.

He had also previously seen the hot-air deicing to the leading edge, though I fail to understand his 'cut out' H – did he mean he had cut a hole in the nacelle to reveal the deicing pipe ?

One or two other items deserve a little explanation. The four big external carriers could each take an SC500 bomb weighing 1102 lb, or various other loads, but I am sure Clark was mistaken in saying they were plumbed for 'long-range fuel tanks'. It is not obvious from the simple word 'HINGE' under the ventral gondola that the rear portion hinged open to serve as the crew entrance and exit, and that the 'TRUNK' in the rear fuselage was actually the fuel jettison pipe.

# BEAUFIGHTER IF

This drawing was published in *The Aeroplane Spotter* of 11 September 1941, and with additional inset details in the parent journal *The Aeroplane* on the following day. Bearing in mind that at this time such aircraft as the Whirlwind and Botha were highly secret, it is quite remarkable that details of this far more important and formidable aircraft should have been published, long before any Beaufighter could have been captured by the enemy. Of course, one feature was not included: airborne radar. The possibility of making radar small enough to fit into a large two-seat fighter was kept secret for a further two years, as explained elsewhere.

Between the wars Britain produced various big twin-engined fighters. One was the Bristol Bagshot of 1927. This had a monoplane wing so deficient in torsional strength that aileron reversal was encountered at under 100 mph; in other words, if you tried to roll to the left, the aircraft rolled to the right ! Bristol then spent years trying to make stiffer monoplane wings, and were so clumsy that when they got to the Type 130 Bombay bomber/transport the only way they could do it was to use seven spars!

They soon got better, as shown by the story of the Blenheim. This, the Type 142M, led to the Type 152 Beaufort, which had a rather broader and much stronger wing, carrying 180 per cent of the Blenheim's weight for only 114 per cent of the wing weight, and needing only half as many manufacturing man-hours. In June 1938 the leaders of the Bristol aircraft and engine design teams, Leslie Frise and Roy Fedden, saw that this wing could be the basis for the answer to a yawning gap in the planned equipment of the RAF. There was no provision for a twin-engined two-seat fighter, to fly long escort missions or carry radar to fight at night. Like so many other great wartime

aircraft, the resulting Type 156 Beaufighter was created at the last possible moment by the private initiative of the aircraft industry.

Apart from local restressing, and fitting it with 0.303 in Browning machine guns, four in one wing and two in the other, the wing was unchanged. The nacelles were strengthened to carry Bristol Hercules 14-cylinder sleeve-valve engines, each rated at 1400 (soon 1590) hp, driving 12 ft 9 in propellers. I think Clark might have drawn one or two propeller blades full-length, or at least pointed out that he had cropped them!

The fuselage was completely new. With hindsight one wonders why Frise did not put the pilot and observer close together. Part of the trouble was the deep front spar, and I found it no easy job, wearing a seat-pack, to climb up the ladder, over the spar and across the seat (even with the seat-back lowered, which is how you left it on getting out). Experienced Beau drivers carried the parachute aboard and put it on the seat before clambering over. As for emergency exit, the two pivoted belly hatches could be opened under hydraulic power to create a useful region of dead air. In a belly landing both crew could get out upwards.

A further factor affecting crew layout is that the main armament was four Hispano 20 mm cannon, two on each side of the floor. Bristol devised two excellent forms of belt feed from 240-round magazines, but the Ministry managed to foul everything up so that the first 400 'Beaus' had to have drum feed. This meant that the observer had to sit far from the pilot behind the wing, and unclip spent drums, take heavy 60-round drums off racks, and clip them accurately on to each of the four guns. Doing this during unpredictable manoeuvres, especially at night, must have been no joke.

First of the RAF's truly effective night-fighters, the Beaufighter IF became operational with No 604 Sqn at Middle Wallop at the end of September 1940. This machine was amongst the initial batch of aircraft delivered to the unit from the Fairey production line, which was building Beaufighters under licence

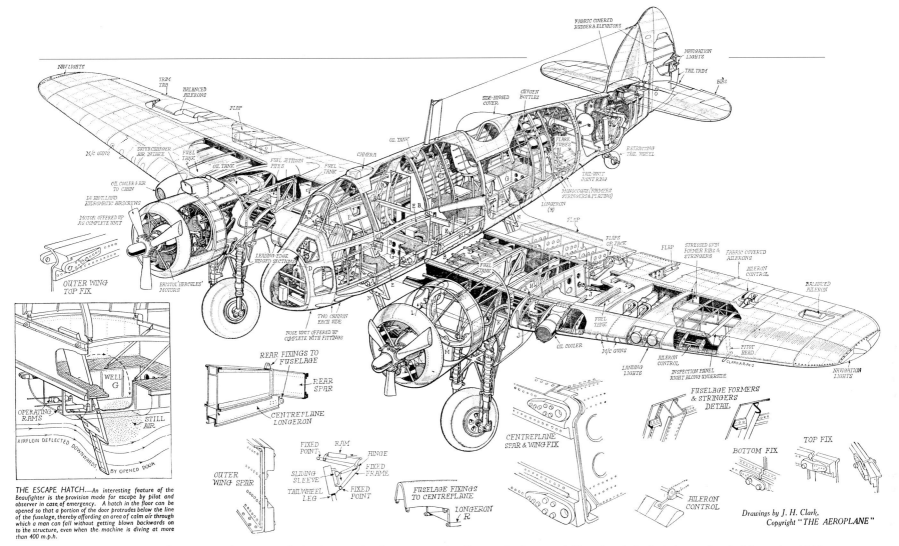

NAV LIGHTS

TRIM TAB

BALANCED AILERONS

FLAP

M/c GUNS

SUPERCHARGER AIR INTAKE

FUEL TANK

OIL TANK

OIL COOLER & AIR TO CABIN

De HAVILLAND HYDROMATIC AIRSCREWS

MOTOR OFFERED UP AS COMPLETE UNIT

OUTER WING TOP FIX

BRISTOL 'HERCULES' MOTORS

LEADING-EDGE HINGED SECTIONS

FUEL JETTISON PIPES

FUEL TANK

CAMERA

OIL TANK

SIDE-HINGED COVER

OXYGEN BOTTLES

FLAME TUBES

RETRACTING TAIL WHEEL

TAIL-UNIT JOINT RING

MONOCOQUE (FORMERS STRINGERS & PLATING)

LONGERON (X)

FLAP

FLAPS OP. JACK

FABRIC COVERED RUDDER & ELEVATORS

NAVIGATION LIGHTS

TAIL TRIM

RIBS

STRESSED SKIN FORMER RIBS & STRINGERS

FABRIC COVERED AILERONS

AILERON CONTROL

BALANCED AILERON

TWO CANNON EACH SIDE

NOSE UNIT OFFERED UP COMPLETE WITH FITTINGS

FUEL TANK

OIL COOLER

M/c GUNS

LANDING LIGHTS

AILERON CONTROL

INSPECTION PANEL RIGHT ALONG UNDERSIDE

PITOT HEAD

Clark A.R. Ae.2

NAVIGATION LIGHTS

REAR FIXINGS TO FUSELAGE

REAR SPAR

CENTREPLANE LONGERON

OUTER WING SPAR

FIXED POINT

RAM

SLIDING SLEEVE

TAILWHEEL LEG

HINGE

FIXED FRAME

FIXED POINT

FUSELAGE FIXINGS TO CENTREPLANE

LONGERON R

CENTREPLANE SPAR & WING FIX

FUSELAGE FORMERS & STRINGERS DETAIL

BOTTOM FIX

TOP FIX

AILERON CONTROL

Drawings by J. H. Clark,
Copyright "THE AEROPLANE"

THE ESCAPE HATCH.—An interesting feature of the Beaufighter is the provision made for escape by pilot and observer in case of emergency. A hatch in the floor can be opened so that a portion of the door protrudes below the line of the fuselage, thereby affording an area of calm air through which a man can fall without getting blown backwards on to the structure, even when the machine is diving at more than 400 m.p.h.

OPERATING RAMS

WELL G

STILL AIR

AIRFLOW DEFLECTED DOWNWARDS

BY OPENED DOOR

The Beau prototype flew on 17 July 1939, and after intense development the Mk I nightfighter became operational in September 1940. It was just what the RAF desperately needed. It was built like a battleship, empty weight being over 14,000 lb compared with about 8100 for a Blenheim. It had adequate engine power, devastating armament and, from November 1940, the vital AI (airborne interception) radar. AI Mk IV boxes were grouped round the observer, and the antennas comprised a double arrowhead transmitter on the nose and dipole azimuth/elevation receivers on the outer wings. After months of near-total impotence at night, the RAF at last had an aircraft which, with a skilled crew, was a lethal killing machine on the darkest night.

Of course, later the 'Beau' went on to carry bombs, rockets and even a torpedo. Its horizontal tail was given 12° dihedral, and a long dorsal fin was added to improve longitudinal stability, especially on climb-out, though on

landing you had to watch like a hawk for incipient swing. In November 1941 a Beaufighter IF made the first flight with short-wavelength (centimetric) radar, the AI Mk VII having its antenna in the form of a power-driven pivoted dish inside a 'thimble nose'.

A total of 5562 Beaufighters were built by many British factories, plus 364 in Australia. Flying overhead it made a deep hushed booming sound, like most Hercules-powered aircraft; the Japanese were said to call it 'whispering death'.

The only points I would criticise in this drawing are wrong perspective on the main wheels, which are slightly too broadside-on, and the fact that the leading edge of the fin and rudder actually formed a smooth continuous curve. Also, if Clark had chosen to view from the starboard (right) side, he could have shown the long flame-damping exhaust pipes.

# AIRACOBRA I

One of the ironies that were sprinkled throughout World War 2 is that the Russians were generally unimpressed by aircraft they were given by the Allies, and in particular were not over the Moon about the Hurricane (too slow) and Spitfire (which they said couldn't stand the harsh environment). But when they got the Bell Airacobra they said 'At last here is a ground-attack fighter we like!' Hundreds of Soviet aces flew this tough machine, and in 1943-44 they moved on to the Kingcobra, which they thought was even better. The irony is that the RAF looked askance at the unconventional Airacobra, and threw it out with hardly even a fair trial.

In the story of the Catalina the point is made that in 1935 Consolidated moved from Buffalo to California. Many of the company's former employees stayed behind, and these included Larry Bell (former general manager), R P Whitman (former assistant general manager) and Robert J Woods (former chief engineer). They quickly formed Bell Aircraft, began designing most unconventional fighters, and started hiring the Consolidated workforce who preferred icy Buffalo to sunny San Diego.

The XP-39 was their second design, and the prototype flew on 6 April 1938. The Putnam *Aircraft of the Royal Air Force Since 1918* tells us that the first flight was in 1939, that the installation of the Allison engine behind the pilot with a long shaft to the propeller reduction gearbox 'gave rise to a good deal of mechanical trouble' (it didn't) and that the mounting of a cannon firing through the propeller hub was 'yet another innovation' (it had been seen on 18 types of fighter since 1917). The same work notes

'A total of 675 Airacobras was ordered for the RAF, but after its *failure* in action (my italics) deliveries ceased at about 80, the remainder going to the US Army'. Part of the trouble was that the General Electric turbo-supercharger had not been cleared for export. Thus, whereas the XP-39 reached 390 mph and climbed to 20,000 ft in 5 min, the RAF aircraft ran out of steam at 355 mph and needed over 11 minutes.

The first aircraft to arrive in Britain were three P-39Cs which a joint

ABOVE Much photographed at the time of its operational debut, the Airacobra was sadly a failure with the RAF, serving very briefly (two months) with No 601 Sqn in late 1941. This marvellous view shows the whole squadron undergoing power checks for the benefit of the assembled media on 17 October 1941

LEFT The censors took the liberty of blotting out the serial of this factory-fresh P-39D before the photo was released to the press by Bell in the autumn of 1941

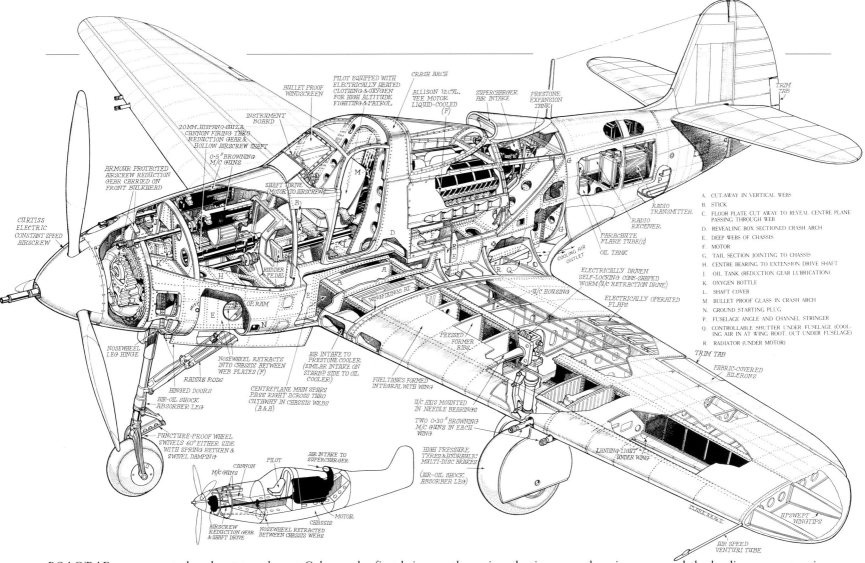

BULLET PROOF WINDSCREEN

PILOT EQUIPPED WITH ELECTRICALLY HEATED CLOTHING & OXYGEN FOR HIGH ALTITUDE FIGHTING & PATROL

CRASH ARCH

ALLISON 12.CYL. VEE MOTOR LIQUID-COOLED (F)

SUPERCHARGER AIR INTAKE

PRESTONE EXPANSION TANK

TRIM TAB

INSTRUMENT BOARD

20MM.HISPANO-SUIZA CANNON FIRING THRO REDUCTION GEAR & HOLLOW AIRSCREW SHAFT

0.5"BROWNING M/C GUNS

SHAFT DRIVE (MOTOR TO AIRSCREW)

RADIO TRANSMITTER

RADIO RECEIVER

ARMOUR PROTECTED AIRSCREW REDUCTION GEAR CARRIED ON FRONT BULKHEAD

PARACHUTE FLARE TUBE(S)

OIL TANK

CURTISS ELECTRIC CONSTANT SPEED AIRSCREW

COOLING AIR OUTLET

RUDDER PEDAL

ELECTRICALLY DRIVEN SELF-LOCKING CONE-SHAPED WORM (U/C RETRACTION DRIVE)

OP. RAM

U/C HOUSING

ELECTRICALLY OPERATED FLAPS

NOSEWHEEL LEG HINGE

WING FIXINGS AT

PRESSED FORMER RIBS

TRIM TAB

NOSEWHEEL RETRACTS INTO CHASSIS BETWEEN WEB PLATES (F)

AIR INTAKE TO PRESTONE COOLER (SIMILAR INTAKE ON STARBD SIDE TO OIL COOLER)

FABRIC-COVERED AILERONS

RADIUS RODS

FUEL TANKS FORMED INTEGRAL WITH WING

HINGED DOORS

AIR-OIL SHOCK ABSORBER LEG

CENTREPLANE MAIN SPARS PASS RIGHT ACROSS THRO CUTAWAY IN CHASSIS WEBS (A & A)

U/C AXIS MOUNTED IN NEEDLE BEARINGS

PUNCTURE-PROOF WHEEL SWIVELS 60° EITHER SIDE WITH SPRING RETURN & SWIVEL DAMPING

TWO 0.30" BROWNING M/C GUNS IN EACH WING

HIGH PRESSURE TYRES & HYDRAULIC MULTI-DISC BRAKES

LANDING LIGHT UNDER WING

CANNON

PILOT

AIR INTAKE TO SUPERCHARGER

(AIR-OIL SHOCK ABSORBER LEG)

UPSWEPT WINGTIPS

M/C GUNS

MOTOR

AIRSCREW REDUCTION GEAR & SHAFT DRIVE

NOSEWHEEL RETRACTED BETWEEN CHASSIS WEBS

CHASSIS

AIR SPEED VENTURI TUBE

A. CUT-AWAY IN VERTICAL WEBS
B. STICK
C. FLOOR PLATE CUT AWAY TO REVEAL CENTRE PLANE PASSING THROUGH WEB
D. REVEALING BOX SECTIONED CRASH ARCH
E. DEEP WEBS OF CHASSIS
F. MOTOR
G. TAIL SECTION JOINTING TO CHASSIS
H. CENTRE BEARING TO EXTENSION DRIVE SHAFT
J. OIL TANK (REDUCTION GEAR LUBRICATION)
K. OXYGEN BOTTLE
L. SHAFT COVER
M. BULLET PROOF GLASS IN CRASH ARCH
N. GROUND STARTING PLUG
P. FUSELAGE ANGLE AND CHANNEL STRINGER
Q. CONTROLLABLE SHUTTER UNDER FUSELAGE (COOLING AIR IN AT WING ROOT. OUT UNDER FUSELAGE)
R. RADIATOR (UNDER MOTOR)

BOAC/RAF crew uncrated and put together at Colerne, the first being flown there by a US Army test pilot on 6 July 1941. No 601 Sqn began to equip with the strange aircraft on 7 August 1941.

It became fashionable to dismiss the machine as a non-starter, though in general pilots thought it a delight to fly. Sadly, prejudice and poor serviceability, resulting from unfamiliarity and shortage of spares, carried the day, and Airacobras flew just two combat missions before being replaced by Spitfire Mk VBs. If anyone still believes the P-39 was rubbish I recommend them to read the type's combat history with 34 Fighter Groups of the USAAF, and particularly the record of the 5000 used by the Soviet Union.

Clark's drawing contains several bits of pure invention, though the parts would have been illustrated in the engineering manuals. Examples are the main reduction gear, the wing spars and the landing-gear retraction mechanism. Incidentally, when the P-39 was designed many American aircraft used electric instead of hydraulic actuators. RAF pilots thought it quaint that such vital actions as selecting gear or flaps should be done by tiny tumbler switches. 'A-A' leaves one wondering whether Clark cut the web away or whether that's how it actually was, while, confusingly, he used the word 'chassis' to mean the centre fuselage instead of the landing gear. Prestone was a brand name for ethylene glycol coolant, which circulated through the radiator inside the bottom of the fuselage and hardly visible externally. The tankage was not integral in the sense understood today; there were six self-sealing bags in each wing, with a total capacity of 100 gal (120 US gal). Finally, was the nosewheel tyre really 'puncture-proof'?

# SPITFIRE I

The original of this classic drawing was done before the War, and showed the initial build-standard of the Mk I Spitfire, as built at Woolston (Southampton). By 1940 the huge Nuffield factory at Castle Bromwich (Birmingham) came on stream, its output far surpassing the little Supermarine works and also Westland, who made a few Mk Is but mainly produced Seafires.

Features of this early standard were the big two-blade fixed-pitch wooden propeller, flat windscreen without the thick bulletproof slab later added on the front, the flat-topped sliding hood which was too low for tall pilots, and the pole-like mast for the wire antenna needed by the old TR 9D radio. By the Battle of Britain VHF radio had begun to arrive, which meant that pilots could actually hear what the controller was saying. By the this rendition appeared in the first issue of *The Aeroplane Spotter* in January 1941, Clark had given the hood a bulged top, and redrawn the propeller as a 'ROTOL V.P' with three-blades. Without changing the drawing, the annotation 'BULLET-PROOF GLASS PANEL' was added to the windscreen. He still omitted the diagonal IFF (identification friend or foe) antenna wires to the tailplane tips, and these may in fact have been secret. Incidentally, the plan-view silhouette (not reproduced here) which accompanied this revised drawing was reversed left-to-right (one could see this from the asymmetric radiators, described later).

One of the odd features is that the wheels look like those of the prototype. The production wheel was forged light alloy with five integral spokes. I think most people would agree the legs are too far apart and a bit on the short side. Another point worth mentioning is that chief designer Reginald Mitchell chose to retain the extraordinary wing construction he had used in earlier monoplanes. The wing had almost all its strength in the D-nose formed by thick skin round the leading edge as far back as the spar. This spar had a plate web with round lightening holes and upper and lower booms in the form of a stack of square-section tubes just fitting inside each other, like a set of Russian dolls! The outermost tube stopped less than half-way to the tip, and the others faded out to leave just the inner member at the tip. Clark did not draw attention to this, yet drew a special detail showing the bridging member that joined the spars across the fuselage, which was quite ordinary!

On a lighter note, how about the language of the times: 'undercart', 'motor' and 'accumulators'. Later the battery compartment was moved to the rear fuselage, and the oxygen bottles also migrated tail-wards. And, of course, by 1944 the Spitfire had been developed by Joe Smith to be a totally different animal.

One of the first things to change was the exposed upper fuel tank. Originally this tank, and the oil tank under the engine, formed part of the exterior skin of the aircraft. The oil tank remained thus until in the final marks, with two-stage Griffon engines, it was relocated behind the engine. A much more important change, in the mass-produced Mk V, was to skin the ailerons with aluminium instead of fabric. Clark's Mk I had fabric, despite his insertion of rows of what look like rivets! Like its great rival the Bf 109, Spifire lateral control (until the Mk 21) almost disappeared in high-speed dives.

Very similar in appearance to the Mk I/II, the Spitfire Mk V was the backbone of Fighter Command during the dark days of 1941/42. These cannon-armed Mk VBs belong to No 72 Sqn, and are seen at Gravesend in October 1941. The unit flew Spitfires throughout the war

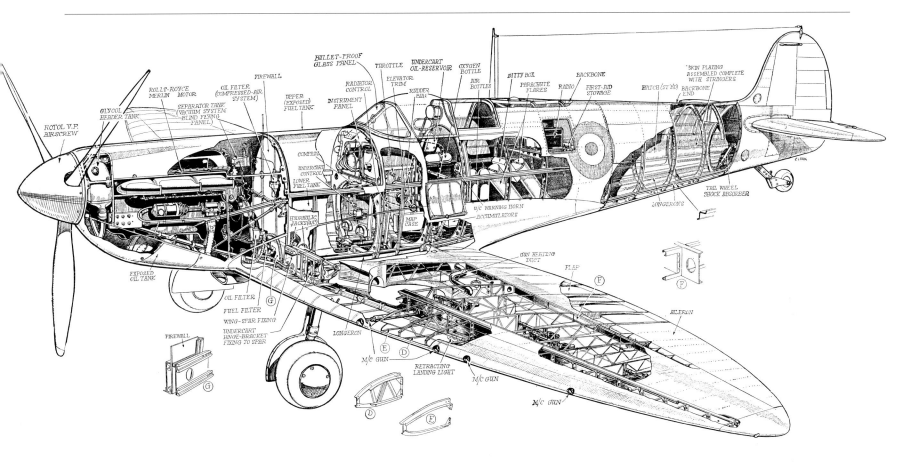

ROTOL V.P.
AIRSCREW

GLYCOL
HEADER TANK

ROLLS-ROYCE
MERLIN MOTOR

SEPARATOR TANK
(VACUUM SYSTEM
BLIND FLYING
PANEL)

OIL FILTER
(COMPRESSED-AIR
SYSTEM)

FIREWALL

UPPER
(EXPOSED)
FUEL TANK

INSTRUMENT
PANEL

BULLET-PROOF
GLASS PANEL

RADIATOR
CONTROL

ELEVATOR
TRIM

THROTTLE

UNDERCART
OIL-RESERVOIR

RUDDER
BIAS

OXYGEN
BOTTLE

AIR
BOTTLES

DITTY BOX

PARACHUTE
FLARES

RADIO

BACKBONE

FIRST-AID
STOWAGE

HATCH (ST'BD)

SKIN PLATING
ASSEMBLED COMPLETE
WITH STRINGERS

BACKBONE
END

CLARK

TAIL WHEEL
SHOCK ABSORBER

LONGERONS

COMPASS

UNDERCART
CONTROL

LOWER
FUEL TANK

HYDRAULIC
JACKS (U/C)

MAP
CASE

U/C WARNING HORN

ACCUMULATORS

EXPOSED
OIL TANK

OIL FILTER

FUEL FILTER

WING-SPAR FIXING

FIREWALL

UNDERCART
HINGE-BRACKET
FIXING TO SPAR

G

LONGERON

M/C GUN

E

D

RETRACTING
LANDING LIGHT

M/C GUN

M/C GUN

GUN HEATING
DUCT

FLAP

F

AILERON

F

D

E

G

Once the war had started, and guns were fired in anger, it was recognised rather quickly that their reliability was a matter of life or death. Accordingly, rectangles of fabric were doped over the muzzles to keep out rain and anything else that might enter, the gun simply blasting a hole on being fired. Usually standard red dope was used, but from September 1941 the outer leading edge of all day fighters was painted yellow. The author always thought, if the idea was to prevent 'own goals', there was no point in having a recognition feature visible only from the front! It may have helped the chaps who couldn't tell one aircraft from another also to have a band in a near-white colour called sky painted round the fuselage just ahead of the tail.

While on this subject, it is odd that Clark appeared to show his Mk I in pre-1937 silver. Even the very first delivery to No 19 Sqn at Duxford was fully camouflaged, and incidentally painted with B-Type (red/blue only) roundels. By 1939 the three-colour roundel had returned, but surrounded by a ring of yellow, to make it stand out better against the green/brown back-

ground. A real puzzle is why the modified drawing of January 1941 had a redrawn roundel with criss-cross shading and no yellow ring! By 1942 the brown camouflage, called dark earth, had been oversprayed with dark sea grey.

Like the Bf 109, the cooling radiators were placed under the inboard wing behind the landing gear. In early aircraft there was an engine radiator under the starboard (right) wing and a small oil cooler in a duct under the port wing. This asymmetry never had the slightest effect on handling, and when the two-stage Merlin was introduced with the Mks VIII and IX the intercooler radiator resulted in a symmetrical arrangement. Clark drew in the curving gun-heating tube, which drew hot air from behind each radiator, but failed to draw in or annotate the radiator itself. He drew what looks like the inlet to the engine radiator (which should have been under the other wing), but lined it up with the retracted leg, whereas actually the inlet was at 90° to the longitudinal axis.

# MOSQUITO II

Apart from the Harvard, this was the aeroplane I knew better than any other. It is part of British folk-lore that, along with military versions of the Albatross, the concept of a high-speed wooden unarmed bomber was suggested by de Havilland in 1939, regarded as nonsensical, repeated until Hatfield got a contract for a prototype flown on 25 November 1940, and then kept alive despite the opposition of production supremo Lord Beaverbrook – who kept cancelling the first production order for 50 Mosquitoes because it might have interfered with established types such as the Blenheim – until eventually 7781 were built in Britain, Canada and Australia to serve with every command, and with the USA and Soviet Union, in every theatre of war.

One of the most exciting days of my life came when, aged 15 in 1942, I was invited by Mr E H Morris, Hon Sec of No 4 Spotters Club, to actually visit the Hatfield factory. Having watched the secret Mosquitoes over Eastcote, suddenly I could climb into a pristine Mk IV day bomber (DK291) and then through the side door of soot-black Mk II nightfighter DD667. When I got home I drew pretty accurate plans of each from memory, and still have them. Of course, nobody in Britain ever doubted we would win the War, but with the 'Mozzie' how could we possibly lose?

Millar drew the Mk II, which was the first dedicated fighter version of the Mosquito to enter RAF service. It was a four machine gun/four cannon derivative of the B IV, the latter originally being designed to carry a bomb load of 1000 lb. This version was then made to operate with a load of 2000 lb, comprising four 500-pounders with shortened tail fins (this became the

AI Mk IV-equipped, DD750 was one of 466 Mosquito II nightfighters built for service with Fighter Command from May 1942

standard bomb of this weight). Finally, the bomb bay was bulged to carry a 4000-lb 'blockbuster'. Not only that, but later bombers, such as the Mk XVI, could carry 4000-pounders all the way to Berlin. Oh yes, and in daylight, and outpace Luftwaffe fighters on the way back!

One is left wondering why the people in positions of executive power – notably excepting Air Marshal Sir Wilfred Freeman – poured such scorn on the concept of a bomber so fast that it didn't need gun turrets, and, even more ridiculous, made of wood! A mere 15 years earlier all RAF aircraft had been made of wood, and efforts were being made to switch to that unfamiliar material, Duralumin, or in Boulton Paul's case, stainless steel. In the supposedly authoritarian Soviet Union nobody poured scorn on Lavochkin or Yakovlev for designing their fastest fighters in wood.

In the case of the Mosquito this material had many advantages. It gave a beautifully smooth and precisely formed exterior profile. It was easy to repair. Because for a given strength a greater volume of wood is needed, compared with metal, a hole made by a bullet or shell splinter may cause proportionately less weakening of the structure. Above all, it avoided consuming scarce raw materials, and brought into the aircraft industry countless big companies which had made furniture, little companies which had made pianos or hay rakes and even locally organised groups of ladies who churned out detail parts.

This was one of Millar's best wartime drawings. It showed all the main features, including the structure of the flaps. These were ply-skinned, whereas the control surfaces were covered in fabric. The fuselage was just wide enough for the pilot and, a bit further back, the navigator. It was packed with even more systems and equipment than Millar was allowed to show, and the only way it could be made was in left and right halves. When these were completely finished and equipped they were joined together, like a plastic model.

The twin-tread tailwheel tyre, invented by Marstrand and made by Dunlop, was later used on the Lancaster and several other aircraft. Of course, it could do nothing to avoid swing, so on take-off you kept the port engine well in advance of the starboard until you had firm rudder control. The landing gear was immensely strong, and the unique rubber-filled legs eliminated the need for precision air/oil seals. I don't know why Mosquito tyres always seemed to have a tread, when so many big wartime tyres were smooth.

The leading-edge radiators were extremely neat, and possibly gave less

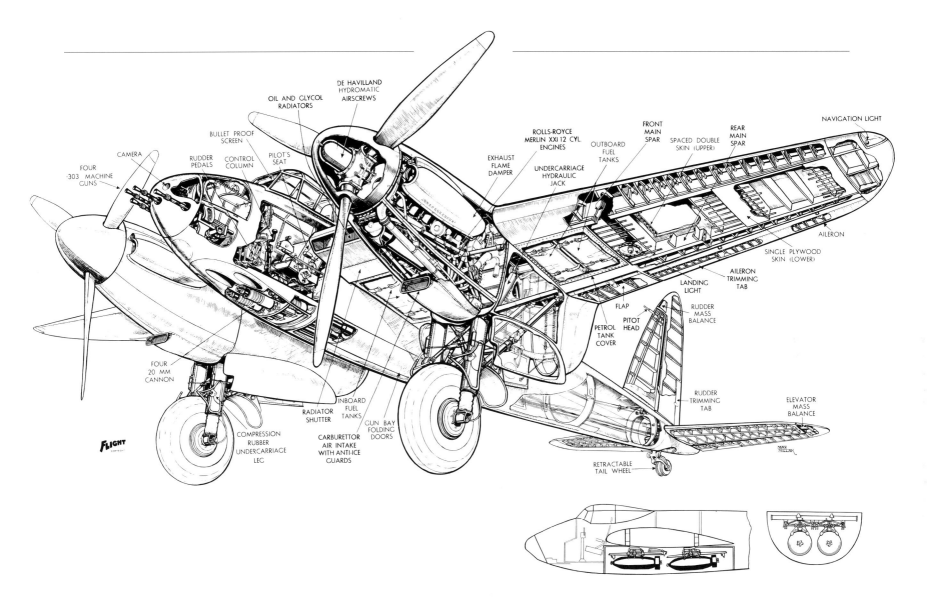

FOUR
·303 MACHINE
GUNS

CAMERA

RUDDER
PEDALS

BULLET PROOF
SCREEN

CONTROL
COLUMN

PILOT'S
SEAT

OIL AND GLYCOL
RADIATORS

DE HAVILLAND
HYDROMATIC
AIRSCREWS

EXHAUST
FLAME
DAMPER

ROLLS-ROYCE
MERLIN XXI 12 CYL
ENGINES

UNDERCARRIAGE
HYDRAULIC
JACK

OUTBOARD
FUEL
TANKS

FRONT
MAIN
SPAR

SPACED DOUBLE
SKIN (UPPER)

REAR
MAIN
SPAR

NAVIGATION LIGHT

AILERON

SINGLE PLYWOOD
SKIN (LOWER)

AILERON
TRIMMING
TAB

LANDING
LIGHT

FLAP

PETROL
TANK
COVER

PITOT
HEAD

RUDDER
MASS
BALANCE

RUDDER
TRIMMING
TAB

ELEVATOR
MASS
BALANCE

FOUR
20 MM
CANNON

RADIATOR
SHUTTER

INBOARD
FUEL
TANKS

GUN BAY
FOLDING
DOORS

COMPRESSION
RUBBER
UNDERCARRIAGE
LEG

CARBURETTOR
AIR INTAKE
WITH ANTI-ICE
GUARDS

RETRACTABLE
TAIL WHEEL

FLIGHT

MAX
MILLAR

drag than the underslung installation of the Beaufighter II and Lancaster. The main coolant section was in the middle, the inner matrix being the cabin heater and the outboard section being the oil cooler. The idea was refined until in the DH 103 Hornet the installation was intended to give positive thrust.

I was once told an amusing story concerning a Mosquito by my colleague H A 'Tony' Taylor, who once found himself in an aircraft with no airspeed reading (and I think it would affect his altimeter and vertical-speed indicator as well). An insect had laid eggs in the static pipe and when these hatched the grubs played havoc with the pressure-sensing. From then on, a flagged stopper had to be pushed into the hole when each aircraft landed.

Published in *Flight* for 6 May 1943, this drawing beat a large cutaway on the Mk IV by Clark by a single day! Millar also showed bomb carriage details of the latter mark through the use of a small, relatively undetailed, side-view which is reproduced here below the main drawing. Conversely, Clark produced a scrap view of the gun-toting nose of a Mk II.

# AUSTER IV

Just after the war I noticed an advertisement for new Auster J-1 Autocrats at a fly-away price of £815. I even wrote off for a brochure. Of course, I could never have scraped together one-tenth of that sum, and this turned out to be a blessing in disguise. I did not get to fly an Auster until I joined *Flight* in 1951, and I then found I couldn't even taxi it nicely. The push/pull throttle knob preferred to be either fully in or fully out, and trying to obtain the power needed meant that you held the throttle while you flew with your left hand. And, of course, to someone who had in Southern Rhodesia had a chance to fly a North American Navion and a Beech Bonanza, the whole thing reminded me of the aeroplanes of the pre-1914 era.

It all stemmed from the classic 1929 design of the Taylor Brothers in Rochester, New York. This was for a neat side-by-side two-seater with any of almost a dozen types of engine of about 40 hp. The fuselage was welded steel tube, the high-mounted wings had parallel plywood spars on to which were slid ribs riveted from rolled steel strip and angle sections, finally nailed in place, and the tail was steel tube welded and brazed by a process called Sifbronze. Everything was then fabric-covered, and doped. The V-struts were oval steel tubes. This product, called the Model A, led not only to a long line of successive Taylor companies but also to Piper.

In 1938 Taylorcraft Aeroplanes (England) was formed, building the Model A under licence. This was made at Thurmaston, north of Leicester. Each machine was trundled for about four miles along ancient Fosse Way to

a small grass airfield at Rearsby. Gradually the 40 hp Model A grew into the Taylorcraft Plus C2 with a 90 hp Cirrus Minor engine. In 1939 one was delivered to the RAF, and used by the Army for a resurrected mission called AOP (Air Observation Post). It was given the Service name of Taylorcraft Auster. From the start, the value of such machines was obvious. Had World War 2 never happened, Taylorcraft Aeroplanes (England) would probably have called in the receiver. As it was, orders came thick and fast, for use by 'brown jobs' (Army pilots and observers) and by the RAF. By 1942 Auster production involved ten small dispersed factories north of Leicester. By the end of the War Rearsby had seen the testing and delivery of 100 Auster Is, 2 Mk IIs, 467 Mk IIIs, 255 Mk IVs and 780 Mk Vs.

The Mk III was the first really capable version, with adequate power from a 130 hp de Havilland Gipsy Major I. Other improvements included Bendix brakes, larger rear areas of transparent Perspex, landing flaps which were pulled down manually by a lever in the cockpit roof, longitudinal trim effected by a small auxiliary surface below the tailplane and, of course, full two-way Army communications radio. The Mk IV, drawn by Clark, was powered by the more compact 130 hp Lycoming O-290-3 engine. It added a third seat in a rear section, with a bulged Perspex roof giving even better all-round vision, as well as a tailwheel on a long leaf-spring instead of the previous tailskid. The Mk V was similar to the IV but had a blind-flying panel, as well as conventional trimmers on the elevators.

Because these aircraft were all so simple, Clark was able to lay bare almost everything. Four years earlier he would just have drawn the aircraft, but by 1944 his standards were much higher, and perhaps because there were no security problems, he really went to town on it. Possibly more than in any other of his drawings, he was able to include a most informative set of inset details which made everything crystal clear.

Today we might conclude that as there are tens of thousands of Lycoming piston engines still in regular use and very few Gipsies, the American horizontally-opposed type was superior. My own belief is that, on balance, it was. I have often wondered whether, had he not started in 1924 with war-surplus engines with four cylinders in line, Frank Halford would not instead have gone for the easier air cooling, better balance and shorter and lighter construction possible with the 'flat four'. During World War 2, however, most British people took it for granted that almost everything we produced was better than any foreign equivalent, so the switch to the Lycoming was possibly because there weren't enough Gipsies?

This Auster IV force-landed near the 8th Army's frontline in January 1945 after sustaining flak damage whilst artillery spotting. Unfortunately, the 'MC' code does not denote its unit

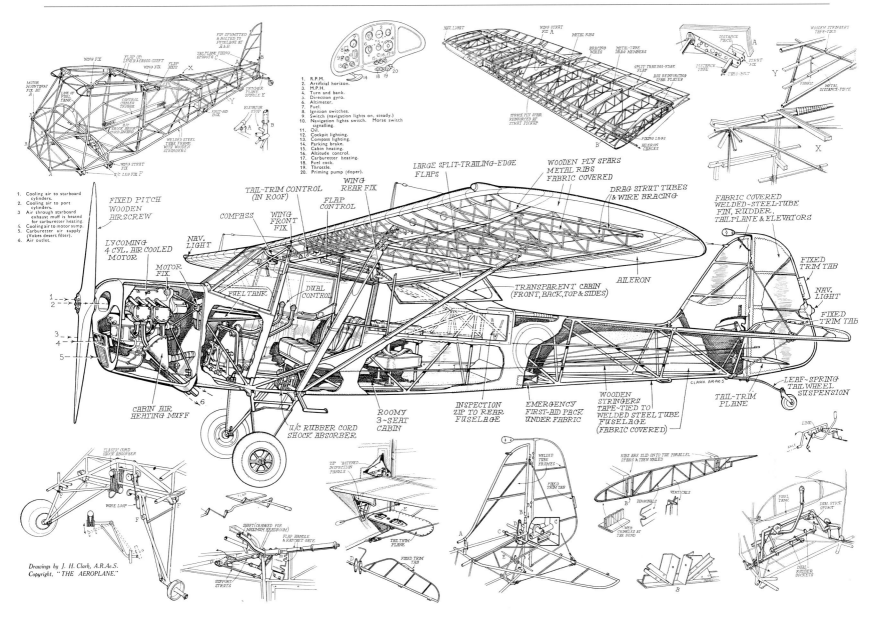

Wartime Austers had various differing instrument panels. As noted, the true RAF 'basic six' blind-flying panel came in with the Mk V, which had an engine-driven vacuum pump. Other aircraft fitted with gyro instruments had a venturi on the left side of the fuselage to provide the suction.

Having regard to the simplicity of the aircraft it is rather surprising that Clark left some things out. Most notably, though he indicated the parking brake pull-lever in the cockpit and showed a tiny bit of pipe near the right wheel, he made no mention of the wheel brakes. Again, though he drew in the antenna mast and wire, he made no mention of the cumbersome Army radio, nor of the possible fit of a reconnaissance camera.

# FIREFLY I

I believe that in World War 2 no company in the world mass-produced a greater range of aircraft than Fairey Aviation. They comprised the Battle, Swordfish, Albacore, Fulmar, Barracuda and Firefly, plus 500 Beaufighters and 662 Halifaxes. Of this mixed bag, the only aircraft that bore a similarity to each other were the Fulmar and Firefly. Both were carrier-based fighters, and in order to get back to that tiny airfield in the middle of the ocean Their Lordships decreed that carrier-based aircraft had to have a navigator.

This inevitably meant that naval fighters came out larger, heavier and less agile than single-seat land-based machines for similar duties. Nowhere was this contrast more marked than with the Fairey Fulmar and Firefly. The former had a low-altitude Merlin and eight machine guns, and with a brochure max speed of 244 mph, was 120-130 mph slower than a Spitfire. The Firefly I had a low-altitude Griffon (initially of 1730 max hp and later of 1990) and four cannon, and with a brochure max speed of 316 mph was again about 130 mph slower than the contemporary Spitfire Mk XIV.

To be fair, the backseater in the Fleet Air Arm's two-seat fighters was also required to act as an observer, for example in shadowing hostile ships or spotting for friendly guns. Moreover, the range and endurance demanded was rather greater than that of a Hurricane or Spitfire, which again reduced the dogfight capability. In the author's opinion there is absolutely no point in mass-producing fighters which are almost certain to come a good second in air combat, and a Firefly pilot would have had to be almost superhuman to beat a Bf 109, Fw 190 or Japanese single-seater.

From 1925 the main Fairey design team had been led by Marcel Lobelle, but he left in 1940 to form M L Aviation, so he only took the Firefly as far as a general-arrangement drawing and mock-up. In 1940 Herbert E Chaplin took over, and the prototype flew on 22 December 1941. It was the last new type to be flown by Chris Staniland, long-time and famous chief test pilot, who was killed shortly afterwards. The Firefly proved to be relatively trouble-free, though it could hardly avoid being caught up in the political problems caused by having so many diverse programmes for aircraft being made at Hayes, Stockport and Errwood Park, and (in the case of the Firefly) also by General Aircraft at Hanworth, with C R (later Sir Richard) Fairey himself permanently stationed in Washington leaving nobody with real authority to take strategic decisions and resolve the many snarl-ups..

Good things about the Firefly I were the simple tough airframe, robust well-cushioned landing gear and, not least, the superb Youngman flaps. Clearly shown by Clark, these were normally retracted flush under the trailing edge of the folding wing, their inboard ends extending under the fuselage to meet at the centreline. For take-off or combat they could be swung down aft of the trailing edge to increase area. For landing, further rotation of bracket (3) pivoted the flap to about 35°. I flew a later version (the T 2 trainer) and was impressed by these flaps.

Bad features certainly started with the fact that, like the Skua seen on earlier pages, the big and heavy wings had to be folded or extended manually. This needed a great deal of muscle-power from a large team of ground handlers to unlatch and extend or fold both wings together. The drawing shows how the wing hinged at oblique axis 'E', so the ground handlers had to

Charles E Brown caught up with an early-production Firefly I on a pre-delivery flight in mid-1943. No 1770 Sqn was the first fleet unit to receive the Firefly I in October 1943

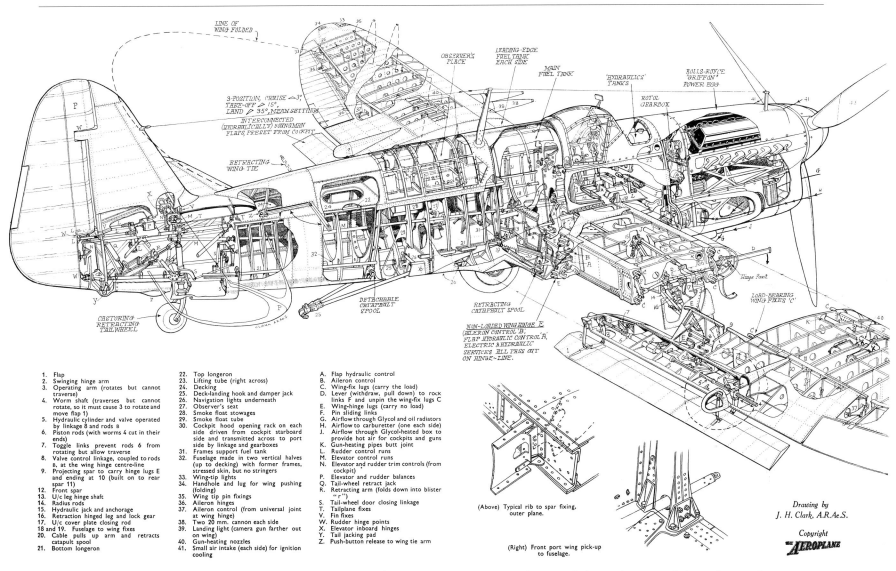

LINE OF WING FOLDED

3-POSITION, CRUISE ⟶3°,
TAKE-OFF ⟶15°,
LAND ⟶35°, MEAN SETTINGS
INTERCONNECTED
(HYDRAULICALLY) YOUNGMAN
FLAPS, PRESET FROM COCKPIT

RETRACTING WING TIE

OBSERVER'S PLACE

LEADING-EDGE FUEL TANK EACH SIDE

MAIN FUEL TANK

'HYDRAULICS' TANKS

ROLLS-ROYCE "GRIFFON" POWER EGG

ROTOL GEARBOX

CLARK ARAES

CASTORING RETRACTING TAILWHEEL

DETACHABLE CATAPULT SPOOL

RETRACTING CATAPULT SPOOL

Hinge Point

LOAD-BEARING WING FIXES 'C'

NON-LOADED WING HINGE E
(AILERON CONTROL 'B',
FLAP HYDRAULIC CONTROL 'A',
ELECTRIC & HYDRAULIC
SERVICES ALL PASS OUT
ON HINGE-LINE.

1. Flap
2. Swinging hinge arm
3. Operating arm (rotates but cannot traverse)
4. Worm shaft (traverses but cannot rotate, so it must cause 3 to rotate and move flap 1)
5. Hydraulic cylinder and valve operated by linkage 8 and rods B
6. Piston rods (with worms 4 cut in their ends)
7. Toggle links prevent rods 6 from rotating but allow traverse
8. Valve control linkage, coupled to rods B, at the wing hinge centre-line
9. Projecting spar to carry hinge lugs E and ending at 10 (built on to rear spar 11)
12. Front spar
13. U/c leg hinge shaft
14. Radius rods
15. Hydraulic jack and anchorage
16. Retraction hinged leg and lock gear
17. U/c cover plate closing rod
18 and 19. Fuselage to wing fixes
20. Cable pulls up arm and retracts catapult spool
21. Bottom longeron

22. Top longeron
23. Lifting tube (right across)
24. Decking
25. Deck-landing hook and damper jack
26. Navigation lights underneath
27. Observer's seat
28. Smoke float stowages
29. Smoke float tube
30. Cockpit hood opening rack on each side driven from cockpit starboard side and transmitted across to port side by linkage and gearboxes
31. Frames support fuel tank
32. Fuselage made in two vertical halves (up to decking) with former frames, stressed skin, but no stringers
33. Wing-tip lights
34. Handhole and lug for wing pushing (folding)
35. Wing tip pin fixings
36. Aileron hinges
37. Aileron control (from universal joint at wing hinge)
38. Two 20 mm. cannon each side
39. Landing light (camera gun farther out on wing)
40. Gun-heating nozzles
41. Small air intake (each side) for ignition cooling

A. Flap hydraulic control
B. Aileron control
C. Wing-fix lugs (carry the load)
D. Lever (withdraw, pull down) to rock links F and unpin the wing-fix lugs C
E. Wing-hinge lugs (carry no load)
F. Pin sliding links
G. Airflow through Glycol and oil radiators
H. Airflow to carburetter (one each side)
J. Airflow through Glycol-heated box to provide hot air for cockpits and guns
K. Gun-heating pipes butt joint
L. Rudder control runs
M. Elevator control runs
N. Elevator and rudder trim controls (from cockpit)
P. Elevator and rudder balances
Q. Tail-wheel retract jack
R. Retracting arm (folds down into blister " r ")
S. Tail-wheel door closing linkage
T. Tailplane fixes
V. Fin fixes
W. Rudder hinge points
X. Elevator inboard hinges
Y. Tail jacking pad
Z. Push-button release to wing tie arm

(Above) Typical rib to spar fixing, outer plane.

(Right) Front port wing pick-up to fuselage.

*Drawing by*
*J. H. Clark, A.R.Ae.S.*

Copyright
THE AEROPLANE

take the entire weight of the wing. Letting it slam down against spar lugs 'C' would have caused serious damage. Not until long after the war, in the course of making 352 Firefly AS.5s, was power-folding added. A minor shortcoming was that the 146-gal main tank separated the two crew-members, and the early Mk I fighters also had poor forward view and a cramped pilot hood. The detail showing the front port (left) wing/fuselage joint also shows part of the push/pull rod driving the rudder.

Altogether, 1702 Fireflies were produced. They included nightfighters, trainers, anti-submarine fighters, three-seat dedicated anti-submarine versions, target tugs and various marks of pilotless target. Clark drew one of the later Mk I fighters, with raised canopy and deeper windscreen, and a most unusual radio wire antenna extended forward to the nose. The drawing was published four days before VE-Day, with the last number (42, the 13-ft Rotol constant-speed propeller) omitted from the key list. By this time Clark was master of his art, and he turned in a drawing so clear it needs little further comment.

# MUSTANG I

I am especially pleased to see this drawing, which was accompanied by an exceptional group of supplementary detail sketches. It shows the type of Mustang which fought through the War on almost every battlefront from 1941 until the beginning of 1944. Only in the final year, when things were getting much easier, did the mass-produced P-51D and P-51K come into action, yet today these are the Mustangs that everyone knows. The original Allison-engined versions are almost forgotten.

In December 1939 the British Purchasing Commission (BPC) suggested to North American Aviation (NAA) – whom they knew as the maker of the Harvard trainer – that they might build under licence Curtiss P-40 Tomahawks for the RAF. NAA President James H 'Dutch' Kindelberger said 'We could build you a much better fighter of our own design'. After five months of talk the BPC ordered an NA-73 prototype and 320 production aircraft. The prototype was rolled out 100 days later. It flew on 26 October 1940, and was an outstanding aircraft from the start.

Those 100 days at the Inglewood, Los Angeles, design office must have been hard work. Clark's detail sketches gave an idea of just how much brilliant aircraft design was done in that short time. Today, when with massive computer power a new fighter design takes ten years, it is salutary to think that five years from the start of design 15,586 Mustangs had been built, and modified versions were still being delivered by Cavalier and Piper into the 1970s.

Why do I call this design brilliant? One reason is that, compared with a 1940 Spitfire, the NA-73 was similar in size and engine power, yet it had heavier armament (eight guns, but four were of 0.5-in calibre) and getting on

for twice as much fuel, yet it had considerably lower aerodynamic drag and at low levels was 25 mph faster. When the second production aircraft, AG346, arrived in England in the summer of 1941 it astonished the pilots at Boscombe Down by its all-round excellence.

Some features, such as the wide track main gear, drum-type radiator (with the oil cooler in the centre) and outstanding elegance of the structure are obvious. Less evident is the so-called 'laminar-flow' wing profile, which reduced camber and moved the point of maximum thickness and peak suction much further back. Almost the only unpopular feature was that, instead of sliding back, the canopy had a top hinged open to the right and a left side that hinged out and down.

The seat was exceptionally comfortable, and the pilot almost lay back on top of the wing with his feet on high pedals. This was relaxing on a long flight (from 1944 Mustangs were often airborne for nine hours) and helped counter high-g loads. In fact, pulling g, as you have to in combat, was the Mustang's only serious weakness. It was all too easy to haul back just that little bit too hard and, with no warning, cause sudden flow breakdown. The 'departure' was wholly uncontrolled, an uncommanded roll of 270° being typical. Of course, if you were trying to escape from an Fw 190 on your tail, this fault might have become a lifesaver!

The Allison engine had a capacity slightly larger than a Merlin (1710 against 1650 cubic inches), but had a longer history of development and in this aircraft was a smooth and quiet engine. Apart from the fact that you had to pay attention to it, there being no automatic boost control, its only drawback was that its power fell away seriously at high altitudes. For this reason,

Mustang I AG345 completed all its flight trials in the US, despite wearing full RAF camouflage and national markings

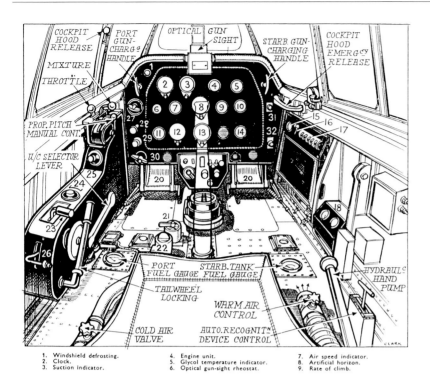

Labels on cockpit diagram:

COCKPIT HOOD RELEASE
PORT GUN-CHARG⁹ HANDLE
OPTICAL GUN SIGHT
STARB GUN-CHARGING HANDLE
COCKPIT HOOD EMERGCY RELEASE
MIXTURE
THROTTLE
PROP. PITCH MANUAL CONT.
U/C SELECTOR LEVER
PORT FUEL GAUGE
STARB. TANK FUEL GAUGE
HYDRAULᶜ HAND PUMP
TAILWHEEL LOCKING
COLD AIR VALVE
WARM AIR CONTROL
AUTO. RECOGNITⁿ DEVICE CONTROL

1. Windshield defrosting.
2. Clock.
3. Suction Indicator.
4. Engine unit.
5. Glycol temperature indicator.
6. Optical gun-sight rheostat.
7. Air speed indicator.
8. Artificial horizon.
9. Rate of climb.

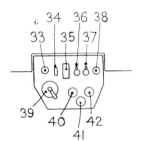

10. Engine r.p.m.
11. Undercarriage position.
12. Altimeter.
13. Turn indicator.
14. Manifold pressure.
15. Generator ammeter.
16. Generator main line.
17. Lights and pressure head heater.
18. Oxygen system regulator.
20. Rudder pedals.
21. Fuel cock.
22. Cold air inlet.
23. Radiator scoops control.
24. Rudder tab control.
25. Port aileron tab control.
26. Wing flap control.
27. Gun selector control.
28. Undercarriage emergency down.
29. Hydraulic system pressure control.
30. Gun heater control.
31. Vacuum system selector switch.
32. Radio control.
33. Airscrew pitch control.
34. Airscrew safety switch.
35. Engine starter.
36. Gun camera safety switch.
37. Oil dilution switch.
38. Undercarriage warning horn cut-out.
39. Ignition safety switch.
40. Instrument panel lights.
41. Cockpit lamps rheostat.
42. Flight instrument lights rheostat.

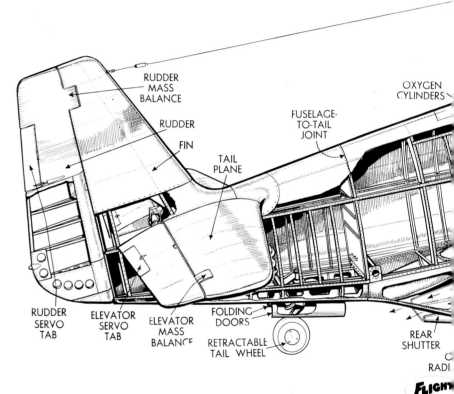

RUDDER MASS BALANCE
RUDDER
FIN
FUSELAGE-TO-TAIL JOINT
OXYGEN CYLINDERS
TAIL PLANE
RUDDER SERVO TAB
ELEVATOR SERVO TAB
ELEVATOR MASS BALANCE
FOLDING DOORS
RETRACTABLE TAIL WHEEL
REAR SHUTTER
RADI
C

FLIGHT
COPYRIGHT

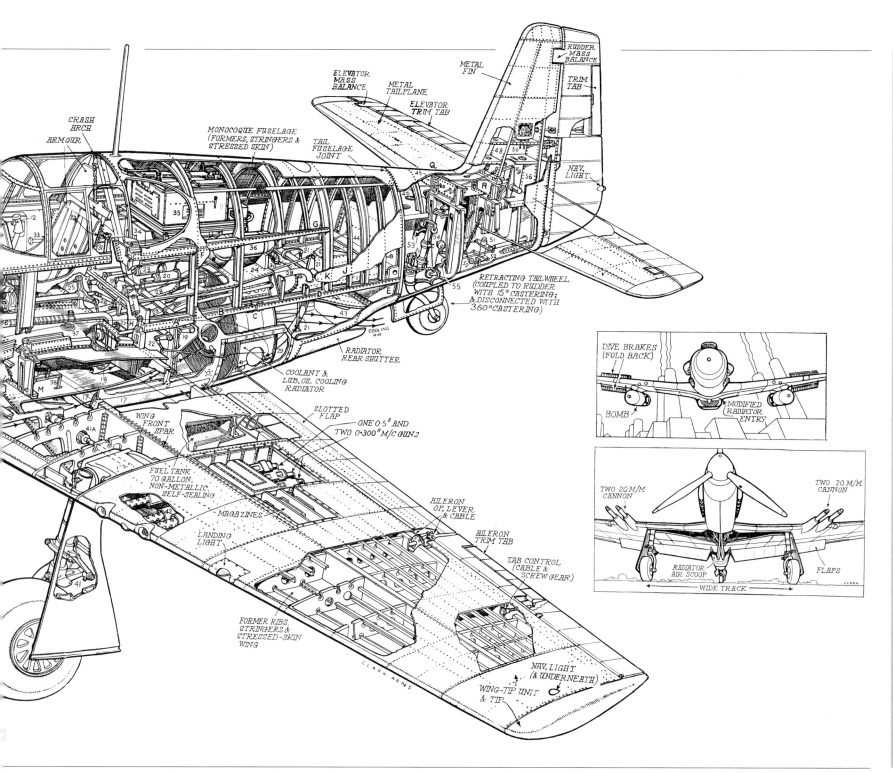

CRASH
ARCH

ARMOUR

MONOCOQUE FUSELAGE
(FORMERS, STRINGERS &
STRESSED SKIN)

ELEVATOR
MASS
BALANCE

METAL
TAILPLANE

METAL
FIN

RUDDER
MASS
BALANCE

TRIM
TAB

ELEVATOR
TRIM TAB

TAIL
FUSELAGE
JOINT

NAV.
LIGHT

RETRACTING TAILWHEEL
(COUPLED TO RUDDER
WITH 15° CASTERING;
& DISCONNECTED WITH
360° CASTERING)

RADIATOR
REAR SHUTTER

COOLING
AIR

COOLANT &
LUB. OIL COOLING
RADIATOR

WING
FRONT
SPAR

SLOTTED
FLAP

ONE 0·5" AND
TWO 0·300" M/C GUNS

FUEL TANK
70 GALLON,
NON-METALLIC,
SELF-SEALING

MAGAZINES

AILERON
OP. LEVER
& CABLE

LANDING
LIGHT

AILERON
TRIM TAB

TAB CONTROL
(CABLE &
SCREW GEAR)

FORMER RIBS,
STRINGERS &
STRESSED-SKIN
WING

NAV. LIGHT
(& UNDERNEATH)

WING-TIP UNIT
& TIP

CLARK ARES

DIVE BRAKES
(FOLD BACK)

BOMB

MODIFIED
RADIATOR
ENTRY

TWO 20 M/M
CANNON

TWO 20 M/M
CANNON

RADIATOR
AIR SCOOP

FLAPS

WIDE TRACK

CLARK

1. Carburetter air intake.
2. Coolant header tank and Fillex plug.
3. Coolant pipe to engine pump.
4. Motor bearer.
5. Motor support block (rubber mounted into bearer 4).
6. Master brake cylinder.
7. Hydraulic tank (connected to 6).
8. Hydraulic filter.
9. Generator control panel.
10. Instrument board.
11. Reflector gun sight.
12. Gun button on stick.
13. Stick locking peg.
14. Starboard rudder pedal.
15. Fuel cock.
16. Cold air to cabin, scooped from cooling air in front shutter 17 by scoop 18.
17. Radiator front shutter controlled by links 19 and hydraulic jack 20.
18. Cold air scoop under wing cut away to show 18-in. shutter passage 17.
19. Shutter control, also control rear shutter through rods 21.
20. Front and rear shutters operating jack under rear floor 24.
21. Rear shutter control rods.
22. Flap rods controlled by operating jack 23.
23. Flap-operating jack under rear floor 24.
24. Rear floor.
25. Aileron links.
26. Elevator link connect to cranks, which ride free on flap shaft 22.
27. Aileron tab control.
28. Coolant and oil pipes to radiator from motor through wing centre-section.
29. Return from radiator to motor through wing centre-section.
30. Cabin warm air scooped out of the heated cooling air in rear shutter and passed along to cockpit valve.
31. Batteries behind pilot.
32. Spring suspension—pilot's seat.
33. Hydraulic hand pump.
34. Radio receiver.
35. Radio transmitter.
36. Oxygen bottles.
37. Port fuel tank gauge.
38. Jack-operated radiator air deflector in front of front shutter 17.
39. Undercarriage cover spring-tensioned return cable.
40. Undercarriage wheel well in wing centre-section.
41. Undercarriage leg torque links.
41a. Undercarriage operating jack.
42. Machine-gun blast tubes.
43. Fuselage air drawn out into rear shutter duct.
44. Cross-tube for fuselage lifting.
45. Tailplane front spar mounted on fuselage frame deck 46.
46. Fuselage decking (extends back to rudder post).
47. Fin front spar.
49. Elevator shaft and levers.
50. Rudder trim tab screw gear and cables.
51. Rudder control.
52. Cables from 51 back to tail wheel to steer tail wheel.
53. Clutch cables disconnect tail wheel from rudder steerage.
54. Tail wheel shock-leg pushed forward (retracted) by a hydraulic jack.
55. Tail wheel hinge.
56. Stern post, carrying rudder

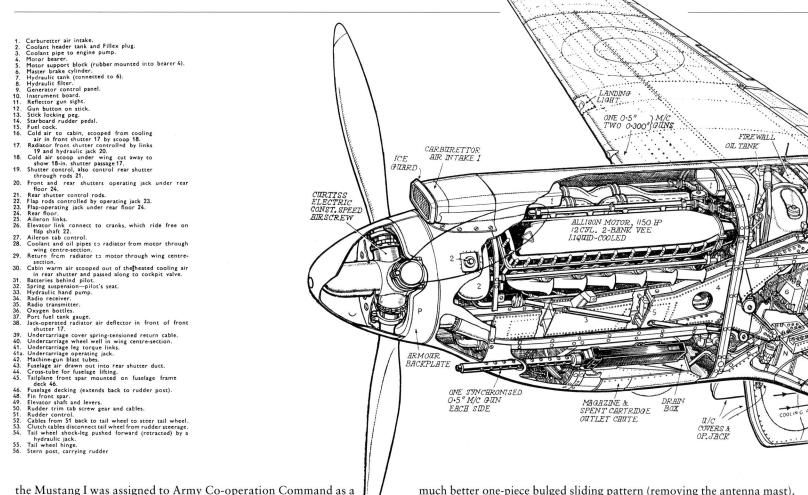

the Mustang I was assigned to Army Co-operation Command as a low-level reconnaissance aircraft, replacing the inferior Tomahawk.

Clark showed the unusual armament, but made the wing guns all look the same size. Under high-g loads the ammunition belts tended to jam. In later versions the nose guns were eliminated and the armament became four, and later six, 0.5 in guns in the wings, all upright and with completely reliable feeds. The P-51 (the first for the USAAF) and Mustang IA had four 20 mm cannon.

All later models could carry underwing bombs, rockets or drop tanks, the A-36A being a ground-attack version with dive brakes. Rolls-Royce fitted several Mustangs with Merlin engines, but NAA did a better conversion to produce the P-51B. This gave a tremendous leap in high-altitude performance, though it had only four 0.5 in guns.

The Malcolm Company in Britain replaced the folding cockpit hood by a much better one-piece bulged sliding pattern (removing the antenna mast). On a visit to Britain Gen Henry H Arnold was impressed at the 'teardrop' canopies of Typhoons and later Spitfires, and he immediately told US fighter manufacturers. Republic quickly produced the P-47D-25, the first example of which Arnold sent to California to show NAA. The result was the P-51D, and Dallas-built P-51K, which are the Mustangs everyone sees today.

The flood of these Merlin-engined versions that came in 1944 were outstanding in all aspects of flight performance. Apart from having six 0.5 in guns in the wings, they had a Hamilton or Aeroproducts propeller with four broad blades, a much better radiator in a different duct, redesigned ailerons, and eventually a dorsal fin to improve the marginal yaw stability. This fell close to zero when an overload tank was put behind the seat, so that bombers could be escorted to Berlin. One took off and climbed with extreme care, relaxing only when the aft tank was empty.

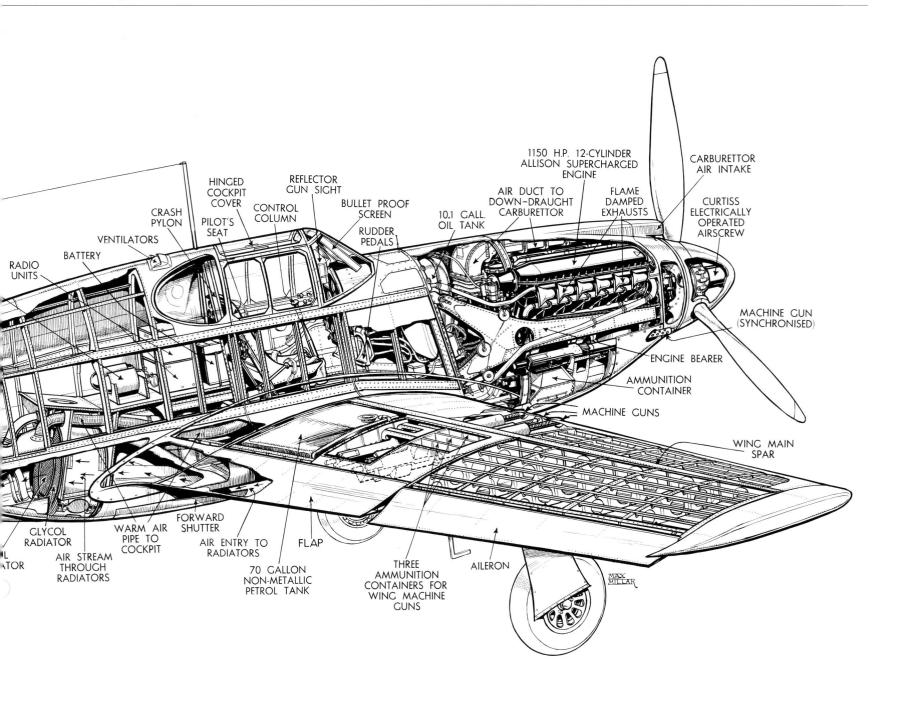

RADIO
UNITS

BATTERY

VENTILATORS

CRASH
PYLON

PILOT'S
SEAT

HINGED
COCKPIT
COVER

CONTROL
COLUMN

REFLECTOR
GUN SIGHT

BULLET PROOF
SCREEN

RUDDER
PEDALS

10.1 GALL.
OIL TANK

AIR DUCT TO
DOWN-DRAUGHT
CARBURETTOR

1150 H.P. 12-CYLINDER
ALLISON SUPERCHARGED
ENGINE

FLAME
DAMPED
EXHAUSTS

CARBURETTOR
AIR INTAKE

CURTISS
ELECTRICALLY
OPERATED
AIRSCREW

MACHINE GUN
(SYNCHRONISED)

ENGINE BEARER

AMMUNITION
CONTAINER

MACHINE GUNS

WING MAIN
SPAR

GLYCOL
RADIATOR

AIR STREAM
THROUGH
RADIATORS

WARM AIR
PIPE TO
COCKPIT

FORWARD
SHUTTER

AIR ENTRY TO
RADIATORS

FLAP

70 GALLON
NON-METALLIC
PETROL TANK

THREE
AMMUNITION
CONTAINERS FOR
WING MACHINE
GUNS

AILERON

MAX
MILLAR

96

TAIL WHEEL FREE.—Pull on cable E swings F about fixed position, an axle H thus raising A and its lug B (through link G and against return spring J) clear of C and D.   C and D (carrying tail wheel) can now castor full 360 degrees independently of rudder.

TAIL WHEEL STEERED BY RUDDER.—Rudder operation swings arm A and its lug B, which rotates tail wheel spindle C by pushing its driving band D. Note play at D, allowing 15 degrees castoring of C and tail wheel.

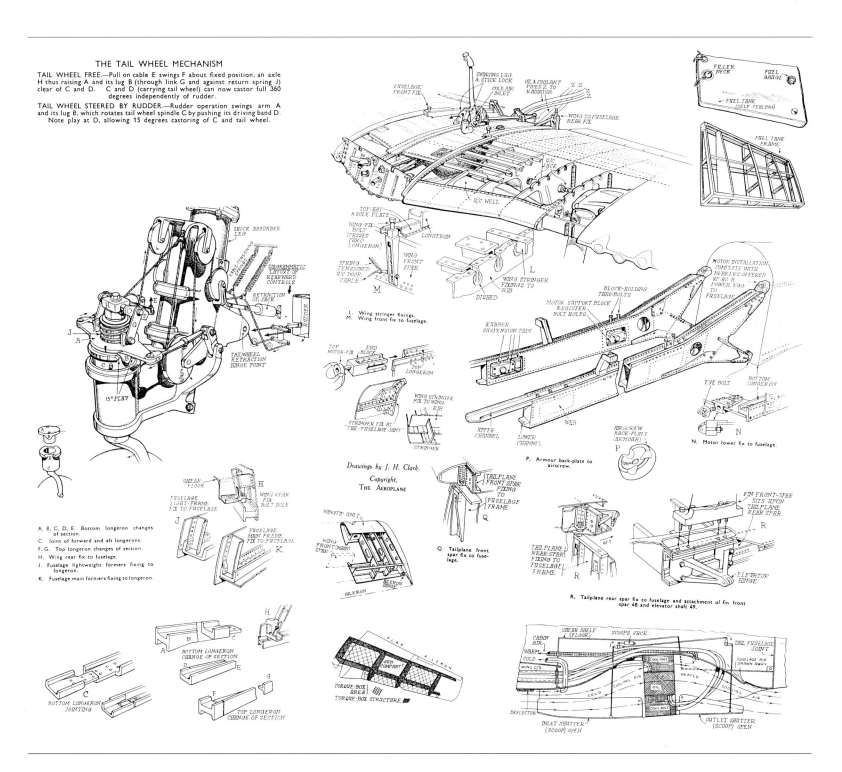

A, B, C, D, E.  Bottom longeron changes of section.
C.  Joint of forward and aft longerons.
F, G.  Top longeron changes of section.
H.  Wing rear fix to fuselage.
J.  Fuselage lightweight formers fixing to longeron.
K.  Fuselage main formers fixing to longeron.

Drawings by J. H. Clark.
Copyright,
THE AEROPLANE

L. Wing stringer fixings.
M. Wing front fix to fuselage.

N. Motor lower fix to fuselage.

P. Armour back-plate to airscrew.

Q. Tailplane front spar fix to fuselage.

R. Tailplane rear spar fix to fuselage and attachment of fin front spar 48 and elevator shaft 49.

# MESSENGER

It is impossible to write about the later products of Miles Aircraft without feeling that there's something wrong with a country which says 'People have to compete in the open marketplace. If a company goes under, too bad. If the entire British aircraft industry ceases to exist, who cares?' Miles went under as far back as 1947, long before this became fashionable. They went under partly because of their unbridled enthusiasm, which drove them on to design, build and flight-test a profusion of prototypes, all exciting and potential winners, when very little money was actually coming in to pay the wages.

It was doubly sad because, like de Havilland, Miles was imbued by a marvellous spirit. Not many people had cars in those days, but if you looked at the small car park at the factory at Woodley, outside Reading, most of the cars were cream and red, the Miles colours. British Aerospace doesn't even have company colours.

F G 'Fred' Miles, his wife Maxine and brother George were the ideal team to run an aircraft company. In sharpest contrast to today's highly paid managements, they were all qualified engineers and designers, and also enthusiastic pilots. After a small series of extremely agile Martlet biplanes, Fred and his wife produced the M.1 Satyr in 1932. This was a tiny sporting biplane which had a long career, and it triggered the launch of Phillips & Powis Ltd on the airfield at Woodley. A year later Miles managed to buy a job lot of 95-hp Cirrus engines at a knockdown price, and this enabled him to put the M.2 Hawk two-seater on the market at £395. It astonished everyone by being a

Although wearing an RAF fin flash, this Messenger is very much a civilianised version of the nimble Miles four-seater

trim cantilever monoplane with folding wings and smooth ply skin. About 100 were built in 22 versions.

There followed a wonderful succession of attractive wooden monoplanes, one specially created for Col Charles Lindbergh, until in 1937 this upstart firm – soon to become Miles Aircraft Ltd – had the effrontery to produce an advanced military trainer with a 745 hp Rolls-Royce Kestrel engine, able to reach 296 mph. Even the officials eventually knew a good thing when they saw it, as the section on the Miles Master shows.

Probably contrary to all kinds of regulations, in 1941 George Miles designed a startlingly beautiful side-by-side cabin trainer with retractable landing gear. This flew in 1942 as the prototype M.28, which on a 140 hp Gipsy carried four adults 500 miles at 160 mph on 25 gallons of fuel. A variety of M.28 versions followed, while the prototype was converted into the first M.38 Messenger, first flown in this form on 12 September 1942.

The Messenger was a STOL (short take-off and landing) version, with fixed landing gear, non-retractable high-lift flaps, a three-finned tail and, in the initial version drawn by Clark, with a pure drag flap (today we would call it an airbrake) hinged under the fuselage. Of course, everything was worked manually, though one might not have expected the human interfaces (items 15, easily confused with 13, and 17) to be designed that way.

Like the M.28 the M.38 was an obvious winner for the postwar era, but initial production had to be for the war effort. Miles were proud of the fact that, unlike rival aircraft such as the Auster, the M.38 carried two adults wearing parachutes plus military communications radio and various other military items, and still met 'all the official trials and several others in addition'. A volume published in early 1945, The Book of Miles Aircraft, showed a Messenger being flown into a large fabric barrier in 'a forced-landing test'. The Messenger was secret at that time, so it was not named in the caption, and did not appear in the type-by-type review.

Of course, it was a simple machine. Postwar Messengers were fitted with various Gipsy, Cirrus Major, Bombardier and Praga engines, always with a fixed-pitch propeller. An 18-gallon fuel tank was in the inboard part of each wing, just where you stood on getting in. Almost all did not have dual control, though RG333, the Messenger used by Gen Sir Bernard (later Field Marshal Lord) Montgomery, did have dual provision because the Deputy Supreme Commander liked to try his hand at it. One of the very few Messengers still flying is today masquerading as this aircraft, replete with D-Day 'invasion stripes'.

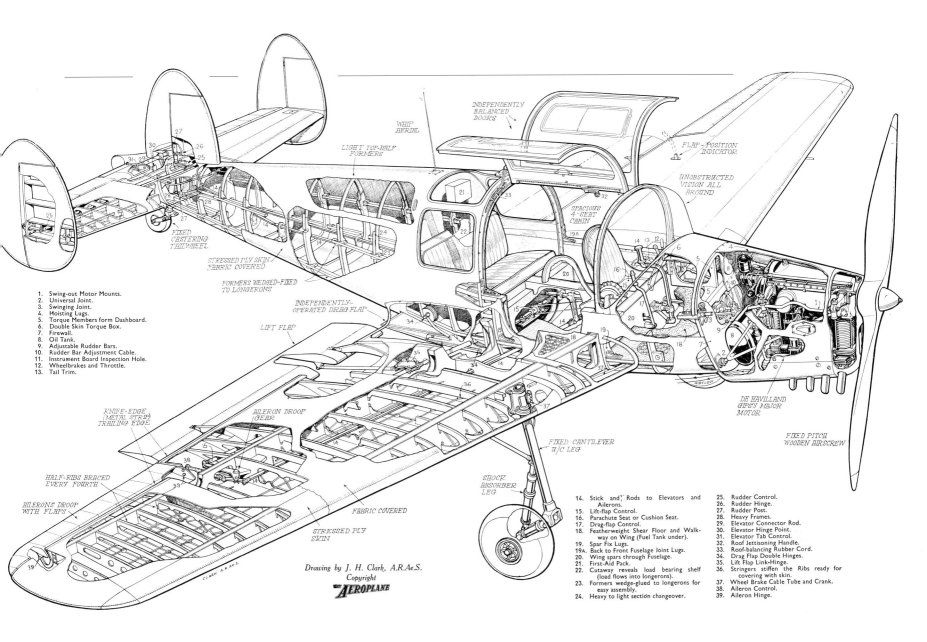

Drawing by J. H. Clark, A.R.Ae.S.
Copyright
*The Aeroplane*

1. Swing-out Motor Mounts.
2. Universal Joint.
3. Swinging Joint.
4. Hoisting Lugs.
5. Torque Members form Dashboard.
6. Double Skin Torque Box.
7. Firewall.
8. Oil Tank.
9. Adjustable Rudder Bars.
10. Rudder Bar Adjustment Cable.
11. Instrument Board Inspection Hole.
12. Wheelbrakes and Throttle.
13. Tail Trim.

14. Stick and Rods to Elevators and Ailerons.
15. Lift-flap Control.
16. Parachute Seat or Cushion Seat.
17. Drag-flap Control.
18. Featherweight Shear Floor and Walkway on Wing (Fuel Tank under).
19. Spar Fix Lugs.
19A. Back to Front Fuselage Joint Lugs.
20. Wing spars through Fuselage.
21. First-Aid Pack.
22. Cutaway reveals load bearing shelf (load flows into longerons).
23. Formers wedge-glued to longerons for easy assembly.
24. Heavy to light section changeover.

25. Rudder Control.
26. Rudder Hinge.
27. Rudder Post.
28. Heavy Frames.
29. Elevator Connector Rod.
30. Elevator Hinge Point.
31. Elevator Tab Control.
32. Roof Jettisoning Handle.
33. Roof-balancing Rubber Cord.
34. Drag Flap Double Hinges.
35. Lift Flap Link-Hinge.
36. Stringers stiffen the Ribs ready for covering with skin.
37. Wheel Brake Cable Tube and Crank.
38. Aileron Control.
39. Aileron Hinge.

When I was Technical Editor of *Flight* in the 1950s we had two successive Miles Geminis as staff hacks. The first had two 100 hp Cirrus Minors, smooth as silk, and the second two 145 hp Gipsy Majors. As the rest of the aircraft was almost pure Messenger (but without the central fin and rudder), but with double the power and electrically retractable landing gear, you can imagine what fun they were to fly, though they were in fact hardworking business tools.

Many people will regret that today we in the United Kingdom seem to find it terribly difficult to produce light aircraft. All we have are tiny teams, with inadequate backing, striving to build in ones and twos. While Cessna, Piper and Beech have for a decade been crippled by product-liability legislation, leaving a worldwide shortfall of many thousands of aircraft, the British industry has left it to its competitors to fill the gap. We don't seem to produce people like the Mileses any more.

# B-17G FLYING FORTRESS

One reason why so few American aircraft appear in this book is that the best way to do such a drawing is to visit the manufacturer, and of course neither Max nor Jimmy could do that where US types were concerned. On the other hand, a significant proportion of the 12,731 Boeing B-17 Fortresses came to England to serve with the Eighth Air Force, and about 200 joined the RAF, so together with access to the descriptive manuals this drawing should have posed few difficulties.

One of the truly great aircraft of World War 2, the B-17 was the eventual winner of a US Army requirement issued in 1934. The demand was for a multi-engined bomber to fly at high altitude. 'Multi' had always been taken to mean 'twin', but with the Model 299 Boeing boldly used four engines purely in order to fly higher. The prototype of this clean stressed-skin aircraft emerged in shining aluminium in July 1935. Initial flight trials were promising, but in October 1935 someone forgot to remove the control locks and this costly prototype crashed, killing the test pilot.

This was hardly the fault of what a journalist had dubbed 'a flying fortress', and soon the Air Corps was learning how to operate the service-test batch of 13 Y1B-17s. Though the prototype had been powered by Pratt & Whitney Hornet engines, all the thousands that followed had Wright R-1820 Cyclones, almost all also being fitted with exhaust-driven turbo-superchargers. These were the key to the B-17's outstanding performance at high altitudes, the service ceiling being an alleged 35,000 ft (though the vast formations of the 'mighty Eighth' seldom even got near to the 30,000 mark). I am astonished that Max didn't choose to draw the aircraft from below, so that the turbos could be illustrated.

Before the War successive versions appeared, culminating in the B-17C. This was expected to be the definitive model, and with 1200 hp R-1820-65 engines had the highest performance of any version, with a maximum speed of 320 mph. The RAF received 20, which – surprisingly, in view of its high security status – were fitted with the complex but exceedingly accurate Norden bombsight. From 8 July 1941 these aircraft, called Fortress Is, were sent on bombing raids in ones and twos in daylight. Results were discouraging, as the US Army had predicted, but these operations did make both the Army Air Force and Boeing do a major rethink.

The immediate result was the B-17E, which introduced much heavier defensive armament. Two of the original seven 0.30 in guns were retained in the nose. To these were added six 0.50 in powered dorsal and ventral turrets and a manual tail turret, plus either one or two 0.5 in in the roof of the radio compartment and a single hand-aimed 0.5 in in each open waist position. Visibly, the main change was a redesign of the tail to increase bombing accuracy at altitude. Armour protection was augmented, but normal internal bombload remained 6000 lb. For short ranges maximum bombload with external racks was 17,600 lb, but this was seldom if ever used on operations.

A mighty production plan was inaugurated, with Boeing's Seattle factories backed up by Douglas at Long Beach and Vega (a Lockheed subsidiary) at Burbank. By the time the BVD complex was operating the production model was the B-17F, with increased weights (caused partly by greater fuel capacity) permitted by stronger main gears, two 0.5 in in the nose and a frameless Plexiglas nosecap. The main production version, available from late 1943 and with the olive-drab paint omitted, was the B-17G seen here. This introduced a power-driven chin turret with twin 0.5 in, bringing the nose guns to four. Quite soon the open waist positions were enclosed, as shown, and a new tail turret adopted with a bigger cone of fire.

These great aircraft would set out from East Anglia and form up in armadas many miles long, climbing until they streamed a trail of ice crystals behind each engine. Together with a few Bomb Wings equipped with the B-24, they played a gigantic role not only in wiping out German factories and cities – don't forget, they hit Dresden four times after the RAF had gone there once – but also in bringing the Luftwaffe up to battle and causing a steady attrition of irreplaceable experienced fighter pilots. We are fortunate that as the B-17 was not British we still have so many preserved specimens flying today.

The B-17 was a true gentleman to fly, though if you approached too fast you'd risk running out of runway. The four throttle levers were formed into an

A shark-mouthed (check out the chin turret) B-17G of the 447th BG undergoes engine maintenance at its Rattlesden base. A second aircraft is on short finals in the background

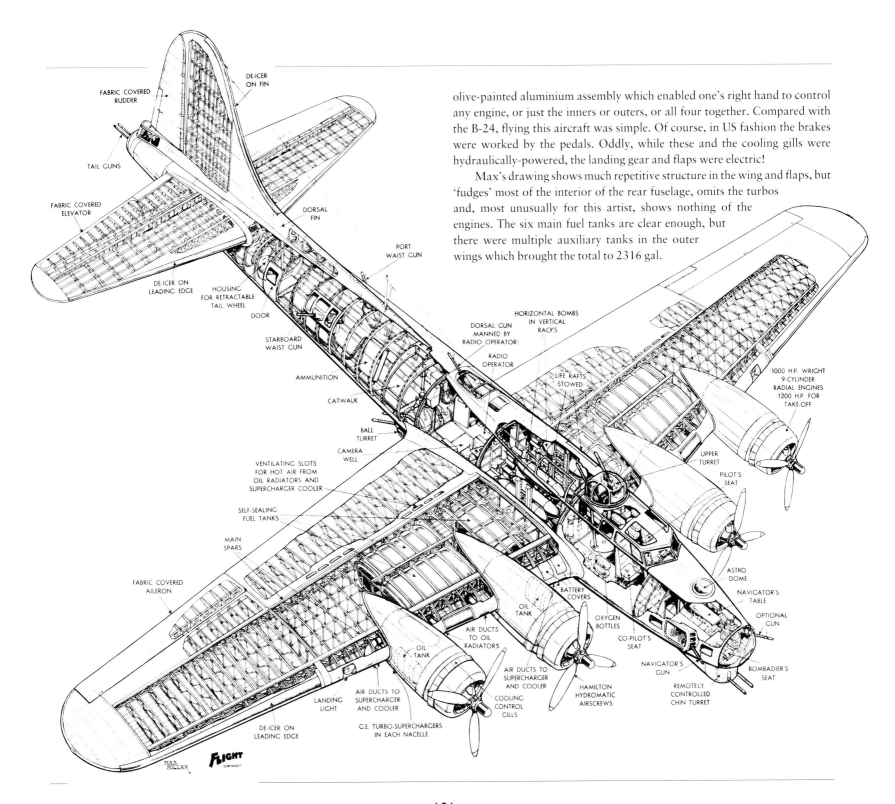

FABRIC COVERED
RUDDER

DE-ICER
ON FIN

TAIL GUNS

FABRIC COVERED
ELEVATOR

DORSAL
FIN

PORT
WAIST GUN

DE-ICER ON
LEADING EDGE

HOUSING
FOR RETRACTABLE
TAIL WHEEL

DOOR

STARBOARD
WAIST GUN

AMMUNITION

CATWALK

DORSAL GUN
MANNED BY
RADIO OPERATOR

HORIZONTAL BOMBS
IN VERTICAL
RACKS

RADIO
OPERATOR

LIFE RAFTS
STOWED

1000 H.P. WRIGHT
9-CYLINDER
RADIAL ENGINES
1200 H.P. FOR
TAKE-OFF

BALL
TURRET

CAMERA
WELL

VENTILATING SLOTS
FOR HOT AIR FROM
OIL RADIATORS AND
SUPERCHARGER COOLER

SELF-SEALING
FUEL TANKS

MAIN
SPARS

FABRIC COVERED
AILERON

UPPER
TURRET

PILOT'S
SEAT

ASTRO
DOME

NAVIGATOR'S
TABLE

BATTERY
COVERS

OIL
TANK

OXYGEN
BOTTLES

CO-PILOT'S
SEAT

OPTIONAL
GUN

OIL
TANK

AIR DUCTS
TO OIL
RADIATORS

AIR DUCTS TO
SUPERCHARGER
AND COOLER

COOLING
CONTROL
GILLS

HAMILTON
HYDROMATIC
AIRSCREWS

NAVIGATOR'S
GUN

REMOTELY
CONTROLLED
CHIN TURRET

BOMBADIER'S
SEAT

LANDING
LIGHT

DE-ICER ON
LEADING EDGE

AIR DUCTS TO
SUPERCHARGER
AND COOLER

G.E. TURBO-SUPERCHARGERS
IN EACH NACELLE

MAX
MILLAR

FLIGHT
COPYRIGHT

olive-painted aluminium assembly which enabled one's right hand to control
any engine, or just the inners or outers, or all four together. Compared with
the B-24, flying this aircraft was simple. Of course, in US fashion the brakes
were worked by the pedals. Oddly, while these and the cooling gills were
hydraulically-powered, the landing gear and flaps were electric!

Max's drawing shows much repetitive structure in the wing and flaps, but
'fudges' most of the interior of the rear fuselage, omits the turbos
and, most unusually for this artist, shows nothing of the
engines. The six main fuel tanks are clear enough, but
there were multiple auxiliary tanks in the outer
wings which brought the total to 2316 gal.

# TOMAHAWK I

In 1995 I am astonished to hear the RAF saying that it wants the C-130 (flying since 1954) instead of the new FLA, the Chinook (1961) instead of the new EH 101 and the Orion (1958) as the replacement for the Nimrod. The reasons given are that these products of foreign factories are supposedly low-risk and proven, and appear to be enticingly cheap. So take a good look at this cutaway, because if that policy had prevailed 60 years ago this is what we'd have had to fight the Battle of Britain with, and we'd have been in some difficulty.

It is strange how fashion comes in cycles. In the 1930s it was absolutely taken for granted that ponderous water-cooled vee engines had been swept away by simple high-performance air-cooled radials such as the Mercury in Britain and the Wasp and Cyclone in the USA. Then the Curtiss XP-37, powered by an Allison liquid-cooled vee-12 turbo-supercharged engine, demonstrated a level speed of 340 mph in April 1937. This led to massive orders for the Hawk 81 series, which the US Army designated the P-40. This was a more practical fighter with the cockpit moved forward and the radiator under the engine, which unfortunately had no turbo-supercharger. Further huge orders were placed by Britain and France, the latter's orders (with metric instruments and a throttle which worked 'the wrong way round', being opened by pulling

it back) being taken over by the RAF after the German invasion of May 1940.

Thus, the British received 1180 Hawk 81s equivalent to the P-40, P-40B and P-40C. They comprised 140 (ex-French) Tomahawk Is, with two 0.5-in guns above the engine and four 0.303 in Brownings (replacing 7.5 mm Darnes) in the wings, 110 Tomahawk IIAs with armour and self-sealing tanks and 930 Tomahawk IIBs with a drop tank, US radio and oxygen, and other detail modifications. In service many of the Tomahawks had the two 'fifties' replaced by 0.303 in Brownings because at that time RAF squadrons could not readily get the far more effective 0.5 in ammunition. None had bomb racks.

After arrival in Britain the Tomahawk Is were, as far as possible, Anglicised, and fitted with a normal type of throttle lever. Despite this, they were judged to be obviously not combat-ready, but did useful work in the advanced training and fighter-affiliation role. The other marks saw a lot of action, at first (fairly briefly) as the fighter of the newly formed Army Co-operation Command, and then throughout the Middle East with the RAF and SAAF. By 1942 Tomahawks were being replaced by the superior Kittyhawk, and many were passed on to China, the Soviet Union, Egypt and Turkey.

This drawing certainly makes the Tomahawk rear fuselage look much too short and stubby, and the landing gears are too far apart. Of course, in RAF

August 1941 saw the newly-formed No 414 RCAF Sqn equipped with Tomahwk I/IIs – plus a small number of Lysander IIIs – at its Croydon base. Much fuss was made of this new outfit, and its American fighter, although in reality the unit, nicknamed the 'Sarnia Imperials', saw little fontline flying in their year-long relationship with the temperamental Tomahawk. This press shot shows AK185, one of the last Mk IIBs delivered, up on a training sortie over Surrey

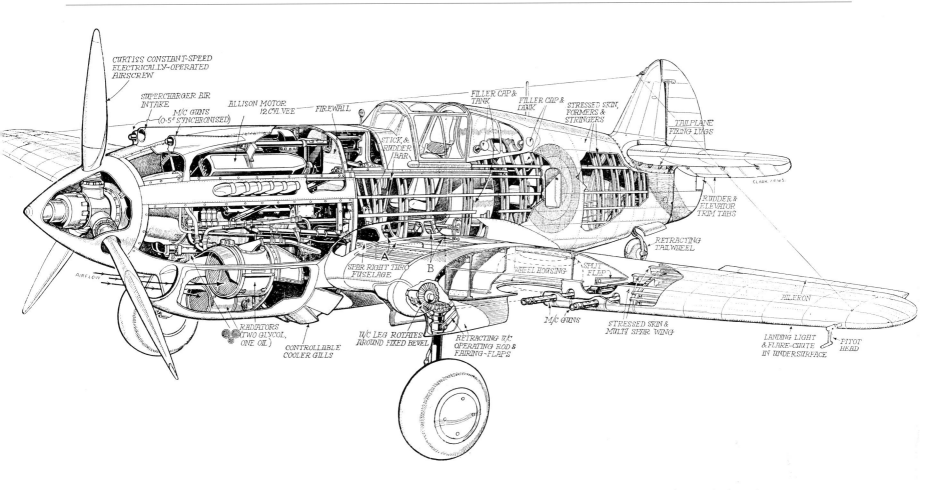

CURTISS CONSTANT-SPEED
ELECTRICALLY-OPERATED
AIRSCREW

SUPERCHARGER AIR
INTAKE

M/C GUNS
(0·5" SYNCHRONISED)

ALLISON MOTOR
12 CYL. VEE

FIREWALL

FILLER CAP &
TANK

FILLER CAP &
TANK

STRESSED SKIN,
FORMERS &
STRINGERS

TAILPLANE
FIXING LUGS

CLARK 1945.

STICK &
RUDDER
BAR

RUDDER &
ELEVATOR
TRIM TABS

AIRFLOW

A

SPAR RIGHT THRO
FUSELAGE

B

WHEEL HOUSING

SPLIT
FLAP

RETRACTING
TAILWHEEL

RADIATORS
(TWO GLYCOL,
ONE OIL)

CONTROLLABLE
COOLER GILLS

U/C LEG ROTATES
AROUND FIXED BEVEL

RETRACTING U/C
OPERATING ROD &
FAIRING~FLAPS

M/C GUNS

STRESSED SKIN &
MULTI SPAR WING

AILERON

LANDING LIGHT
& FLARE-CHUTE
IN UNDERSURFACE

PITOT
HEAD

service a reflector gunsight was fitted, not just a ring and bead. Clark forgot to include the bead, which was attached above the firewall, and he also failed to include the large magazines for the 0.5 in guns which were immediately behind the firewall. His rendering of the huge bevel gears that rotated the lower part of the main undercarriage legs through 90° during retraction to the rear suggests that he never actually saw it. The gears were much smaller, and the fixed bevel was only a short segment.

One also feels he never asked about the fuel system. Compared with British fighters, American ones tended to have much greater internal fuel capacity – a tradition that still persists. The Tomahawk's fuel filler behind the sliding canopy could take on board 132 gal, 55 per cent more than a Spitfire. Two of the three fuel tanks were in the wings, not shown in this drawing. The second filler, further back, was for lubricating oil; it was most unusual not to

have the oil tank close to the engine, and I wonder how the Russians got on with those long oil pipes at -40° (Celsius or Fahrenheit, it's just as cold, and makes oil very thick). Incidentally, the filler caps were in holes cut in two panes of transparent Plexiglas which faired over a cutaway recess that gave the pilot a better view to the rear.

During the war many people were puzzled by Curtiss Electric (a registered name) propellers. It simply meant that the propeller hub contained an electric motor which, via reduction gears, varied the pitch of the blades. Power was taken through slip-ring connections from the aircraft DC supply.

Whether using 'THRO' as an abbreviation for through is significant, one feels that Clark was either under extreme pressure with this drawing or else he wasn't really very interested. A much later cutaway of the same type of aircraft done by a rival firm has a key list of 130 items.

# WHITLEY III

Sir W G Armstrong Whitworth Aircraft, who grew to occupy many factories in and around Coventry, were among the first British companies to 'bite the bullet' and follow the Germans, Russians and Americans into the challenging world of all-metal stressed-skin construction. At the same time, the design team under John Lloyd outdid Tupolev in choosing severe shapes

Relegated from frontline duties in the summer of 1940, Whitley III K8948 found a new lease of life as paratroop transport, although with exactly which unit remains a mystery

made up of straight lines, with no concessions to aesthetic beauty. Their brutish box-like structures reached a pinnacle in the AW 23 bomber transport, flown in June 1935. This had a cantilever monoplane wing based on a huge all-metal box, so deep a short man could stand upright inside the root. Aft of this box the wing was skinned in traditional fabric.

Cut down to 84 ft span, almost the same wing was used in the Whitley heavy bomber, but this also had a stressed-skin fuselage. The prototype flew in March 1936, the same month as the very different Spitfire. The one thing people remember about the Whitley is that it flew startlingly nose-down. This is because Lloyd knew little about putting flaps on the wings, so the deep wing was set at a considerable positive angle of incidence. This setting did not change even when production aircraft were fitted with split flaps. Thus, when the wing was flying at cruising speed, the fuselage was tilted downwards, and in a beat-up at maximum speed the attitude was even more startling. The effect was further accentuated by the fact that the Whitley's fuselage began at full depth at the front and continued with straight lines to the tail.

To the pilot, the Whitley was a gentle giant, a kind of half-way house between the biplanes and the heavily loaded Mosquito and Lancaster. It tended to take-off and land by itself, with the fuselage at what appeared to be totally wrong attitudes.

All early Whitleys were powered by the Armstrong Siddeley Tiger, a 14-cylinder radial which gave 795 hp in the Mk I aircraft and 920 hp in the Mks II and III. It was in all respects an unimpressive engine, which in the giant Ensign airliner was replaced by the Wright Cyclone. In the Whitley it was replaced, from the Mk IV onwards, by the Merlin. I don't blame Clark for ignoring the engines, but he might have drawn the propellers properly. They were de Havilland Hamilton bracket-type, which had just two pitch settings. Though these were only 10° apart, going from fine to coarse made the engines shudder and cough, the rpm falling momentarily 'off the clock'. The Merlin-Whitleys had the far superior constant-speed Rotol, which if necessary could be feathered. While on the subject of engines, the Tiger VIII fitted to the Whitley II and III was the first engine in the RAF to have a two-speed supercharger. Some standard books incorrectly call this a two-stage supercharger, which is totally different.

Clark showed the crude oil cooler above the nacelle, and also the daft location of the three fuel tanks, which had a total capacity of 519 gallons (less than half as much as a PR 34 Mosquito). For a bomber, which gets shot at, why put a tank in the fuselage when you have that vast empty space (Clark

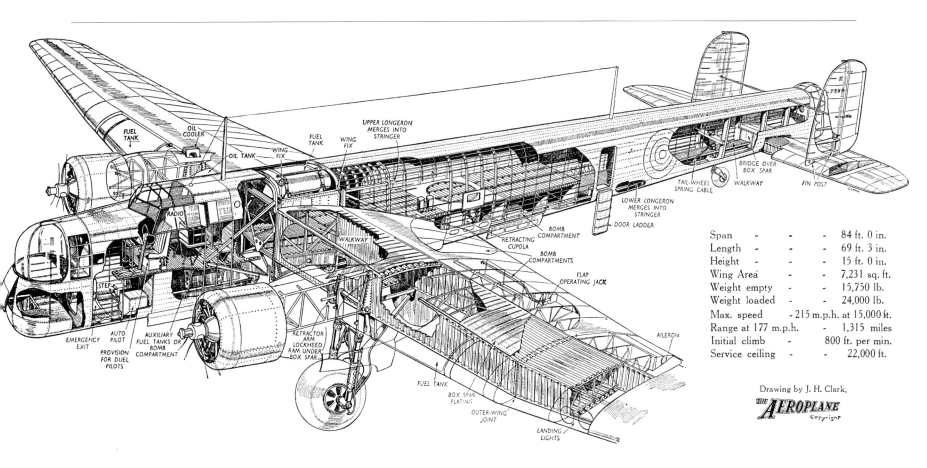

Labels on drawing:

FUEL TANK
OIL COOLER
OIL TANK
WING FIX
FUEL TANK
WING FIX
UPPER LONGERON MERGES INTO STRINGER
RADIO
WALKWAY
RETRACTING CUPOLA
BOMB COMPARTMENT
BOMB COMPARTMENTS
FLAP OPERATING JACK
BRIDGE OVER BOX SPAR
TAIL-WHEEL SPRING CABLE
WALKWAY
FIN POST
LOWER LONGERON MERGES INTO STRINGER
DOOR LADDER
EMERGENCY EXIT
AUTO PILOT
AUXILIARY FUEL TANKS OR BOMB COMPARTMENT
PROVISION FOR DUEL PILOTS
STEP
RETRACTOR ARM LOCKHEED RAM UNDER BOX SPAR
FUEL TANK
BOX SPAR PLATING
OUTER-WING JOINT
LANDING LIGHTS
AILERON

| Span | - | - | - | 84 ft. 0 in. |
| Length | - | - | - | 69 ft. 3 in. |
| Height | - | - | - | 15 ft. 0 in. |
| Wing Area | - | - | - | 7,231 sq. ft. |
| Weight empty | - | - | - | 15,750 lb. |
| Weight loaded | - | - | - | 24,000 lb. |
| Max. speed | - | - | 215 m.p.h. at 15,000 ft. |
| Range at 177 m.p.h. | - | - | 1,315 miles |
| Initial climb | - | - | 800 ft. per min. |
| Service ceiling | - | - | 22,000 ft. |

Drawing by J. H. Clark,
THE AEROPLANE
Copyright

labelled it 'WALKWAY') inside the main box spar? He might have labelled the fabric covering behind the spar, and on the tail, as well as showing how the flaps worked. Again, while the geometry of the undercarriage was obvious, the reader cannot see how the 'retractor arm' operated.

Early Whitleys had Armstrong Whitworth manual turrets with Lewis guns, but the Mk III introduced Nash and Thompson hydraulic turrets, with Browning guns, including the FN17 ventral turret with two Browning Mk Is. Clark was obviously told not to show any details of armament, but he did annotate the FN17 as a 'RETRACTING CUPOLA'. RAF policy soon forgot about defence against attack from below, and the big hole left when the FN17 was removed came in useful when from mid-1940 the early Whitleys were at last taken off operations and used as the trainers for our first parachute troops, at what is today Manchester airport.

By the time war came, in September 1939, the production Whitley was the Mk V, with the excellent Merlin XX engine, normal fuel capacity of 837

gal, redesigned fins and rudders, and a four-gun FN4 tail turret carried on a 15-in extension of the rear fuselage to improve the field of fire to the beam. These aircraft did marvellous work, including taking quite heavy bomb loads across the Alps to Turin and Milan, one operation landing in the about-to-be-occupied Channel Islands to refuel from petrol cans!

In contrast to the crowded interiors of bombers at the end of the war, the main impression left by this drawing is that the interior of a Whitley was almost empty. Such a belief is not far wrong for the earliest versions, though things had changed with the Whitley V, and they changed even more with the radar-equipped Mk VII for Coastal Command. A typical Mk VII had an empty weight of 21,020 lb, which was almost the same as the loaded weight of a Mk I! The Whitley was designed to a load factor of 4.9, compared with 4.5 for the Wellington and Lancaster, and the wing loading of the Mk I was only 17.6 lb/sq ft, compared with the Lanc's 52.5, so it is hardly surprising that its percentage structure weight came out at the unimpressive value of 44.

# BATTLE

Today the Battle is remembered as the death-trap in which hundreds of gallant men went to their deaths in France in five short weeks in the early summer of 1940. Less memorable is the fact that when it first appeared it caused gasps of astonishment. Here was an RAF light day bomber in the form of an all-metal stressed-skin monoplane with retractable undercarriage, flaps and a transparent canopy over the cockpits! Compared with the aircraft it

replaced, the Hawker Hind biplane, it carried double the bomb load twice as far at a speed 50 per cent faster. What people at that time failed to notice is that such an aircraft, lacking any effective defence, was going to be a sitting duck for such aircraft as the Bf 109E. So, because nobody stopped them, several factories churned out 2201 Battles, each with a Merlin which might have gone into a fighter.

When Clark first drew the Battle it was customary to add national Service markings, and sometimes even a serial number. Clark drew the roundels appropriate to a camouflaged aircraft (getting the proportions of the B-Type roundel above the wings completely wrong). He also got some of the basic shape surprisingly incorrect. For example, the nose was nothing like that on the actual aircraft, and instead of the wing having most of the taper on the leading edge, it was actually almost entirely on the trailing edge!

Again, the front spar is clearly shown (though with a lot of dihedral, whereas actually the spar upper boom was horizontal from tip to tip) together with the prominent bulkhead in the fuselage at this location. But it is far from obvious that, whereas the fuselage ahead of this point was welded steel tubes with quick-release access panels, the rest of the fuselage was stressed-skin

K7650 was a Battle I of No 63 Sqn, based at Upwood, near Peterborough, in 1939

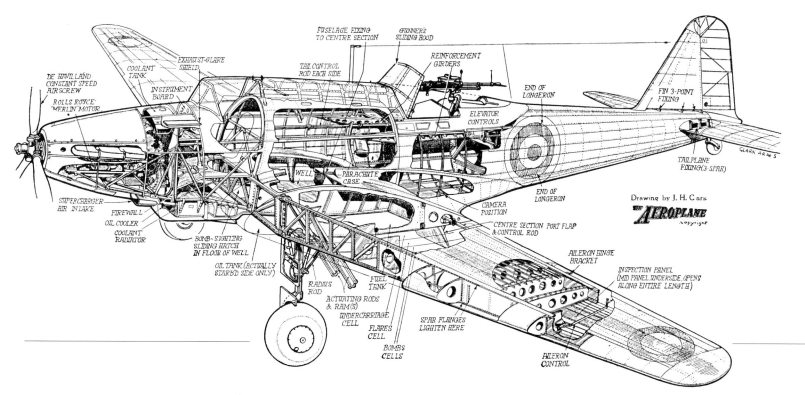

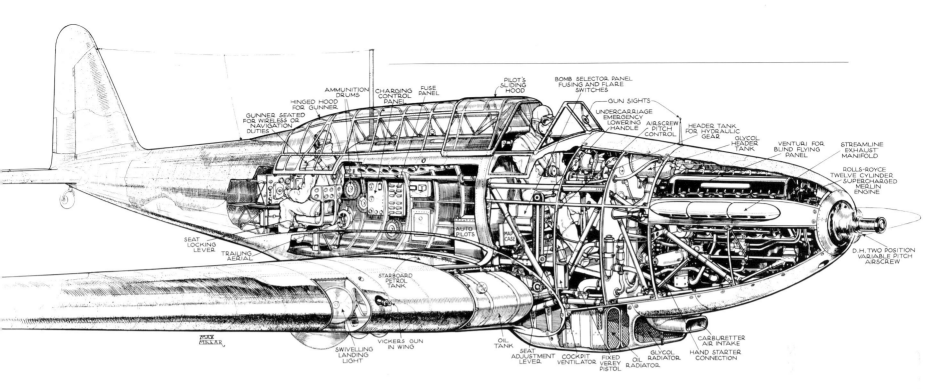

semi-monocoque. Again, Clark wrote 'FUEL TANK', but drew the arrow pointing to an empty void which looked as though it would be occupied by the retracted landing gear.

Outboard of the mis-positioned 'UNDERCARRIAGE CELL' we find 'FLARES CELL' and then 'BOMBS CELL'. Nobody would have guessed that all four large cells were for 250-lb bombs, which were attached to racks extended below the wing by hydraulic jacks which then raised the bombs into their cells (and could be extended in the air for dive attacks). Flares were carried in separate small cells, two on each side, and for short ranges an additional 250-lb bomb could be carried under each wing externally.

In typical Clark style, he drew the aircraft from the left side and then found he had to point out that the oil tank was actually in the leading edge of the other wing. He did not even make the point that also in the starboard (right) wing was a fixed Browning machine gun, aimed by the pilot, with a 400-round magazine and a combat ciné camera alongside. Perhaps the most prominent feature of the drawing was the gun behind the 'GUNNERS' hood (which pivoted rather than slid), which Clark rightly drew as a Vickers K (gas-operated) but did not identify – early Battles had a Lewis.

Even when this drawing was republished in *The Aeroplane Spotter* for 3 July 1941 Clark did not indicate the aft-facing ventral gun which was hastily added during the Battle for France. This was just aft of the wing, aimed by the third crew-member with a mirror sight.

Many details in this drawing were confused (such as the flap, which inboard is clearly of the split type but outboard looks like a plain or slotted variety), while such items as the bomb sight and camera leave the reader looking at empty space. Battles came in different marks (I, II, III and V), reflecting the mark number of Rolls-Royce Merlin fitted. The drawing shows the 1030-hp Merlin III, with ejector exhausts, but earlier installations simply let the exhaust escape through narrow slits. The propeller was certainly not of the constant-speed type, but was a licensed Hamilton bracket-type unit which had only two pitch settings 20° apart, fully fine or fully coarse. After climbing away, selecting coarse made the Merlin go all quiet, cutting rpm by half.

The anti-glare shield which he did insert was not a standard fitting on any Battle before autumn 1940, by which time these vulnerable aircraft were no longer operated in the bombing role (though poor No 98 Sqn were isolated in the anti-U-boat role in Iceland). Yet another criticism is that the crew of a Battle was normally three. The third man was the observer/bomb-aimer, but it is by no means clear where he sat behind the pilot. As noted, his prone bomb-aiming position enabled him to slide back a D-shaped hatch and use his optical sight, but our James was forbidden to show this!

Max's drawing is of a Mk I, and as with most of his work, has a more 'human' feel to it, right down to the figures of the two-man (where's the observer/bomb aimer again?!) crew. He has exposed more cockpit detail than Clarke, plus employed a typically thorough approach to drawing the Battle I's early-build Merlin I – Millar has ignored the wing structure, however. This drawing was first published in the 19 August 1937 edition.

# WELLINGTON II

The British are undoubtedly the world's worst preservers of famous aircraft – I mean when we were surrounded by them. Today, not a single Wellington is flying anywhere in the world, and many aviation enthusiasts around the globe have probably never heard of it, yet it was the most numerous British multi-engined aircraft of all time, 11,461 being built. Almost everyone who fought in RAF Bomber Command in World War 2 crewed Wellingtons at some point or another, either on a squadron or, in the second half of the War, at an Operational Training Unit. They also served all over the world in many roles. Structurally extraordinary, Wellingtons were incredibly tough, nice to fly and generated a feeling of confidence.

The story begins in the early 1920s when a structural engineer working for Vickers named B N Wallis began to design the huge R.100 airship. He devised a kind of basketwork made from thousands of strips of aluminium alloy, some flat but most rolled into simple angle or channel sections. The result was strong, light, slightly flexible and very easy to repair after damage. He called this Geodetic construction, because almost all the structural members were disposed around the curved outer shape of the airship. Apart from the Warren-type zig-zag bracing of the main nose-to-tail girders there was no internal structure at all, so everywhere was available for gasbags and fuel.

By 1930 he had translated Geodetic construction into aeroplanes. Here, the only internal members were the zig-zag spar webs and the strong fuselage frames to which the wing root ribs were attached. Apart from a few parts such as the cowlings, everything was covered in fabric. The first result was the Wellesley long-range bomber of 1935. This was followed by the twin-engined

B.9/32, first flown on 15 June 1936. A young designer named George Edwards was told to do the vertical tail, and he used that of the twin-finned Stranraer flying boat as a basis. Later he became Sir George Edwards, while the Geodetic pioneer became Sir Barnes Wallis, whom even ordinary members of the public have heard of!

After near-total redesign the B.9/32 became the Wellington, with a power-driven gun turret at each end and a different vertical tail. Early versions had fairly useless Vickers turrets, but better ones arrived by 1939, and these are shown in Clark's drawing. A few Mk I aircraft had the FN25 retractable ventral turret, but this was soon discontinued because nobody ever imagined Luftwaffe nightfighters would be so unsporting as to attack from below. By 1941 the tail turret was the FN20, with four Brownings fed from magazines which could accommodate 2500 rounds per gun (usually less was carried).

In the late 1930s, cartoon character Popeye had a friend named J Wellington Wimpey. Somehow the second name was adopted, and more than half Bomber Command aircrew in the mid-war years would say they flew Wimpeys. The Mk I had Pegasus engines, a modest batch of 400 had the Merlin and were called the Mk II, and 220 Mk IVs had the American Twin Wasp, driving Curtiss Electric propellers. From 1942 to the end of the war the dominant engine was the sleeve-valve Hercules, typically rated at 1675 hp, driving broad-blade Rotols with electric pitch change. I once saw an unfortunate 'Erk' put on a charge for allowing his 'trolley acc' to run into a depression in the grass and take a chip (just big enough to put the aircraft unserviceable) out of a Mk X's propeller just as it was about to go 'gardening' (laying mines).

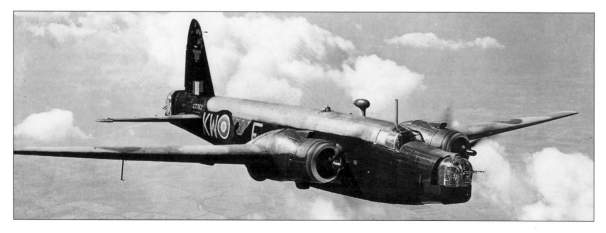

A Dishforth-based Wellington III of No 425 RCAF Sqn formates with the photographer during a rare daylight flight in the autumn of 1942. The Mk III was the backbone of Bomber Command during that year, thanks to its sheer numbers – 1519 were built and despatched to squadrons across Britain in short order

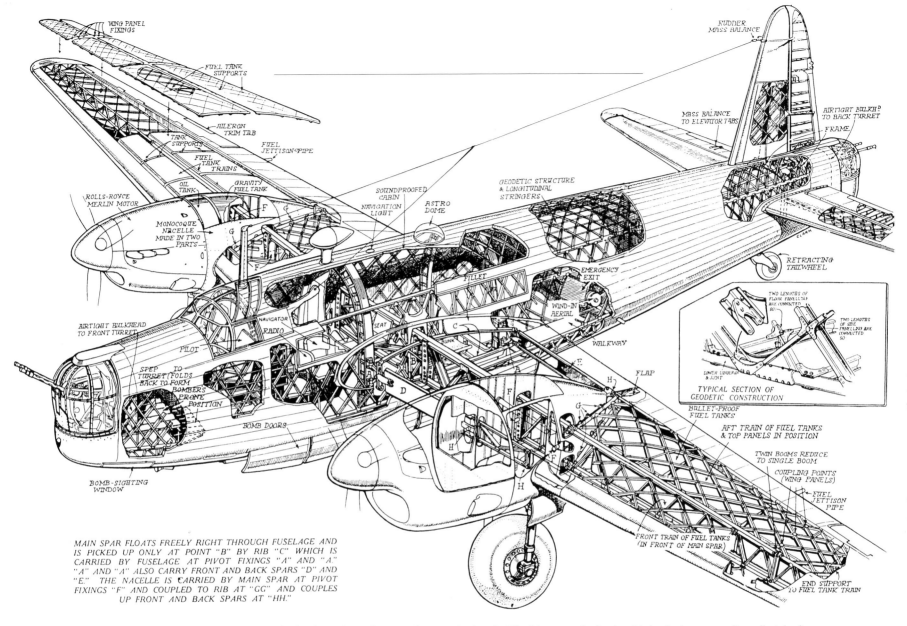

WING PANEL FIXINGS

FUEL TANK SUPPORTS

AILERON TRIM TAB

TANK SUPPORTS

FUEL TANK TRAINS

FUEL JETTISON PIPE

OIL TANK

GRAVITY FUEL TANK

ROLLS-ROYCE MERLIN MOTOR

MONOCOQUE NACELLE MADE IN TWO PARTS

AIRTIGHT BULKHEAD TO FRONT TURRET

PILOT

STEP TO TURRET (FOLDS BACK TO FORM BOMBERS PRONE POSITION)

BOMB-SIGHTING WINDOW

BOMB DOORS

NAVIGATOR RADIO

SOUNDPROOFED CABIN

NAVIGATION LIGHT

ASTRO DOME

GEODETIC STRUCTURE & LONGITUDINAL STRINGERS

SEAT

BUNK

FILLET

EMERGENCY EXIT

WIND-IN AERIAL

WALKWAY

FLAP

RUDDER MASS BALANCE

MASS BALANCE TO ELEVATOR TABS

AIRTIGHT BULKH'D TO BACK TURRET

FRAME

CLARK

RETRACTING TAILWHEEL

TWO LENGTHS OF FLOOR PANELLING ARE CONNECTED SO

TWO LENGTHS OF SIDE PANELLING ARE CONNECTED SO

LOWER LONGERON & JOINT

TYPICAL SECTION OF GEODETIC CONSTRUCTION

BULLET-PROOF FUEL TANKS

AFT TRAIN OF FUEL TANKS & TOP PANELS IN POSITION

TWIN BOOMS REDUCE TO SINGLE BOOM

COUPLING POINTS (WING PANELS)

FUEL JETTISON PIPE

FRONT TRAIN OF FUEL TANKS (IN FRONT OF MAIN SPAR)

END SUPPORT TO FUEL TANK TRAIN

MAIN SPAR FLOATS FREELY RIGHT THROUGH FUSELAGE AND IS PICKED UP ONLY AT POINT "B" BY RIB "C" WHICH IS CARRIED BY FUSELAGE AT PIVOT FIXINGS "A" AND "A" "A" AND "A" ALSO CARRY FRONT AND BACK SPARS "D" AND "E." THE NACELLE IS CARRIED BY MAIN SPAR AT PIVOT FIXINGS "F" AND COUPLED TO RIB AT "GG" AND COUPLES UP FRONT AND BACK SPARS AT "HH."

Early versions had funny windows along the fuselage above the wing, but the Mk III and most later versions replaced these with triangular beam windows in the rear fuselage through which could poke a 0.303-in Browning. In the floor below was the main door (Clark labelled it 'EMERGENCY EXIT'), beside which was clipped a short ladder. Standard fuel capacity was 750 gal, in 12 wing cells and two in the humpbacked nacelles. With most marks the propellers were close enough for a long-armed pilot to touch them, as happened to a luckless Pole I was about to fly with.

The Wimpey was nothing if not soft, bouncy on the ground and smooth in the air. The big control wheel, with brake levers needing all eight fingers, rocked gently to front and rear throughout each flight. A wag once said that one should never quote a dimension such as 'span 86 ft 2 in' without also stating the time, because the dimensions changed from one moment to the next!

This was one of Jimmy's earlier drawings, not up to his later standard, though the small inset did at least make Geodetic construction clear. Fortunately, someone recently found the original rolling-mill dies used during the War to make Geodetic parts, and this has helped the rebuilding of a 'Wimpey' salvaged from Loch Ness which is now going on at Brooklands.

# BLENHEIM IV

One of Jimmy Clark's very first full cutaway aircraft was a drawing of the Blenheim I published in *The Aeroplane* of 16 June 1937. He then produced this much better drawing of the 'long-nosed' Mk IV, which appeared on 24 April 1941. The Blenheim was a fast day bomber which Bristol derived from the Type 142, a private-venture executive transport built for newspaper tycoon Lord Rothermere. In 1934 the company accepted the order for this aircraft only after much heart-searching because they were afraid that building a modern stressed-skin cantilever monoplane would offend their chief customer, the Air Ministry, which only bought fabric-covered biplanes!

In June 1935 the Type 142, named *Britain First*, proved to have a level speed of 307 mph, 80 mph faster than the fastest fighters in the RAF. Far from being outraged, the Air Ministry said 'Turn it into a bomber'. The wing was raised 16 in to leave room underneath for a small bomb bay for a load of 1000 lb, a Browning gun was fixed firing ahead, a Vickers K gun was put in a retractable turret, and the glazed nose was occupied by the pilot on the left and the navigator/bomb-aimer on the right. To say they were cramped is an understatement. When one pilot looked into the cockpit for the first time his immediate thought was 'What a horrible place in which to die'. Many crews did die in 1939-41, and smaller numbers followed later in the Mediterranean and the Far East. Like most RAF aircraft of the day, Blenheims were vulnerable.

To aim bombs the navigator undid his harness, unfolded a second seat from the right wall and lay on this, sliding it forward until he was in the best position for using the sight, on the right side of the extreme nose. The whole scheme was most inconvenient. By the time 1134 Blenheim I bombers had

been built someone had thought of a better arrangement, which of course ought to have been done at the mock-up stage.

The first idea was merely to extend the nose by 3 ft. This was tested on K7072, an early Mk I which was then renamed the Bolingbroke. Not unnaturally, test pilot Cyril Uwins didn't like the windscreen so far from his eyes, so the windscreen was then brought back immediately in front of him. Finally, so that he could see the airfield ahead when landing, the top of the nose was lowered on the left side. The result was a strange asymmetric shape, but it worked. At last the poor navigator could sit in comfort on the right side of the nose, with barely adequate head room, facing to the left to plot courses on a chart table. His bombsight was unchanged.

This odd nose came with the Blenheim IV, of which no fewer than 3297 were built. Including production by Fairchild in Canada, most of which differed only in detail but were named Bolingbroke, the total was 3813. Compared with the Mk I they had more powerful Bristol Mercury XV engines rated at 920 hp, additional fuel tanks in the outer wings, better protection, and a turret with two belt-fed Brownings. Many were used for trial installations of armament and other equipment. Blenheims were the first nightfighters to carry radar. Coastal Command used the Mk IVF with four fixed Brownings in place of a bomb load, while by 1941 those remaining in Bomber Command had either a single Vickers K or twin Brownings firing to the rear from a mirror-sighted blister under the nose. Clark showed the single under-nose installation, and the original single-gun dorsal turret.

Unlike his Mk I drawing, Clark did at least show the starboard engine this

The distinctive nose contours, and later chin turret, are clearly visible in this view of a No 13 OTU Blenheim IV in mid-1942. By this stage in the conflict, the training units in the UK were producing crews principally for units in North Africa and the Far East, as the type had been all but retired from frontline use by Bomber Command in Europe

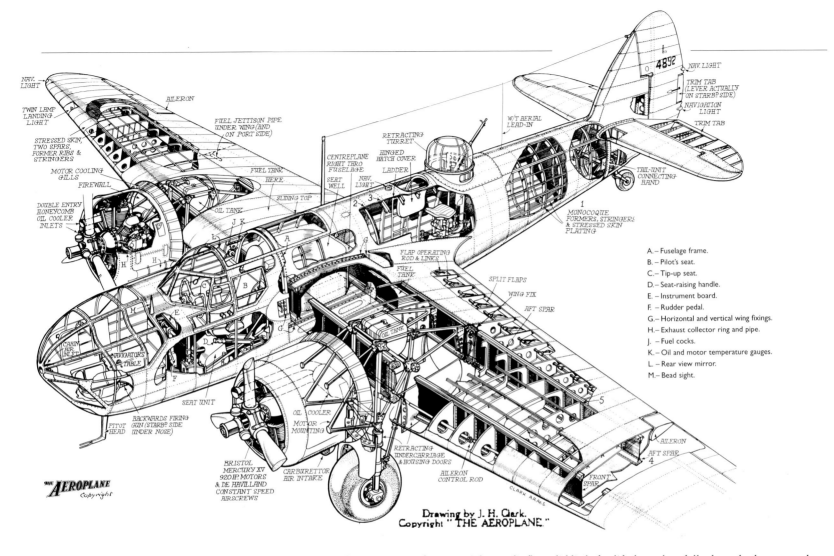

NAV. LIGHT

TWIN LAMP LANDING LIGHT

STRESSED SKIN, TWO SPARS, FORMER RIBS & STRINGERS

MOTOR COOLING GILLS

FIREWALL

DOUBLE ENTRY HONEYCOMB OIL COOLER INLETS

AILERON

FUEL JETTISON PIPE UNDER WING (AND ON PORT SIDE)

FUEL TANK HERE

SLIDING TOP

OIL TANK

CENTREPLANE RIGHT THRO FUSELAGE

SEAT WELL

NAV. LIGHT

RETRACTING TURRET

HINGED HATCH COVER

LADDER

W/T AERIAL LEAD-IN

NAV. LIGHT

TRIM TAB (LEVER ACTUALLY ON STARBD SIDE)

NAVIGATION LIGHT

TRIM TAB

TAIL-UNIT CONNECTING BAND

MONOCOQUE FORMERS, STRINGERS & STRESSED SKIN PLATING

FLAP OPERATING ROD & LINKS

FUEL TANK

SPLIT FLAPS

WING FIX

AFT SPAR

A. – Fuselage frame.
B. – Pilot's seat.
C. – Tip-up seat.
D. – Seat-raising handle.
E. – Instrument board.
F. – Rudder pedal.
G. – Horizontal and vertical wing fixings.
H. – Exhaust collector ring and pipe.
J. – Fuel cocks.
K. – Oil and motor temperature gauges.
L. – Rear view mirror.
M. – Bead sight.

CABIN AIR INLET

NAVIGATORS TABLE

SEAT UNIT

BACKWARDS FIRING GUN (STARBD SIDE UNDER NOSE)

PITOT HEAD

BRISTOL MERCURY XV 920 H.P. MOTORS & DE HAVILLAND CONSTANT SPEED AIRSCREWS

CARBURETTOR AIR INTAKE

OIL COOLER MOTOR MOUNTING

RETRACTING UNDERCARRIAGE & HOUSING DOORS

AILERON CONTROL ROD

AILERON

AFT SPAR

FRONT SPAR

THE AEROPLANE Copyright

Drawing by J. H. Clark.
Copyright " THE AEROPLANE."

time, though he cut off most of the blades of the propellers. These were not of the constant-speed type, but licensed Hamiltons of the simple bracket design which could adopt only two pitch angles, fine or coarse. Clark may have been forbidden to show the outer-wing tanks, though there was nothing the Germans didn't know about the Blenheim. These tanks increased take-off weight to 14,400 lb, and in the later Mk V it reached 17,000 lb, which was too much for the engines – we get an idea of how aircraft have developed by noting that today's fighter-like Tornado is four times heavier! The Mk IV could take off at maximum weight and then, in emergency, land immediately, but the run was excessively long. Accordingly, fuel-jettison pipes were added under the outer tanks. Clark showed only one of these, and put it too far back, under the starboard flap!

These split flaps did little for lift, but when fully down had a tremendous effect on drag. If it didn't have to go to war the Blenheim was quite an enjoyable machine, with performance and agility that in 1937 was very exciting. Sadly, like so many other aircraft, by 1940 it was a different story, and hundreds of gallant men paid the price in having to meet the enemy in a vulnerable aircraft. It was a time of near-panic, trying to make up for years of inactivity, and one had to settle everywhere for second-best answers.

Likewise, Clark would not have wanted posterity to judge his artistry by this drawing, even though it was more detailed than his even earlier Blenheim I. For example, he failed to show any of the mass of equipment in the nose, and in later years he would have connected up the push/pull rod in the left leading edge to show how it drove the aileron.

# MASTER I

Before World War 2 – indeed for 10 years after it as well – the British aircraft industry was made up of some 30 companies enjoying varying degrees of size and prosperity. Aircraft for the RAF were the jealously guarded preserve of a mere 18, and even these tended to be pigeonholed into clearly defined categories. One of the outsiders was the little firm of Phillips and Powis at Woodley aerodrome, just east of Reading. They were un-British. For example, they built streamlined monoplanes, which they even fitted with flaps. On 3 June 1937 they had the effrontery to fly, on their own initiative, an advanced trainer which reached 296 mph!

The officials were outraged. Miles were supposed to build light sporting machines, and had no business to meddle with the training of pilots to fly Hurricanes and Spitfires. But when the officially ordered advanced trainer – the de Havilland Don – proved to be the victim of a misguided specification, with extreme reluctance discussions were opened with Fred and George Miles to investigate how the M.9 Kestrel Trainer might be turned into an aircraft that would meet RAF requirements. The result was the M.9A Master I, which is the version Clark drew.

The basic wooden structure, with thick and sharply cranked wings, remained almost unchanged. Covering was plywood throughout, overlain by Madapolam fabric, except for the control surfaces which were fabric-skinned. The wide-track landing gear retracted backwards. The wheels rotated through 90° to lie flat in the kink of the wings, immediately in front of the split flaps. Like the landing gear and wheel brakes, the flaps were powered hydraulically, and they could be depressed to 90° for landing. Whereas the Kestrel Trainer had had a 745-hp Rolls-Royce Kestrel XVI, the Master I had a Kestrel XXX de-rated to 715 hp. The radiator was moved from a neat instal-lation immediately below the engine to a deep "bathtub" further back. These changes, and a redesign of the canopy and addition of blind-flying gear, oxygen and radio, reduced maximum speed by 70 mph to 226 mph.

This was of little consequence, and the Master I proved to be a very satisfactory machine which trained its first pupils in time for the Battle of Britain in 1940. The new canopy was much deeper than before, with a tall flat windscreen suitable for a reflector sight with which to aim a Vickers or Browning gun in the starboard wing, but this armament was not normally fitted. The pupil in the front cockpit could be shrouded under a blind-flying hood, and the instructor could swing open a roof panel to form a windscreen through which he could look after raising his seat by 12 in, simultaneously moving the rudder pedals, to get a good view for landing (Clark showed this as a detail).

Miles, used to making cheap lightplanes (you could fly away a trim Hawk two-seater for £395) in ones and twos, suddenly received a huge order for the complex Master. They quadrupled the size of the factory and set up tracked assembly lines, one of which constructed the centre wings upside-down. In 1939-41 Miles delivered 900 Master Is, as well as 1293 Magisters.

During the critical summer of 1940 the Woodley factory completed 25 Master Is as fighters. Designated the M.24, they had single-seat cockpits, four Browning guns, VHF radio and IFF, and the radiator moved back under the engine. These must be the least-known of all RAF fighters. In a matter of days Miles also produced a completely new purpose-designed M.20 fighter with many good features.

As Kestrel stocks were running out, Miles switched to the 870-hp Bristol Mercury XXX radial, clipped the wings from 39 ft to 35 ft 7in and built 1747 with the designation Master II. On the ball, *The Aeroplane Spotter* published

The first production-standard Master I was this machine, N7408, and it was delivered to the RAF in May 1939. Another 899 Mk Is would duly follow before production switched the Mercury XX-powered Mk II

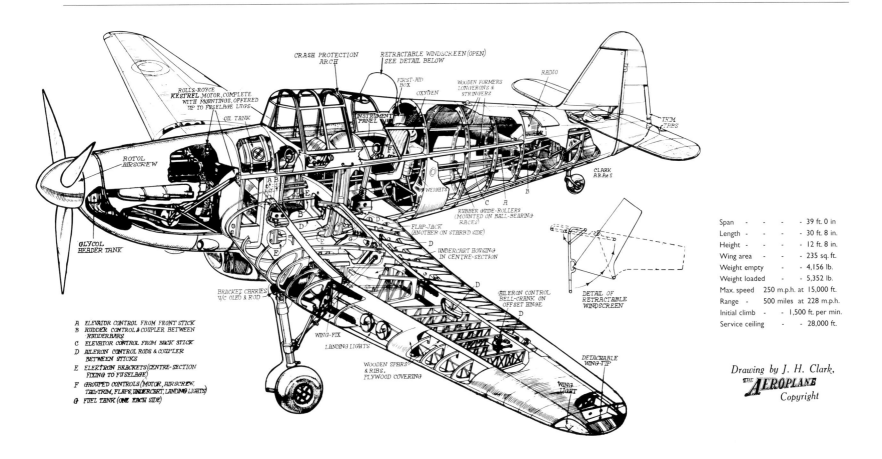

CRASH PROTECTION ARCH

RETRACTABLE WINDSCREEN (OPEN) SEE DETAIL BELOW

FIRST-AID BOX

OXYGEN

WOODEN FORMERS LONGERONS & STRINGERS

RADIO

ROLLS-ROYCE KESTREL MOTOR, COMPLETE WITH MOUNTINGS, OFFERED UP TO FUSELAGE LUGS

OIL TANK

INSTRUMENT PANEL

TRIM TABS

ROT'OL AIRSCREW

CLARK A.R.Ae.S

WEIGHTS

RUBBER GUIDE-ROLLERS (MOUNTED ON BALL-BEARING RACES)

GLYCOL HEADER TANK

FLAP-JACK (ANOTHER ON STARB'D SIDE)

UNDERCART HOUSING IN CENTRE-SECTION

DETAIL OF RETRACTABLE WINDSCREEN

AILERON CONTROL BELL-CRANK ON OFFSET HINGE

BRACKET CARRIES U/C OLEO & ROD

WING-FIX

LANDING LIGHTS

WOODEN SPARS & RIBS, PLYWOOD COVERING

DETACHABLE WING-TIP

WING LIGHT

| | |
|---|---|
| Span - - - | 39 ft. 0 in |
| Length - - - | 30 ft. 8 in. |
| Height - - - | 12 ft. 8 in. |
| Wing area - - | 235 sq. ft. |
| Weight empty - - | 4,156 lb. |
| Weight loaded - - | 5,352 lb. |
| Max. speed 250 m.p.h. at 15,000 ft. | |
| Range - 500 miles at 228 m.p.h. | |
| Initial climb - - 1,500 ft. per min. | |
| Service ceiling - - 28,000 ft. | |

A ELEVATOR CONTROL FROM FRONT STICK
B RUDDER CONTROL & COUPLER BETWEEN RUDDERBARS
C ELEVATOR CONTROL FROM BACK STICK
D AILERON CONTROL RODS & COUPLER BETWEEN STICKS
E ELEKTRON BRACKETS (CENTRE-SECTION FIXING TO FUSELAGE)
F GROUPED CONTROLS (MOTOR, AIRSCREW, TAIL-TRIM, FLAPS, UNDERCART, LANDING LIGHTS)
G FUEL TANK (ONE EACH SIDE)

*Drawing by J. H. Clark,*
**THE AEROPLANE**
*Copyright*

a picture of this new version. A week or so later they admitted the picture should really have been captioned 'Master 1¹/₂'. Lacking a photograph of the Mk II, they had used a picture of the Mk I on which their artists had air-brushed in the radial engine, but had forgotten to remove the radiator!

The Mk II was the fastest production Master, reaching 260 mph at medium altitudes. Some had the lower part of the rudder removed to enable them to tow Hotspur III gliders. Then, to guard against a possible shortage of Mercuries, Miles kept the airframe unchanged but fitted the 825-hp Pratt & Whitney R-1535-SB4G Twin Wasp Junior. This was a beautifully smooth engine, and its reduced diameter improved the view ahead. Master IIIs were built until trainer production stopped at the 3450th aircraft in 1942. Then the Woodley factory, besides making a host of prototypes, churned out 1724 Martinet target tugs, plus 11 radio-controlled Queen Martinets. These were

based on the Master II but had greater span, extra tanks in the outer wings (increasing loaded weight from around 5600 lb to 6750 lb), different cockpits and towing gear. Some were specially equipped air/sea rescue machines. Like Masters, they were pleasant to fly.

Apart from the propeller, and the confusing 'hole' which he drew to show the front wing/fuselage bracket (labelled E), there is little to criticise in Clark's drawing, which shows a machine typical of the main run of Master I aircraft. He did not label the carburettor air inlet at the base of the cowling (there was one on each side), nor the combined coolant and oil radiators, though their presence was obvious. He drew the metal fishplates joining the front and rear spars of the centre and outer wings in solid black. Of course the engine mounting was also metal, as were several other parts bearing concentrated local stress. Sadly not a single Master or Martinet survives today.

# ALBEMARLE I

During World War 2 cadets in the Air Training Corps could spend lots of time flying in things like Dragon Rapides and Ansons, and if they were lucky enough to be in East Anglia they were likely to put in their fold-out logbooks the B-17 and B-24, but the most one could hope for among operational RAF aircraft were OTU machines such as the Wellington. So I was among an excited group from No 628 (Pinner County School) Sqn when for Easter Camp 1944 we descended on Brize Norton and found it absolutely stuffed with Albemarles towing Horsa gliders.

This was in the amazing build-up to D-Day, when if the Luftwaffe had thought of dropping a bomb anywhere on southern England it would almost certainly have hit an aircraft, tank, field hospital or mobile radar. Every field was packed with war material. Everywhere was activity, and nobody worked harder than the Heavy Glider Conversion Unit at Brize. From before dawn until dark the operative runway, usually 26 (26°), thundered to the sound of Hercules engines and the whoosh of huge gliders.

I am glad that Clark found time to draw the Albemarle. I wonder how many aviation buffs in the USA, or even in Britain, have ever heard of it? Like the Warwick, Buckingham and other types, this aircraft never made it as a bomber. What made this one different is that it was planned as the Bristol 155, to be derived from the Beaufort to specification B.18/38. Moreover, to save scarce light alloys it was designed to be made almost entirely from steel and wood, as Clark makes clear in this outstanding drawing. It was to have had a nosewheel undercarriage – almost the first in Britain – and dorsal and ventral turrets each with two 20 mm cannon. But after the death of designer Barnwell, in the August 1938 crash of his own ultralight, the project was transferred to Armstrong Whitworth at Coventry, becoming the AW 41 Albemarle.

Despite countless problems, and inevitable weight growth which called for the 1100 hp Taurus engines to be replaced by the Hercules, the prototype was flown as early as 20 March 1940. Then followed a typically British series of procrastinations, indecisions and general foul-ups, compounded by the amazing production arrangement. As a firm of the Hawker Siddeley Group, Armstrong Whitworth gathered together over 1000 small companies who knew little or nothing about aircraft and got them to make all the parts. The

ABOVE An impressive line up of newly-completed Albemarle Is at Brockworth, in Gloucester, in late 1943, awaiting the arrival of their ATA ferry crews. In the field behind them sit six Typhoons, also ready for despatch to the frontline

LEFT This D-Day-striped Albemarle V was part of No 297 Sqn, based at Brize Norton. It was later lost in a crash near Bretton, in Wiltshire, during a glider-towing practice mission on 22 December 1944

# YORK I

After World War 2 we British excused our failure to compete with the Constellation and DC-6 by saying that there had been an agreement that, while we built combat aircraft, the Americans could build the transport aircraft needed. In fact, the postwar situation was merely a continuation of the pre-war position, when we had failed to compete except with small aircraft such as the Dragon Rapide. In fact, no restriction was placed on our industry, and in the Avro 685 York we built a simple but effective low-cost transport conversion of the Lancaster bomber.

As Clark indicated, most of the wing, engines, landing gear and tail were almost unchanged from the bomber. The fuselage had to be completely new, and lack of pressurisation made possible a useful square cross-section. The obvious dimensions to quote are cabin width and height, but I

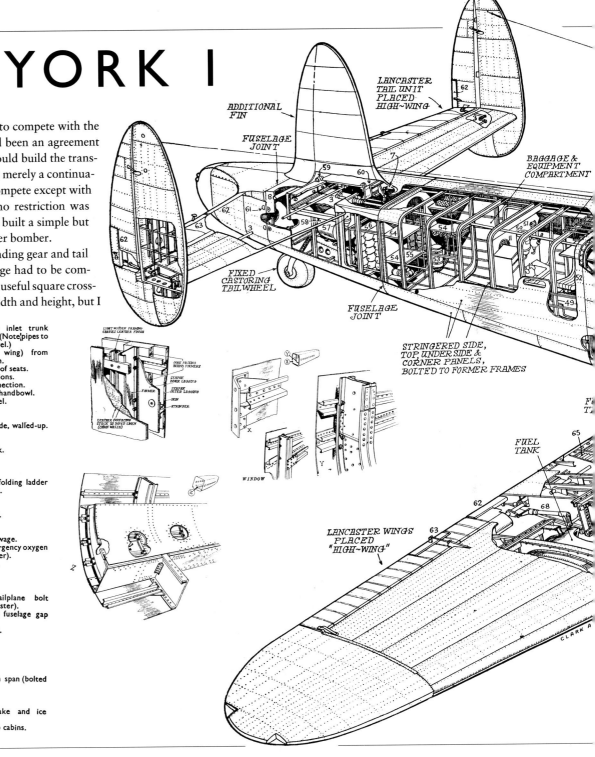

1. Hinged nose with headlamp (access to electric circuits terminal panel 2 and controls).
3. Rudder pedals and rod along (above) cabin ceiling to tail.
4. Hobson control box, engine controls, flaps, undercarriage, etc., and cable-runs above ceiling.
5. Two pilots.
6. Elevator control from sticks, along (above) cabin ceiling to tail.
6A. Elevator quadrant and servo motor.
7. Elevator control cranked to pass under tailplane.
8. Elevator shaft.
9. Navigator's table and floor.
9A. Navigator's instrument panel.
10. "Standing air" fan on door.
11. "Standing air" fan in galley (cabin cooling when aircraft is grounded).
12. Radio operator's seat and window.
13. Astro-dome.
14. Navigator's observation blister window.
15. Drift meter.
16. Oxygen stowage.
17. Di-pole aerial.
18. Aerial mast.
19. Windscreen anti-icing nozzle(s).
20. Portable oxygen stowage.
21. Immersion switch (operating emergency dinghy).
22. Rudder and elevator and aileron gyros.
23. Flare stowage.
24. Fuel control panel (starboard pilot).
25. Rudder servo motor.
26. Cabin air extractor and duct.
27. Cold air inlet, filter and duct.
28. Water tank.
29. Cabin ceiling.
30. Hydraulic tank (flaps and undercarriage op.) in roof.
31. Port warm air inlet trunk supplies forward cabin.

32. Starboard warm air inlet trunk supplies rear cabin. (Note pipes to discharge at floor level.)
33. Passageway (under wing) from forward to rear cabin.
34. Rail carries wall-side of seats.
35. Air charging connections.
36. Ground starting connection.
37. Lavatory and folding handbowl.
37A. Main power fuse panel.
38. Cloakroom.
39. Entrance door.
40. Door on starboard side, walled-up.
41. Fuel tank.
42. DF loop.
43. Line of wing fuel tank.
44. Hot-water tank.
45. Cold-water tank.
46. Flap op. cylinder.
47. Emergency exit and folding ladder above door in ceiling.
48. Refrigerator.
49. Electric hay boxes.
50. Electric water heater.
51. Water filter.
52. Steward's seat.
53. Frequency meter stowage.
54. Dinghy stowage (emergency oxygen bottles stowage, under).
55. Tropical kit stowage.
56. Oxygen stowage.
57. Compass repeater.
58. De-icing fluid tank.
59. Two halves of tailplane bolt together (as in Lancaster).
60. Tailplane drops into fuselage gap and bolted home.
61. Tailpiece bolted joint.
62. Hand trim tabs.
63. Servo trim tabs.
64. Motor oil tanks.
65. Outer wing flap.
66. Centre plane flap.
67. Wing trailing section span (bolted to wing rear spar).
68. Aileron control.
69. Outer-wing fix.
70. Carburetter air intake and ice guard.
71. Lagged double skin to cabins.

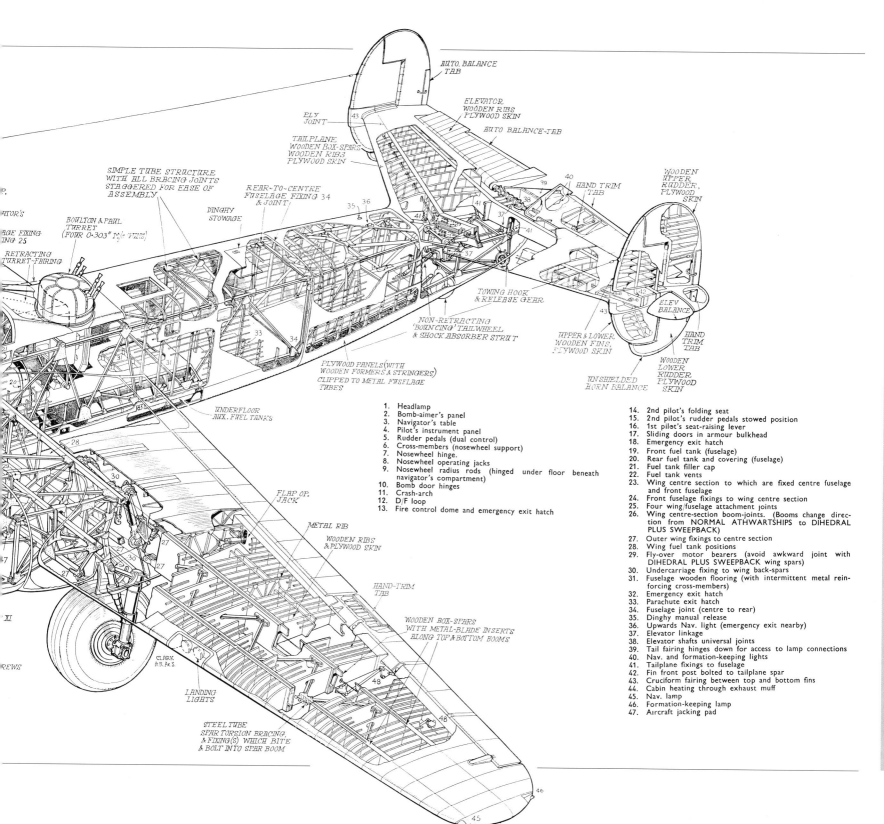

AUTO. BALANCE TAB

ELEVATOR
WOODEN RIBS
PLYWOOD SKIN

AUTO BALANCE-TAB

PLY JOINT

TAILPLANE
WOODEN BOX-SPARS
WOODEN RIBS
PLYWOOD SKIN

HAND TRIM TAB

WOODEN UPPER RUDDER, PLYWOOD SKIN

SIMPLE TUBE STRUCTURE
WITH ALL BRACING JOINTS
STAGGERED FOR EASE OF
ASSEMBLY

REAR-TO-CENTRE
FUSELAGE FIXING 34
& JOINT

DINGHY STOWAGE

BOULTON & PAUL TURRET
(FOUR 0·303" M/c GUNS)

RETRACTING
TURRET-FAIRING

TOWING HOOK
& RELEASE GEAR

NON-RETRACTING
'BOUNCING' TAILWHEEL
& SHOCK ABSORBER STRUT

UPPER & LOWER
WOODEN FINS,
PLYWOOD SKIN

ELEV BALANCE

HAND TRIM TAB

WOODEN LOWER RUDDER PLYWOOD SKIN

UNSHIELDED HORN BALANCE

PLYWOOD PANELS (WITH
WOODEN FORMERS & STRINGERS)
CLIPPED TO METAL FUSELAGE
TUBES

UNDERFLOOR
AUX. FUEL TANKS

METAL RIB

WOODEN RIBS
& PLYWOOD SKIN

FLAP OP. JACK

HAND-TRIM TAB

WOODEN BOX-SPARS
WITH METAL-BLADE INSERTS
ALONG TOP & BOTTOM BOOMS

CLARK A.R.Ae.S.

LANDING LIGHTS

STEEL TUBE
SPAR TORSION BRACING,
& FIXING(S) WHICH BITE
& BOLT INTO SPAR BOOM

1. Headlamp
2. Bomb-aimer's panel
3. Navigator's table
4. Pilot's instrument panel
5. Rudder pedals (dual control)
6. Cross-members (nosewheel support)
7. Nosewheel hinge.
8. Nosewheel operating jacks
9. Nosewheel radius rods (hinged under floor beneath navigator's compartment)
10. Bomb door hinges
11. Crash-arch
12. D/F loop
13. Fire control dome and emergency exit hatch

14. 2nd pilot's folding seat
15. 2nd pilot's rudder pedals stowed position
16. 1st pilot's seat-raising lever
17. Sliding doors in armour bulkhead
18. Emergency exit hatch
19. Front fuel tank (fuselage)
20. Rear fuel tank and covering (fuselage)
21. Fuel tank filler cap
22. Fuel tank vents
23. Wing centre section to which are fixed centre fuselage and front fuselage
24. Front fuselage fixings to wing centre section
25. Four wing/fuselage attachment joints
26. Wing centre-section boom-joints. (Booms change direction from NORMAL ATHWARTSHIPS to DIHEDRAL PLUS SWEEPBACK)
27. Outer wing fixings to centre section
28. Wing fuel tank positions
29. Fly-over motor bearers (avoid awkward joint with DIHEDRAL PLUS SWEEPBACK wing spars)
30. Undercarriage fixing to wing back-spars
31. Fuselage wooden flooring (with intermittent metal reinforcing cross-members)
32. Emergency exit hatch
33. Parachute exit hatch
34. Fuselage joint (centre to rear)
35. Dinghy manual release
36. Upwards Nav. light (emergency exit nearby)
37. Elevator linkage
38. Elevator shafts universal joints
39. Tail fairing hinges down for access to lamp connections
40. Nav. and formation-keeping lights
41. Tailplane fixings to fuselage
42. Fin front post bolted to tailplane spar
43. Cruciform fairing between top and bottom fins
44. Cabin heating through exhaust muff
45. Nav. lamp
46. Formation-keeping lamp
47. Aircraft jacking pad

only big subassemblies were the wing centre section (Rover Car Co), front fuselage (MG Motors) and tail (Harris Lebus Furniture). The parts were then taken by truck to a big hangar at Brockworth, Gloucester, and put together by a specially created company called A W Hawksley. There may have been someone there who knew about aeroplanes, but I know visiting Americans were utterly incredulous that such an arrangement could work.

From September 1941 this 'Hawksley' company began by delivering 158 Albemarles as bombers, with a four-gun Boulton Paul dorsal turret, but all were converted into various kinds of glider tug and special transport. Production then continued to the 600th aircraft, plus the two prototypes made at Coventry. There were eight marks, one (the Merlin-engined Mk III) never being built. Some batches went to the Soviet Union, but nearly all went to No 295-297 and 570 Sqns, the ones I flew in belonging to Nos 296 and 297.

Though it was hardly a great war-winner, it is harsh and wrong to call the Albemarle a failure. It flew many thousands of exceedingly effective missions pulling Horsas (bigger than the tug) to Sicily, Normandy, Arnhem and across the Rhine, and doing countless challenging duties in support of the French Maquis resistance fighters.

Each morning at Brize hundreds of manila hemp towropes would be stretched along the downwind end of the runway. On each end were massive forgings which clipped in the tail of the Albemarle and under the nose of a Horsa II. The Horsa I needed a bifurcated rope, attached to each wing leading edge. The tug would move off at a walking pace while a batsman would give signals. As the line became taut and rose off the ground he would signal, and the pilot would then open up to full power. Of course, the Horsa would be airborne all the way down the runway, but not the tug.

Most wartime aircraft had nitpicking faults. With a glider in tow, the tug pilot wanted to retract the gear as quickly as possible, but to do this he had to bend right down to find the lever, when he should have been looking ahead. ATC cadets were helpful here. After the sortie the glider would cast off, and the tug would dive at about 300 mph on a field where the pilot (or ATC passenger) would pull the towrope release. The massive chunk of metal on the front would bury itself in the ground within a few feet of the recovery crew, who in each half-hour would fill a truck with ropes. Meanwhile, the tug would return to Brize, the pilot braking with his right thumb, and taxi round for the next trip. Above each tug would be two rising pillars of bluish oil smoke from the engines, which were designed for cruise power at 250 kts instead of maximum-continuous power at 90 kts! The 'fire-control dome' enabled one to watch the wingtips when taxiing through crowds of parked aircraft.

This drawing is beyond criticism, apart from 'astral dome' and joining all the cooling-gill petals into a continuous ring! And the casual reader might think the Albemarle was a bomber.

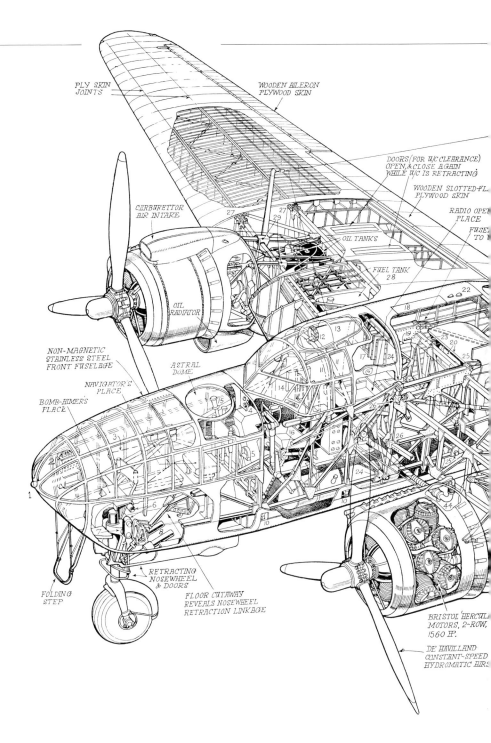

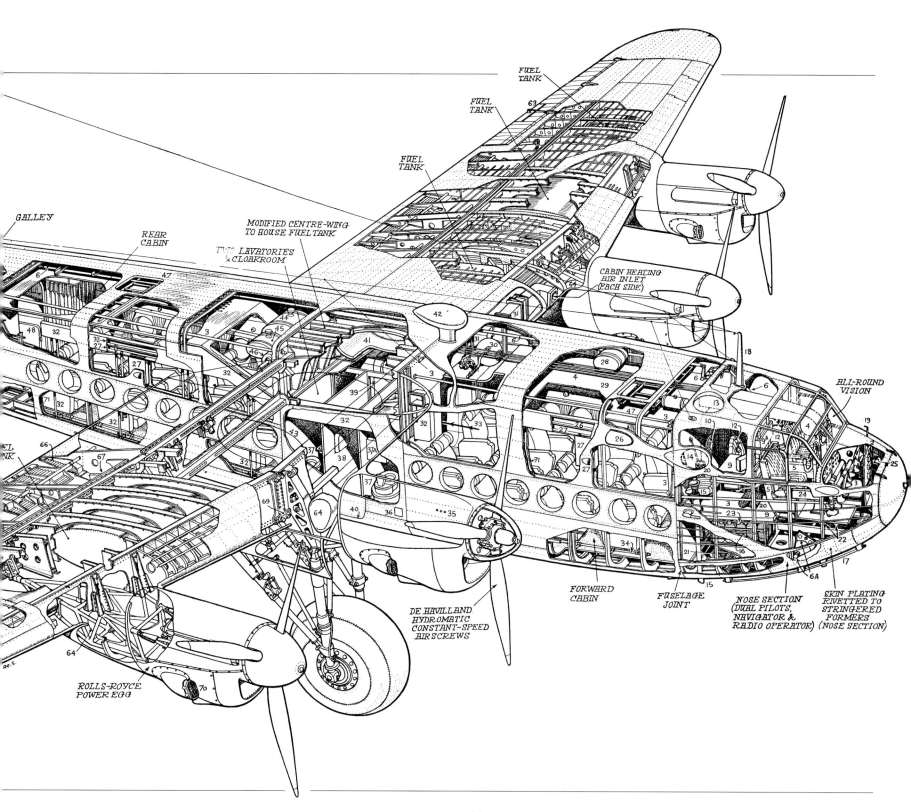

FUEL TANK

FUEL TANK

63

FUEL TANK

GALLEY

MODIFIED CENTRE-WING TO HOUSE FUEL TANK

REAR CABIN

TWO LAVATORIES & CLOAKROOM

CABIN HEATING AIR INLET (EACH SIDE)

6

47

64

6

ALL-ROUND VISION

48

32

32

27

44

45

31

42

41

3

46

3

18

27

32

32

31

30

28

13

10

12

19

71

32

39

3

4

29

47

3

6

25

32

32

33

71

26

26

3

14

12

9

5

FUEL TANK

66

43

38

37A

36

35

27

27

24

20

23

9

22

6A

67

32

37

37

69

40

64

34

21

16

15

15

6A

FORWARD CABIN

FUSELAGE JOINT

NOSE SECTION (DUAL PILOTS, NAVIGATOR & RADIO OPERATOR)

SKIN PLATING RIVETTED TO STRINGERED FORMERS (NOSE SECTION)

DE HAVILLAND HYDROMATIC CONSTANT-SPEED AIRSCREWS

64

ROLLS-ROYCE POWER EGG

70

Ae.S.

failed to find these data in 19 books and magazine articles which purported to describe the York! The only relevant supposed fact that appears everywhere is that fuselage volume was 'twice that of the Lancaster'. At a guess the interior was about 90 inches square, except for height under the wing spars. This was adequate for pairs of seats on each side of a central aisle, each with its own oxygen mask. The floor (on some Yorks at least) was thick plywood. The porthole-type windows were close together, and did not line up with seat rows. The third York had a much smaller number of slightly larger square windows.

It is ironic that, whereas the Hastings, designed from the outset specifically as a transport, should have been extremely difficult to load with cargo, the quick lash-up York had an almost level floor at a convenient height. Driving four Jeeps inside was no problem. Fuselage length was 78 ft 6 in, 9 ft longer than a Lancaster. The first time I boarded a York I walked forward and immediately saw I was abreast the main wheels. There still seemed to be half the fuselage between me and the cockpit, and over the last few feet I was sure the aircraft would tip up!

The entire York programme was A V Roe Ltd's own idea, so the project proceeded very quickly. LV626, the prototype, flew at what today is Manchester Airport on 5 July 1942, only five months after the first drawing had been issued. Later this aircraft was tested with Bristol Hercules engines, in an installation identical with the Lancaster II, and it was found that the different nacelles required a third fin to be added. No more Hercules-Yorks were built, but the third fin was retained. Many sources say the central fin was demanded by the larger forward fuselage, but the first two prototypes flew perfectly well with the original Lancaster tail. The wider fuselage slightly reduced wing area (from 1258 to 1190 square feet) and the span of the flaps, and there were significant differences in the fuel and cabin-heat systems.

The cockpit was so far in the nose there was not even room to stow a suitcase in front. The instrument panel went right across, and dual control was standard, as it usually is in large transports. Throttle, mixture and pitch controls were on the centreline above the windscreen. Flight crew was completed by a navigator, with a plotting table, a few instruments, drift sight and astro dome for taking sextant 'shots' of heavenly bodies, and a radio operator who had primitive communications, such as TR.1154/1155.

At first little effort could be spared to build Yorks, and only three were delivered in 1943, rising to nine in 1944. These were camouflaged, and from the outset worked hard taking Allied leaders to conferences and war theatres. Production really got under way in 1945, and in October that year the assembly jigs were transferred to Yeadon (today Leeds/Bradford airport) where the last 77 of a total of 257 Yorks were built. A total of 208 went to the RAF, five of these then being lent to BOAC. Some had 12 seats but carried mainly cargo, while others had sleeper accommodation for 12 VIPs. Passenger Yorks had the door under the wing and a square baggage hatch in front of the tail, but cargo versions had a stripped interior accessed via two enormous doors in the left of the rear fuselage. On the Berlin Airlift in 1948-49 most Yorks, civil and RAF, served round the clock flying over 29,000 sorties laden with anything from coal and flour to livestock. Flights were at low-level, and windscreens became coated with flies.

Eventually, after 1950, many Yorks were bought secondhand by small carriers. Most were furnished for as many as 65 passengers. Cheap to build, and not particularly costly to operate, these rather outdated workhorses did an impressive job in all parts of the world even into the 1960s. A tiny detail is that if you look carefully (as scale modellers do) you will see numerous visible differences between the radiator, radiator duct, carburettor inlets (No 70 in this drawing), exhaust pipes and many other details between different batches of Lancasters, Lancastrians and Yorks. Here, Clark did not even bother to draw an engine, and he put flame-damping shrouds over the exhausts. I can't blame him for re-using chunks of the left wing, tail and other parts from his drawing of the Lancaster.

Still to be issued to a Transport Command unit, a virginous York I basks in the spring sun at Yeadon in 1945. Just how low the passengers sat in the fuselage is plainly obvious from the window line

# TYPHOON IB

Both Clark of *The Aeroplane* and Max Millar of *Flight* did wartime cutaways of the Hawker Typhoon. We have chosen Max's merely in order to try to even out the balance somewhat. One can get an excellent idea of what Clark's was like by studying his Tempest, which we have used.

Dealing with the aircraft first, Chief Designer Sydney Camm was extremely pleased with the Hurricane, but was under no illusions regarding its speedy obsolescence. In fact he once told me he was astonished that it was still in major frontline service (admittedly, not in North West Europe) to the end of the War. By 1938 he had roughed out a next generation fighter, to meet specification F.18/37 and be powered by a 2000 hp engine.

There were three possible engines. The eventual winner was the superb Bristol Centaurus sleeve-valve radial, but at the outset nobody bothered much about it, apart from Rex Pierson who wanted it for the Warwick bomber. The Fw 190 had yet to hit us between the eyes and show what a radial engine could do, so Camm's attention was polarized around two extremely complicated and troublesome 24-cylinder liquid-cooled engines. He called his new fighter the N, for Napier (with the Sabre engine) and the R, for Rolls-Royce (with the Vulture). In my opinion it's a pity both engines were not drowned at birth. In fact, the Sabre proved that if you put enough effort into an engine for long enough, it can eventually be made more or less to work.

The R prototype, by this time called the Hawker Tornado, flew on 6 October 1939. The N, called the Typhoon, followed on 24 February 1940. Plans were made for Avro to build the Tornado in quantity and Gloster

Aircraft the Typhoon. If only things had gone well this would have given the RAF a lot more muscle much more quickly. And I can't help contrasting this situation, where we had a choice of two great new fighters with a choice of three engines, with today when the RAF may perhaps get a new fighter provided the three foreign partners don't pull out.

The Vulture is remembered by Rolls-Royce as the worst thing they ever did until the original RB.211. Though it didn't bankrupt the company it caused endless hassle, and also the loss of many Manchester aircrew, and in July 1941 it was at last abandoned. This left just the otherwise very similar Typhoon to battle on against a sea of troubles. As well as the basic unreliability of the engine, these difficulties included stability and control problems in high-speed dives, inadequate rear view, delays in the belt-fed version of the four 20 mm Hispano guns, and, most dangerous of all, a tendency for the tail to come off.

There are cures to most things. The Sabre very gradually became an acceptable frontline engine. The long-barrel Hispano Mk II gun eventually matured with its belt feed, each box magazine holding 140 rounds. In early aircraft the barrels and massive recoil springs were exposed, as in the similarly armed versions of the Hurricane, but by the time Max did his drawing the guns were faired in. Prolonged testing led to a ring of doublers, a joint strap and external fishplates round the rear fuselage which pretty well ensured that the tail would stay on. I have to say, the rest of the Typhoon was built like a tank, and chaps walked away from awesone pile-ups.

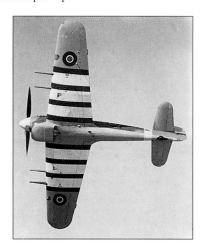

LEFT Fresh off the production line, and ready for its first check flight, a definitive Typhoon IB poses with assorted Hawker staff for a company publicity shot in mid-1944

RIGHT Although wearing full D-Day style invasion stripes, this Typhoon IB (EK286) was not amongst the dozens employed in support of the landings. Indeed, very few 'old' EK-series aircraft were still in frontline service by June 1944, most having been passed on to OTUs or simply struck off charge

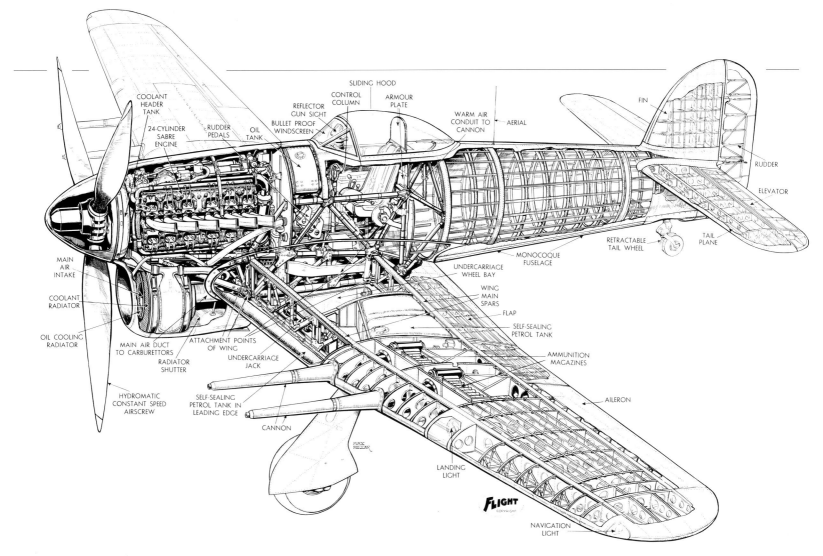

COOLANT
HEADER
TANK

24-CYLINDER
SABRE
ENGINE

RUDDER
PEDALS

OIL
TANK

REFLECTOR
GUN SIGHT

BULLET PROOF
WINDSCREEN

SLIDING HOOD

CONTROL
COLUMN

ARMOUR
PLATE

WARM AIR
CONDUIT TO
CANNON

AERIAL

FIN

RUDDER

ELEVATOR

MAIN
AIR
INTAKE

COOLANT
RADIATOR

OIL COOLING
RADIATOR

MAIN AIR DUCT
TO CARBURETTORS

ATTACHMENT POINTS
OF WING

RADIATOR
SHUTTER

UNDERCARRIAGE
JACK

HYDROMATIC
CONSTANT SPEED
AIRSCREW

SELF-SEALING
PETROL TANK IN
LEADING EDGE

CANNON

MONOCOQUE
FUSELAGE

RETRACTABLE
TAIL WHEEL

TAIL
PLANE

UNDERCARRIAGE
WHEEL BAY

WING
MAIN
SPARS

FLAP

SELF-SEALING
PETROL TANK

AMMUNITION
MAGAZINES

AILERON

LANDING
LIGHT

NAVIGATION
LIGHT

The original cockpit had a car-type door on the left and a long metal fairing behind the pilot's head. Hawker's test pilots were amongst the most experienced, and gifted, aviators in Britain, and might have been expected to suggest that the Kingston designers might think again. To cut a long story short, by the time Gloster really got into mass production in 1943 the 'Tiffy' had matured into a far better aircraft, with a sliding bubble canopy which really impressed USAAF Chief of Staff Arnold when he saw it (so the same thing soon appeared on US fighters). The 1944 Typhoon IB also usually had a four-blade DH propeller, though the diameter remained an impressive 13 ft.

Thus, by attacking each fault, Hawker Aircraft and D Napier & Son at last got something unexpected. The Typhoon had explicitly been planned as a high-altitude dogfighter. Nothing could be done about the buffeting and control problems in high-speed dives, caused by the great thickness of the wing.

This demanded a new thinner wing, as explained on the Tempest pages. Again, not much could be done to make the Sabre give high power at high altitude. What could be done was make the Typhoon carry eight rockets with 60-lb warheads, or the 25-lb armour-piercing variety. Alternatively, it first carried two 500-lb bombs and later two bombs of 1000 lb.

The unexpected result was the greatest ground-attack aircraft of the European war. Their work with 23 squadrons of the 2nd Tactical Air Force, played down by the government at the time (but very much appreciated by the 'brown jobs') has become legendary. 'You want a bridge taken out? A particular building? A Panzer division? Certainly, no problem.'

Max's drawing used typeset annotation. I think he gave the wing too much dihedral, and he might have commented that, most unusually, the rudder was the only part covered in fabric.

# BARRACUDA II

Scattered all over the world are a dwindling bunch of courageous men who went to war in the 'Barra'. Most of the rest of the world, even aviation buffs, have probably never heard of it. So I am especially glad to help various other authors who think the Fairey Barracuda ought to have its place in history.

In fact, while it was hardly an inspired aircraft, it was certainly not a disaster either. The one ironic thing that does stick in the mind is that Rolls-Royce were specifically told to build the Exe in order to power the Barracuda. This engine was as unusual as the aircraft it was intended for, with 24 air-cooled sleeve-valve cylinders arranged in X-formation. It was a most successful engine which would soon have been rated in the 1500 hp class. Sadly, it was cancelled at the start of the War (for no very good reason), but was so troublefree it continued to drive the Rolls-Royce Battle, used as a 'hack' transport, to the end of the War. So the Barracuda had a low-rated Merlin, and never had quite enough power.

Without being told, you can see that the Barracuda was a carrier-based torpedo bomber for the Fleet Air Arm. It was also a dive bomber. Like the Firefly, its folding wings were fitted with Youngman flaps, though in this case they could not be retracted under the wings. At the neutral setting they gave lift, acting as extra wing area. For take-off they were set to 20°, for landing they were driven hydraulically to 45°, and for steep dive bombing they were rotated to a negative angle of -30°. These flaps were one of the striking features, the others being the odd location of the wing, with huge windows but

no internal weapon bay under it, the funny bent landing gears (you can imagine them extended) and the high tailplane. In the early 1940s such a tail seemed much stranger than it does to us today.

The wings did not have power folding, but deck crews seem to have managed quite well. Under each outer wing was a flush-fitting V-shaped handle which, when released, came down to a convenient height above the deck (this was omitted from Max's drawing). But before you could rotate the wings back alongside the fuselage, you first had to fold not only the flaps but the entire bit of wing to which they were attached upwards about hinges along the top of the rear spar. When these were lying inverted on top of the wing, the actual folding of the wings could take place. They rotated back about vertical hinges, and so were stowed with the leading edge facing outwards.

The normal crew comprised the pilot above the leading edge, with a remarkably good view, the observer/navigator amidships and the radio operator/gunner at the back. All sat under a long greenhouse, but the middle and rear men could get down into different locations lower in the fuselage. The Barracuda had to do so many different things and carry so much equipment it could easily have been rubbish, but in fact I only heard it spoken of with a kind of bemused affection.

Apart from the 18 in torpedo illustrated – which I do not believe was ever used in action – the external stores racks under the fuselage and wings could carry an amazing array of bombs, mines, depth charges and even an air/sea rescue lifeboat. Wing racks made successful live drops with four paratroops

LEFT The first Barracuda II built by Fairey, P9667 is seen being put through its paces with an underslung torpedo – this weapon was rarely used by the aircraft in combat, Barracuda squadrons preferring to attack targets with 500 and 1000 lb bombs in steep diving attacks

RIGHT Battered and weather-beaten, a war-weary Barracuda II from No 774 Sqn is deftly flown aboard the training carrier HMS *Ravager* in early 1944. Deck landing qualification was the final challenge facing a pilot under training, prior to him being given a frontline posting

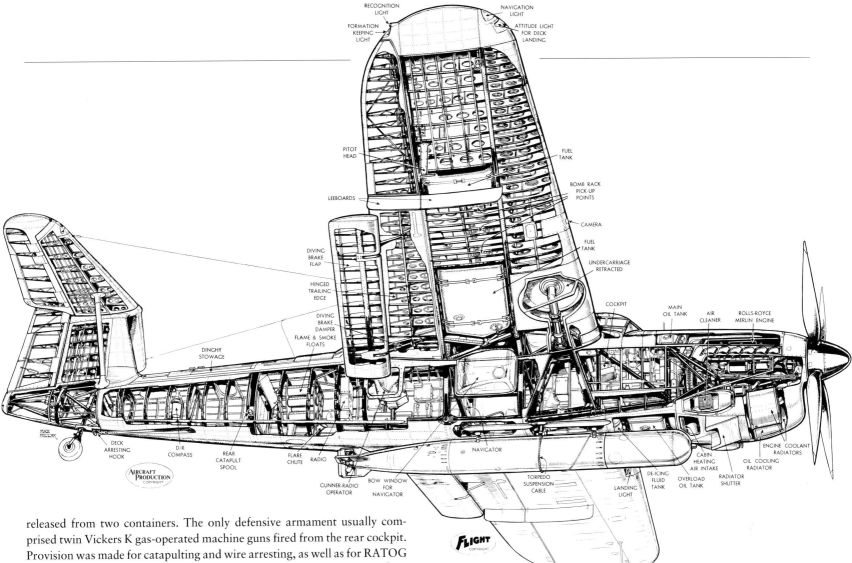

RECOGNITION LIGHT

NAVIGATION LIGHT

FORMATION KEEPING LIGHT

ATTITUDE LIGHT FOR DECK LANDING

PITOT HEAD

FUEL TANK

LEEBOARDS

BOMB RACK PICK-UP POINTS

CAMERA

DIVING BRAKE FLAP

FUEL TANK

UNDERCARRIAGE RETRACTED

HINGED TRAILING EDGE

DIVING BRAKE DAMPER

FLAME & SMOKE FLOATS

COCKPIT

MAIN OIL TANK

AIR CLEANER

ROLLS-ROYCE MERLIN ENGINE

DINGHY STOWAGE

DECK ARRESTING HOOK

D/R COMPASS

REAR CATAPULT SPOOL

FLARE CHUTE

RADIO

NAVICATOR

ENGINE COOLANT RADIATORS

CABIN HEATING AIR INTAKE

OIL COOLING RADIATOR

RADIATOR SHUTTER

GUNNER-RADIO OPERATOR

BOW WINDOW FOR NAVIGATOR

TORPEDO SUSPENSION CABLE

DE-ICING FLUID TANK

OVERLOAD OIL TANK

LANDING LIGHT

AIRCRAFT PRODUCTION COPYRIGHT

FLIGHT COPYRIGHT

released from two containers. The only defensive armament usually comprised twin Vickers K gas-operated machine guns fired from the rear cockpit. Provision was made for catapulting and wire arresting, as well as for RATOG (rocket-assisted take-off gear) to blast off escort carriers.

The Mk I had a 1260 hp Merlin and a three-blade propeller, 30 being built. The Mk II, the main variant used for dive bombing, had the 1640 hp Merlin 32 and a four-blade propeller. Fairey made 675, and a further 1013 were added by Westland, Blackburn and Boulton Paul. The Mk III, intended mainly for ASW (anti-submarine warfare), was distinguished by a giant blister under the rear fuselage for the Mk X radar. Fairey delivered 460 of this version, Boulton Paul providing another 392, to bring the overall total to 2572 including the two prototypes.

Though Barracudas did many unsung operations, for example at Salerno in 1943 and in the Pacific from April 1944 until VJ-Day, its main moment of glory came on 3 April 1944. On that day aircraft from *Victorious* and *Furious*

scored 15 direct hits with 250 and 500-lb armour-piercing bombs on the *Tirpitz*, lying in Kaa fjord. On 24 August 1944 another attack scored a hit with a 1000-lb bomb. Too late to see action came the Barracuda V, with a much more powerful Griffon engine and many other changes including a new wing and tail.

Max Millar seemed to like drawing aircraft from below, and in this case he probably did choose the best viewpoint. The aerodynamic fences, called leeboards, were occasionally absent from production aircraft. '"D/R" COMPASS' meant distant-reading, the dial being in the cockpit, and of course 'BOW WINDOW' rhymed with 'no', not with 'now'.

# P-38 LIGHTNING

Few military aircraft have been so distinctive as the Lockheed P-38 Lightning, because it had a short central nacelle and large booms – almost twin fuselages – to carry the tail. The only other machine in the World War 2 sky that looked even vaguely similar (Fokker G.1s being grounded) was the Fw 189, which was a much slower frontline reconnaissance aircraft unlikely to be seen outside Germany and the Soviet Union.

In 1937 the US Army Air Corps issued a requirement for 'an experimental pursuit having the tactical mission of interception and attack of hostile aircraft at high altitude'. A height of 20,000 ft was to be reached in six minutes, and level speed was to be 360 mph. Under Robert E Gross, Lockheed's president, design engineers Hall L Hibbard and C L 'Kelly' Johnson roughed out six configurations for a twin-engined fighter (not actually requested). All had typical Lockheed high wing-loading, and all had two liquid-cooled Allison engines with turbo-superchargers. Three had the tail carried on twin booms, No 4 having tractor engines and a central nacelle, No 5 being the same but with the cockpit in the left boom and armament in the centre wing, and No 6 having push/pull engines on the centreline. The choice fell on No 4, the only remaining decision on the basic layout being to tunnel-test and finally reject a canard elevator on the nose.

Fresh off the boat from Burbank, California, natural metal P-38J-15-LO fuselages are stripped of their protective coverings in preparation for wing mating in April 1944

Only one XP-38 prototype was built, flying on 27 January 1939. From the start the five-piece wing was unusual in being stiffened by spanwise and chordwise internal corrugations, the rear ribs being reinforced to handle heavy loads from the powerful Fowler flaps. These flaps were needed to counter the wing-loading, which in later versions reached 67 lb/sq ft (compared with, for example, 26.5 for a Spitfire Mk V). Like the tricycle landing gear, which was a novelty in 1939, the flaps were moved hydraulically.

A few early aircraft had a 37 mm cannon and two 0.30 in and two 0.5 in machine guns, but almost all had the arrangement shown in Max Millar's drawing. The magazines held 150 rounds of 20 mm and 4 x 500 of 0.5 in. The most interesting part of the P-38 was the powerplant. By adding or removing a gearwheel the engines could be made to turn in either direction (thus each aircraft had left and right engines of different sub-types), the Curtiss electrically-controlled propellers always turning outwards at the top. This made take-offs and landings easier than driving a car, with no trace of swing.

Max showed how the white-hot exhaust gas was piped back to drive the General Electric turbo-supercharger, which gave the aircraft excellent performance at all altitudes. Compressed air from the supercharger was ducted to the intercooler under the engine and thence to the gear-driven supercharger inside the rear of the engine. On each side of the intercooler was an oil radiator. More pipes carried the Prestone engine coolant a long way back to the radiators on each side of the tail boom. Auxiliary inlets on top cooled the turbine disc and provided air which, heated by the exhaust, was piped to the cockpit.

The latter was comfortable and, like everything about the P-38, extremely fully equipped and finished like a Cadillac. You got aboard by raising a hinged catch above the tail of the nacelle, which released a beautifully made ladder which pivoted out immediately below, thence crossing the wing to the canopy. Each side panel could hinge out, and the roof hinged up and back. So far as I know all P-38s had a wheel on top of a massive control column pivoted fore/aft on the right side of the cockpit, but despite this and the span of 52 ft the rate of roll was nothing to be ashamed of.

All-round manoeuvrability was astonishingly good for so large and heavy an aircraft. In dives to very high speeds P-38s were among the first aircraft to encounter a compressibility (high Mach number) problem. To overcome this the final blocks of P-38J and all the P-38Ls had special electrically-driven flaps, hinged at the front under the main spar, which pivoted down immediately beyond the nacelle on each side. Equally important was that the same

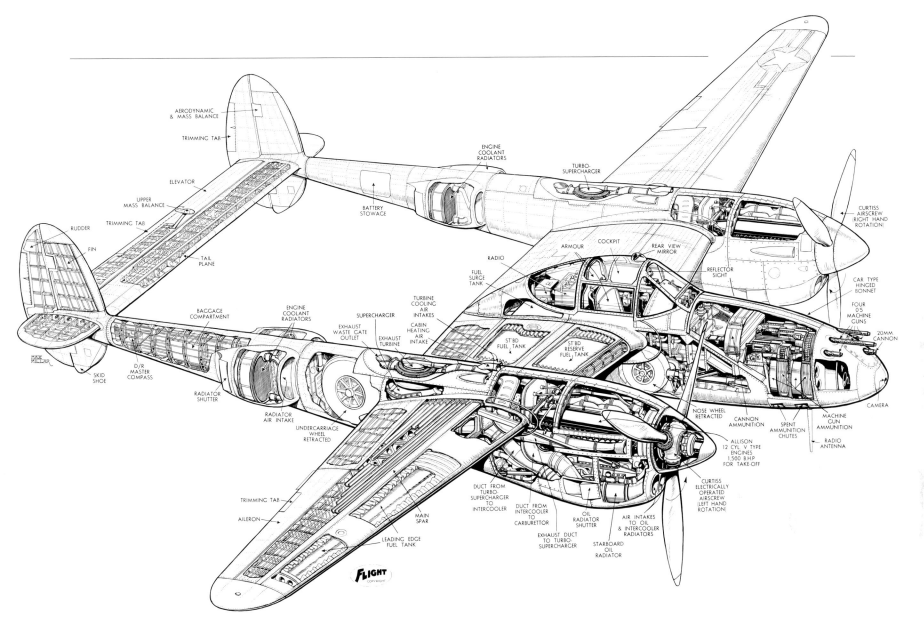

AERODYNAMIC
& MASS BALANCE

TRIMMING TAB

ELEVATOR

UPPER
MASS BALANCE

TRIMMING TAB

RUDDER

FIN

TAIL
PLANE

MAX
MILLAR

SKID
SHOE

D/R
MASTER
COMPASS

BAGGAGE
COMPARTMENT

ENGINE
COOLANT
RADIATORS

RADIATOR
SHUTTER

RADIATOR
AIR INTAKE

EXHAUST
WASTE GATE
OUTLET

SUPERCHARGER

EXHAUST
TURBINE

TURBINE
COOLING
AIR INTAKES

CABIN
HEATING
AIR INTAKE

ENGINE
COOLANT
RADIATORS

TURBO-
SUPERCHARGER

BATTERY
STOWAGE

RADIO

FUEL
SURGE
TANK

ST BD
FUEL TANK

ST BD
RESERVE
FUEL TANK

ARMOUR

COCKPIT

REAR VIEW
MIRROR

REFLECTOR
SIGHT

CURTISS
AIRSCREW
(RIGHT HAND
ROTATION)

CAR TYPE
HINGED
BONNET

FOUR
0·5
MACHINE
GUNS

20MM
CANNON

CAMERA

NOSE WHEEL
RETRACTED

CANNON
AMMUNITION

SPENT
AMMUNITION
CHUTES

MACHINE
GUN
AMMUNITION

RADIO
ANTENNA

ALLISON
12 CYL V TYPE
ENGINES
1,500 B.H.P.
FOR TAKE-OFF

UNDERCARRIAGE
WHEEL
RETRACTED

TRIMMING TAB

AILERON

MAIN
SPAR

LEADING EDGE
FUEL TANK

FLIGHT
COPYRIGHT

DUCT FROM
TURBO-
SUPERCHARGER
TO
INTERCOOLER

DUCT FROM
INTERCOOLER
TO
CARBURETTOR

EXHAUST DUCT
TO TURBO-
SUPERCHARGER

OIL
RADIATOR
SHUTTER

STARBOARD
OIL
RADIATOR

AIR INTAKES
TO OIL
& INTERCOOLER
RADIATORS

CURTISS
ELECTRICALLY
OPERATED
AIRSCREW
(LEFT HAND
ROTATION)

late-war versions had the first hydraulically boosted ailerons fitted to any fighter. Not least, though it inevitably increased drag slightly, a special combat setting of the main flaps was introduced, which added wing area and a little camber. I can confirm that this enabled one easily to black out in level turns, but some idiot put the flap lever on the right instead of the left, and most people like to fly right-handed.

Max's overall shape was perfect, but he may not have had time to do justice to this unique fighter, every part of which was packed with goodies for an artist. For example, it would not have been difficult to add another 27 items inside the tail booms alone, from oxygen bottles to flare tubes. One's abiding memory of these graceful aircraft is of their uncanny silence. Thanks to the fact that the exhaust had to do so much work to get out, all one heard in a low-level beat-up was a gently murmuring whoosh! Sadly, some of the few examples flying today have no turbos, and so are noisier.

# HAMILCAR

My memories of the Hamilcar are just a bit more pleasant than those of the Horsa, which isn't saying much. The Horsa smelt of wood (it would, naturally), creaked and groaned, and lurched about sickeningly. The Hamilcar might have been the same, but this time I was able to sit in the cockpit and fly it, and in any case its sheer size inspired a feeling of confidence.

Apart from the Douglas C-54, which could carry a Locust light tank slung externally underneath, the Hamilcar was the only Allied aircraft able to transport a tank. Unlike the C-54, the British glider could deliver it to the battlefront. Of course, the tanks were tiddlers, with two types being available – the Locust and the British Tetrarch – both weighing about 7½ long tons. They were useful, provided they didn't encounter a Panzer division!

Germany designed a giant all-wing wooden glider to carry tanks, the

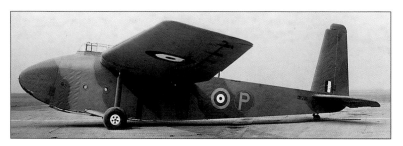

TOP The prototype Hamilcar photographed at Snaith in March 1942
ABOVE Showing how it's done for the Press, a light Tetrarch tank is carefully driven out of the Hamilcar's hold following a successful landing – 31 Hamilcars were used on D-Day

Junkers 322 Mammut, which was a total disaster. In contrast, General Aircraft Ltd, under chief designer Crocombe and chief engineer Hollis Williams, created a thoroughly conventional wooden glider which was a total success. For its day the Hamilcar was big; the late Charles Prower believes it was the largest wooden aircraft ever put into production, though in span and wing area it was outclassed by the Handley Page V/1500 and Zeppelin Staaken R-series of 1917-18. Span was actually 110 ft, the same as a B-24, but the wing area of 1658 sq ft was more than 50 per cent greater. The prototype flew on 27 March 1942. General Aircraft at Hanworth built 10 for trials and 10 for service, assembling them at North Luffenham, while a specially formed group of companies built 390, assembled at various RAF stations.

The original idea had been to drive the tank on to a platform on a low wing and connect the flying controls to the tank's driving position. This might have solved many problems, but would have created even bigger ones. As actually built, the Hamilcar was conventional. The tank just reversed inside through the nose, while the two pilots came in the same way, or via a door amidships, climbed a ladder inside the right wall to a roof hatch, climbed up the wing to the canopy (it seemed a long way to the ground, especially with slippery ice on the walkway) and with relief opened either the front or rear left-half canopy, which was hinged like a door, and got inside. There were two pilots partly because one pilot would become tired on a long tow and partly because one might be killed before landing, though the windscreen was bulletproof, the rear seat bulkhead was armour and there was a tank underneath!

The nose was hinged on the right and bolted shut on the left. Jettisoning the main gears on take-off proved to have drawbacks. The massive gears soon blocked the departure airfield, dropping them in itself was a dangerous business, and an arrival on the skids resembled a controlled crash. In any case, later arrivals on skids couldn't steer past a crowd of gliders already there. In the end, everything was made to work, as follows.

The tug had to be a Stirling IV or a Halifax V, VII or IX. The special towrope (I believe seven-inch-circumference manila), was bifurcated to massive anchorages which were attached by a man riding on a truck to sockets under the main spar at each end of the centre section. Both pilots had control on take-off, holding the glider right down so as not to lift the tail of the straining tug, which would have been lethal. In the air the manual flight controls were not particularly heavy. It was usual to adopt the high-tow position, above the tug's slipstream.

After casting off near the LZ (landing zone) the objective was to get on the ground in as few seconds as possible. The big flaps were essential, driven by compressed-air bottles. These were firmly anchored so that they could not fly about if punctured by enemy fire. On landing, either pilot could steer using the powerful air-bottle wheel brakes, and thus avoid obstructions on a crowded LZ. Either pilot could then unlatch and pull up a lever to deflate the main landing-gear struts as the monster came to rest. The glider would then rapidly sink on to its skids.

The tank driver started his engine in the air, exhaust being extracted through fuselage side vents. The tank was restrained against possibly violent impact deceleration by floor lashings at the rear. The driver could disconnect these from the cab, so that he could drive forward, pushing a leather strap to unlatch and open the nose door.

Both weeklies did cutaway Hamilcars, and the contrast could not have been more complete. For *Flight*, R E Poulton's drawing was a beautiful picture, complete with tank and invasion stripes. It was much, much easier to follow than Jimmy's, but on the other hand it didn't show half as many details.

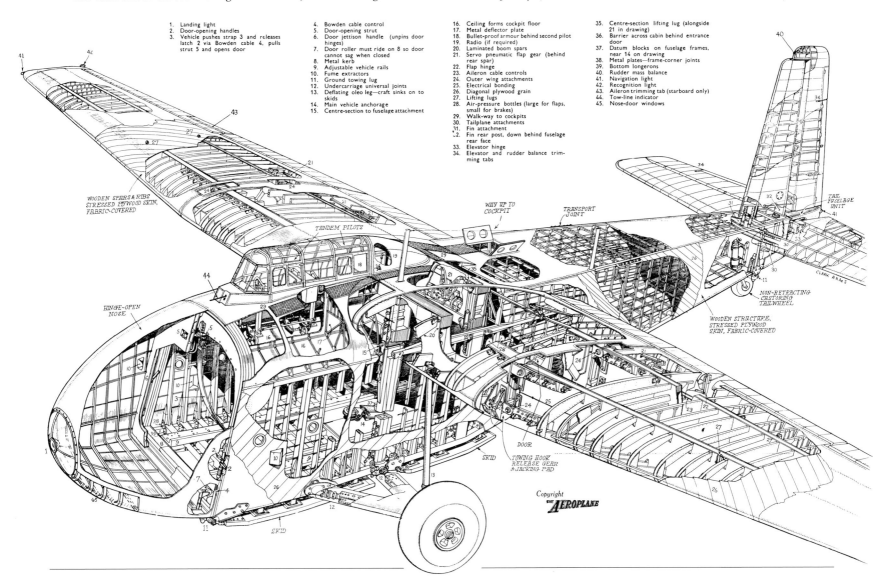

1. Landing light
2. Door-opening handles
3. Vehicle pushes strap 3 and releases latch 2 via Bowden cable 4, pulls strut 5 and opens door
4. Bowden cable control
5. Door-opening strut
6. Door jettison handle (unpins door hinges)
7. Door roller must ride on 8 so door cannot sag when closed
8. Metal kerb
9. Adjustable vehicle rails
10. Fume extractors
11. Ground towing lug
12. Undercarriage universal joints
13. Deflating oleo leg—craft sinks on to skids
14. Main vehicle anchorage
15. Centre-section to fuselage attachment
16. Ceiling forms cockpit floor
17. Metal deflector plate
18. Bullet-proof armour behind second pilot
19. Radio (if required)
20. Laminated boom spars
21. Servo pneumatic flap gear (behind rear spar)
22. Flap hinge
23. Aileron cable controls
24. Outer wing attachments
25. Electrical bonding
26. Diagonal plywood grain
27. Lifting lugs
28. Air-pressure bottles (large for flaps, small for brakes)
29. Walk-way to cockpits
30. Tailplane attachments
31. Fin attachment
32. Fin rear post, down behind fuselage rear face
33. Elevator hinge
34. Elevator and rudder balance trimming tabs
35. Centre-section lifting lug (alongside 21 in drawing)
36. Barrier across cabin behind entrance door
37. Datum blocks on fuselage frames, near 14 on drawing
38. Metal plates—frame-corner joints
39. Bottom longerons
40. Rudder mass balance
41. Navigation light
42. Recognition light
43. Aileron trimming tab (starboard only)
44. Tow-line indicator
45. Nose-door windows

# HERCULES XVI

One could study this drawing for an hour, and doing so would emphasise how long it must have taken Clark to complete it. He just drew a typical wartime Hercules, basing his work on the Mk XVI. These 14-cylinder sleeve-valve radial engines were in my view second only to the Merlin in importance among wartime British engines. Unlike the strident Merlin, the 'Herc' just murmured with a deep booming sound suggestive of awesome power.

I was honoured to be asked by Sir Roy Fedden to write his biography. Called *By Jupiter*, it has long been out of print, but I am delighted to find that it is to be republished soon by the Rolls-Royce Heritage Trust, who I am sure will provide copies for sale. It is a fact-packed tale of singleminded drive by a most remarkable man. In the 1920s he made the Bristol Jupiter the world No 1 engine, getting it produced by both Bristol and 17 other licensees to power 262 types of aircraft. Had he merely continued with the Pegasus and Mercury, and then switched to two-valve cylinders in order to make two-row engines (like the rival Duplex Cyclone and Double Wasp) he would have saved himself and the Bristol firm a lot of bother.

Unfortunately, for good breathing he used four valves per cylinder, and

An uncowled and 'propless' 1650 hp Hercules VI, as fitted to a Beaufighter VI during construction. The nose of the aircraft has been masked out in this November 1943 shot

this made it very difficult to design an elegant engine with two rows of cylinders. He became hooked on the kind of cylinder in which the piston slides up and down inside a single sleeve with ports (apertures) cut in it which, on each stroke, rotate to line up with either inlet or exhaust ports in the surrounding barrel. Clark's drawing, with the insets, makes it all clear. Whereas the barrel was forged aluminium alloy, with deeply machined cooling fins, the sleeve was nitrided steel, so the cylinder and sleeve expanded at different rates. The sleeve had to have a wall thickness like cardboard, yet withstand the pressures of the white-hot gas on each firing stroke. The piston's rings had to fit tightly inside the sleeve, and the sleeve had to fit precisely in the barrel, yet the engine might have to start in an Arctic winter and then run smoothly to full power. And everything had to be lubricated without the oil forming a hydraulic lock.

Fedden's first sleeve-valve cylinder ran in 1927, and the first complete engine, a Perseus, was started in July 1932. The Perseus had nine cylinders with a bore of $5^3/4$ in and stroke of $6^1/2$ in, and by World War 2 it had been developed from its initial 480 hp up to 905 hp. The Hercules had 14 similar cylinders, giving a capacity of 2360 cu in (38.7 litres). It first ran in January 1936 at 1290 hp, and was eventually developed to give almost twice this power. Fedden also created the Aquila, Taurus and the magnificent Centaurus in the 3000 hp class, but most unfortunately he had to leave Bristol in 1942 before he had completed even the prototype of the 4000 hp Orion.

The many gearwheels between the engine and the propeller reduction gear was the simplest way the sleeves could be driven. Just as in steam locomotives, the valve gear caused more arguments than anything else. The author suggested to Fedden that a peripheral ring, such as that used with poppet-valve engines, could have rotated the 14 drive shafts (all at the same speed) more elegantly, but this was merely to draw out his reasons for preferring the 56 gearwheels.

By far the most difficult task in developing an acceptable sleeve-valve engine was to make it so that one could pick components for each cylinder at random. Making an engine from parts hand-fitted together was easy (once a way had been found to make sleeves truly round, which took ten years), but handbuilt prototypes are useless in a war! Fedden eventually succeeded, and by the time the 'Herc' was in production in 1940 it was ready to be mass-produced by a complex network of Shadow factories, the biggest being at Accrington. By the end of the war they had delivered 57,400 engines, rated at 1490-1800 hp. A few thousand more, most rated at over 2000 hp, were produced postwar. The chief applications were the Beaufighter, Wellington,

Stirling, Halifax, Albemarle, Lancaster II, Hastings, Hermes and Viking.

To make life easier Clark did not show the fat exhaust pipes that would be bolted on apertures 'E'. In most wartime installations these went to a collector ring round the front of the surrounding cowling, from where a pipe with dozens of small fishtail apertures would let the gas escape without any flames or visibly hot metal showing at night. By 1944 (initially with the Centaurus in the Tempest II) the pipes were curved back between the cylinders to exhaust on the sides of the fuselage or nacelle behind the engine.

In order to give a clear view of the Farman-type propeller reduction gear, Clark chose a viewpoint from the front, and so was unable to show the rear of the engine. This was covered in pumps for fuel, oil, vacuum and hydraulics, an air compressor, starter, electric generator, tachometer and many other things. He showed one of the two magnetos whose 28 radio-screened leads served the two plugs in the centre of each cylinder junkhead, which extended inside each sleeve at the top of its stroke. You have to look carefully at 'No 3 CYL (REAR BANK)'; at first sight the rings appear to be on the sleeve, but they are actually on the junkhead which extends down inside it.

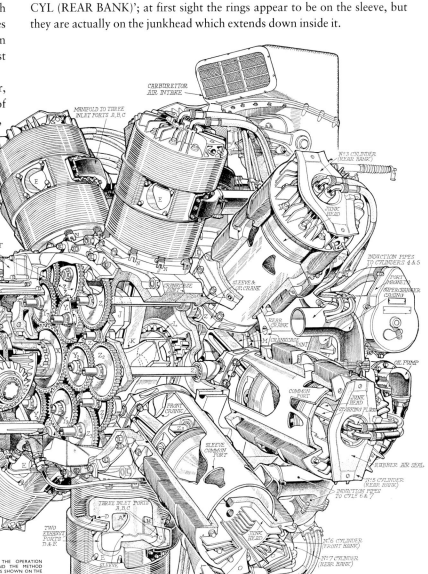

F.   SPIDER SHAFT (ONE PIECE WITH AIRSCREW DRIVE-SHAFT).

G.   ROLLER BEARING (REDUCTION GEAR DRIVING WHEEL).

H.   BALL BEARING (REDUCTION GEAR THRUST).

J.   CRANKSHAFT BALANCE WEIGHT.

K.   MASTER ROD (NO. 4 CYLINDER FRONT BANK).

L.   CRANKSHAFT SELF-ALIGNING CENTRE BEARING.

M.   CRANKSHAFT REAR BEARING.

N.   SPRING-HELD LOCK WASHERS  CYLINDER RETAINING NUTS).

| | |
|---|---|
| BORE | 5.75 INS. |
| STROKE | 6.5 INS. |
| DIAM. | 52 INS. |
| CAPACITY | 38.7 LITRES |

TIMING GEAR SYSTEM WORKS THUS:

SHAFT WHEEL X DRIVES 7 INTERMEDIATE WHEELS AND PINIONS $Y_1$ $Y_2$—$Y_7$.

EACH INTERMEDIATE WHEEL PINION (Y) DRIVES TWO WHEELS, AS $Y_1$ DRIVES $Z_1$ $Z_1$.

EACH PAIR OF DRIVEN WHEELS Z DRIVE TWO SLEEVE CRANKS, ONE TO FRONT BANK, ONE TO REAR BANK.

THE PRINCIPLE OF THE OPERATION OF THE SLEEVES AND THE METHOD OF DRIVE TO THEM IS SHOWN ON THE LEFT. FROM THIS PURELY DIAGRAMMATIC VIEW THE WAY IN WHICH THE TRAIN IS BUILT INTO THE MOTOR CAN BE TRACED ON THE DETAIL DRAWING. THE SLEEVES RECIPROCATE AND TURN IN THE CYLINDERS, AT THE SAME TIME EXPOSING THE PORTS AS SHOWN IN THE "EXHAUST" AND "INDUCTION" DIAGRAMS.

Drawing by J. H. Clark, A.R.Ae.S., Copyright THE AEROPLANE.

# PEGASUS X

Today's Harrier family are all powered by engines designed and made at Bristol, and named Pegasus. They have little in common with the Bristol Pegasus used in over 90 types of aircraft in 1931-45, the original Pegasus being simply a new name given to an improved version of the Jupiter, which young Roy Fedden and 'Bunny' Butler had designed at the Brazil Straker company in 1917.

In 1920 Fedden and his team were taken on as second-class citizens by the autocratic board of the Bristol Aeroplane Co. Fedden's relentless drive forced the Jupiter, and its team, not merely to survive but far outstrip the aeroplane part of the firm in time. By 1930 he had signed up 17 foreign licensees, and 7100 Jupiters had flown in 262 different types of aircraft! This air-cooled

A pre-war Bristol publicity photograph shows the compact nature of one of the company's most successful engines

radial, with nine big cylinders (5 3/4 in/146 mm bore and 7 1/2 in/190.5 mm stroke) had become almost the standard engine of the RAF and Imperial Airways, though the latest Hawker biplanes used the Rolls-Royce Kestrel.

Features included cylinders with separate forged heads housing two inlet valves and two exhaust valves, a one-piece master rod driving a crankpin on a split crankshaft (Clark could have annotated the big bolt pinching the crank web tightly round the crankpin, which he showed clearly) and, in most versions, a high-speed centrifugal supercharger and a Farman-type reduction gear to the propeller. Unlike his rivals, Fedden devoted great effort to installations, appointing Freddy Mayer to do nothing else. After 1930 he put Jupiters inside Townend ring cowls.

A version of the Jupiter with stroke reduced to 6.5 in was called the Mercury, finding a big market in fighters and high-speed bombers. This quickly developed cylinders with enclosed valve gear, more and deeper cooling fins, a lighter reduction gear and quick-start fuel and oil systems. Fedden put these features into an engine with Jupiter-size cylinders, calling it the Mercury V, but soon changed to the new name Pegasus. It began life in 1932 around 500-640 hp, but soon climbed to 750 hp on 87-octane fuel. By 1939 the Pegasus XXII was giving 1010 hp on 100-grade fuel, for a weight of 1030 lb – an outstanding performance.

The Pegasus powered many important aircraft, including dozens of foreign types. In Britain the Supermarine Walrus and Vickers Victoria, Valentia, Vildebeest and Vincent used it uncowled, whilst the Bristol Bombay, Fairey Swordfish, Hawker Swedish Hart and Iraqi Audax (also called Hawker Nisr), Supermarine Stranraer, Vickers Wellesley and Westland Wallace used it with a Townend ring, the Boulton Paul Overstrand and Saro London had twin 'Peggies' in odd nine-sided cowls, and the Handley Page Harrow and Hampden, Short C-Class 'Empire' and Sunderland, and Vickers-Armstrongs Wellington had Pegasus in long-chord cowlings with an exhaust collector ring at the front and adjustable cooling gills round the back.

Production in England totalled just over 17,000, ending in 1942. Of these, 14,400 were delivered after October 1936, which was when 'Shadowing' began.

In September 1935 Air Marshal Sir Hugh Dowding, the great leader of RAF Fighter Command in the Battle of Britain, took Fedden aside and said 'I think you will be relieved to learn that the Air Staff have come to the conclusion that we are going to have a war with Germany. Quite when it will come we cannot say. But what we must do is precisely what you have been advocating, and that is to build up a vast increase in our production potential. We have decided to choose an established manufacturer and create exact replicas, or "shadows" of his production process. Where engines are concerned, we have chosen you. With Bristol engines we are minimising the risk'.

Fedden invited to Bristol the heads of seven car firms. Six scorned the idea and showed no interest. Billy (later Lord) Rootes showed such enthusiasm he almost launched the vast Shadow industry single-handed, and before long the Shadow engine firms were being run not only by Bristol and Rootes but also by Daimler, Austin, Rover and Standard. They began with the Mercury, and six engines were tested assembled from parts from all the participating factories shuffled at random. They soon made the Pegasus and finally, in much greater numbers, the Hercules (which is on pages 126 and 127).

At the start the car firms thought they knew better than Fedden, and introduced often seemingly trivial changes to crucial production processes, such as gear grinding. It took dozens of often fatal crashes to get across the idea that the hard-won Bristol technology should not be departed from in the slightest degree without careful consultation. Of course, a basic requirement was that any engine should run perfectly after being assembled from parts made by a random selection from Bristol and any of the Shadow factories.

Clark's drawing shows a typical Pegasus as mass-produced at the start of the War.

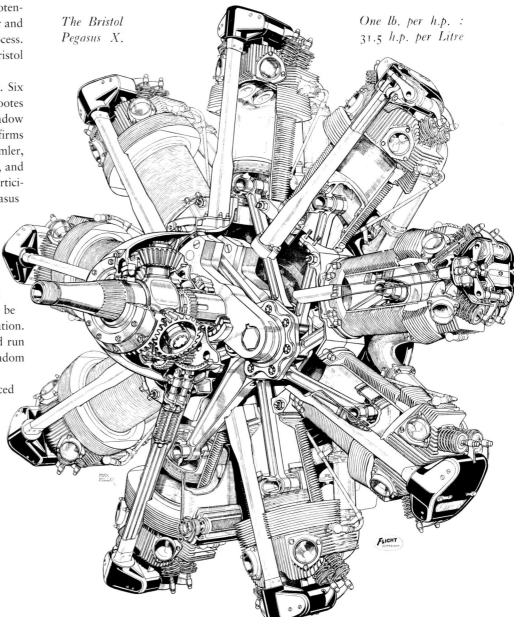

*The Bristol Pegasus X.*

*One lb. per h.p. : 31.5 h.p. per Litre*

A part-sectioned view of a Bristol 900 h.p. engine. The master connecting-rod goes to the piston of No. 6 cylinder (lower left) The airscrew reduction gear is of the type having two crown wheels and three bevel pinions. The cam sleeve which operates the valves is located between the reduction gear and the crank throw. The rocker boxes on top of the cylinders pivot about two pillars, and the front end of the box is linked to the crank case by a tie-rod lying between the two push-rods. This compensation gear maintains correct valve clearances.

# DAGGER

D. Napier & Son, of Acton, West London, achieved a smash hit with their first aero engine, the Lion. Designed by Arthur J Rowledge, the Lion was an outstanding engine for April 1917. It had three banks of four water-cooled cylinders arranged in the so-called W or fan layout. It soon gave 500 hp, and in the 1927 Schneider Trophy race was boosted to deliver 1400 hp. In 1921 Napier were silly enough to fall out with Rowledge, who went to Rolls-Royce and played a key role in developing the Kestrel. Not knowing how to stay competitive, the Acton management commissioned a gifted freelance designer, Maj Frank B.Halford, to create some new Napier engines in 1928.

I have always wondered if Halford had a brainstorm, or merely thought that this provided an opportunity to try out some funny ideas. Instead of carrying on where the Lion left off, he decided to make engines with lots of small aircooled cylinders, running at exceptionally high speed. He began with the Rapier, with 16 cylinders in H-formation. The H layout has four banks of cylinders driving two crankshafts, each crankshaft having an upright row of cylinders on top and an inverted row underneath. At the front the two crankshafts each have a small gearwheel driving a larger gear on the propeller shaft on the centreline.

An overly complex piece of machinery for its day, the Dagger was not one of Napier's more successful powerplants

Halford followed the Rapier with the Dagger. This had no fewer than 24 slightly larger cylinders, each of 3.8125-in bore x 3.75-in stroke, giving a capacity of 1027 cubic inches (16.84 litres). In 1934 Daggers were giving 635 hp, and in 1936 an improved version was cleared for production at a speed of 4200 rpm, giving 950 hp for take-off. The later version drawn by Clark was the Dagger VIII, which powered the Handley Page Hereford bomber. This had a maximum rating of 1000 hp at 8750 ft, or a remarkable one horsepower per cubic inch of capacity.

Clark erred in labelling the crankshafts '12-throw'. Though each was driven by 12 cylinders, there were only six crankpins, each driven by a fork-ended connecting rod from above and an intermeshing narrow blade rod from below. A 12-throw crankshaft would have required the upper and lower cylinders on each side to have been displaced relative to each other.

Several design features are particularly interesting. On the front of the engine were two magnetos above and two distributors below, arranged like a letter X. The 12 sparking plugs on the right, visible in the drawing, were supplied by a screened ignition harness from the distributor on the left. The screened harness from the right distributor can be seen going vertically up and disappearing at the top to feed the left-hand plugs, even though on its way it brushed against the other harness! Why not cut out a lot of weight and potential trouble by letting each distributor feed the plugs immediately behind it?

Another unusual feature was the use of a double-sided centrifugal supercharger impeller (spelt here 'impellor'). The fact that in this engine there had to be two big pipes feeding the compressed air to the engine, one to the upper 12 cylinders and the other to the lower 12, is immaterial. Whittle used a double-sided centrifugal compressor in all his pioneer turbojets, yet, perversely, when in 1941 Halford came to design turbojets (for de Havilland), needing a far greater airflow, he did an about-face and used a single-sided compressor! There are good and bad features in both arrangements.

Though Halford was a great man, and nobody can take away from him the record of the Cirrus and Gipsy engines for light aircraft, when it came to high-power engines I feel he got carried away by his own enthusiasm. Even with the Gipsy series he eventually produced the Gipsy Twelve (called Gipsy King by the RAF) which, compared with other ways of getting 525 hp, was complex, heavy and expensive. His culminating piston engine was the Sabre, included in this album.

Clark's Dagger appeared in *The Aeroplane* for 11 January 1939. In those days the aviation weeklies were poles apart from today's periodicals, which

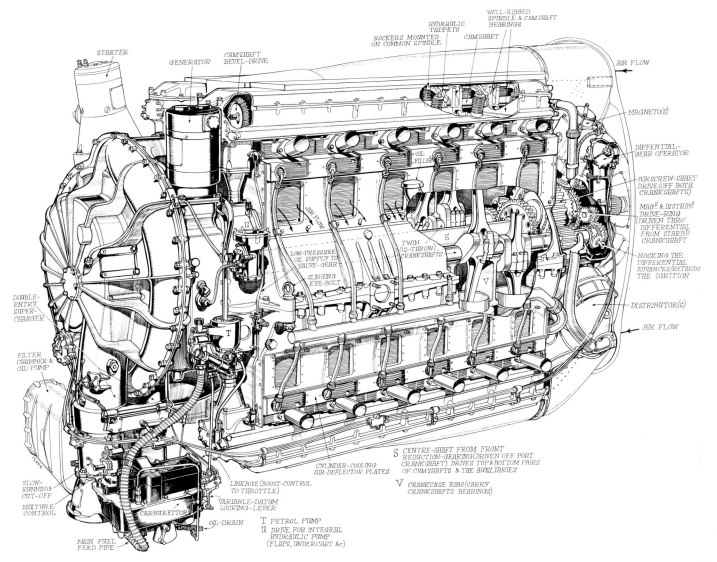

STARTER

GENERATOR

CAMSHAFT
BEVEL~DRIVE

ROCKERS MOUNTED
ON COMMON SPINDLE

HYDRAULIC
TAPPETS

WELL-RIBBED
SPINDLE & CAMSHAFT
BEARINGS

CAMSHAFT

AIR FLOW

MAGNETO(S)

DIFFERENTIAL~
GEAR OPERATOR

AIRSCREW-SHAFT
DRIVE (OFF BOTH
CRANKSHAFTS)

MAG.S & DISTRIB.R
DRIVE-RING
(DRIVEN THRO'
DIFFERENTIAL
FROM STARB.D
CRANKSHAFT

OIL
FILLER

ROCKING THE
DIFFERENTIAL
ADVANCES/RETARDS
THE IGNITION

TWIN
(12-THROW)
CRANKSHAFTS

LOW-PRESSURE
OIL SUPPLY TO
VALVE-GEAR

SLINGING
EYE-BOLT

DISTRIBUTOR(S)

AIR FLOW

DOUBLE-
ENTRY
SUPER-
CHARGER

FILTER
CHAMBER &
OIL-PUMP

SLOW-
RUNNING
CUT-OFF

MIXTURE
CONTROL

CARBURETTOR

OIL-DRAIN

MAIN FUEL
FEED PIPE

LINKAGE (BOOST-CONTROL
TO THROTTLE)

VARIABLE-DATUM
LOCKING-LEVER

CYLINDER-COOLING
AIR-DEFLECTOR PLATES

S CENTRE-SHAFT FROM FRONT
REDUCTION~GEARING (DRIVEN OFF PORT
CRANKSHAFT) DRIVES TOP & BOTTOM PAIRS
OF CAMSHAFTS & THE AUXILIARIES

V CRANKCASE RIBS (CARRY
CRANKSHAFTS BEARINGS)

T PETROL PUMP
U DRIVE FOR INTEGRAL
HYDRAULIC PUMP
(FLAPS, UNDERCART &c)

aim to tell it like it is. I don't know whether it was Thurstan James, Freddie Meacock or editor C G Grey who visited Acton, but they wrote 'We had the good fortune to be taken round the works by . . . , who is well known throughout . . . , so what he has to say is well worth listening to. When we first described the Dagger in 1935 we remarked that one might expect its life to be long because each cylinder produces a lower proportion of the total power. This has been borne out in a remarkable way. Such reliability is an attribute of aero-motors designed by Maj F B Halford. The Hereford is expected to be a very swift bomber indeed. One begins to see why the installation of the Dagger VIII in a bomber should be so interesting'.

It was all a load of sycophantic drivel. Apart from being loathed by the engine fitters, the Dagger make a shrieking noise which deafened Hereford crews. Worse still, it had a tendency to fall silent. Its record of reliability was even worse than that of the Rolls-Royce Vulture, in the Manchester. Production of the Hereford was quickly stopped, many were junked and the rest were fitted with Pegasus engines and returned to the RAF as Hampdens.

# SABRE II

Most people either loved the Sabre or hated it. My feeling is that, while it did eventually become a great engine, doing a fine job in the Hawker Typhoon and Tempest, we in Britain would have saved a lot of bother, and not a few pilots, if we had relied instead on the Griffon and Centaurus. On the other hand, there was no more thrilling sound than the take-off of a Sabre-powered aircraft – unless it was a whole squadron. This was partly because takeoff speed was 3700 rpm in the Mk II and 3850 rpm in later versions.

I had a few observations to make on designer Maj Frank Halford in connection with the Napier Dagger. This had 24 small cylinders arranged in upright H configuration. In 1935, while the Dagger was still in all kinds of trouble (indeed, it never got out of it), Halford embarked on the next generation, which became the Sabre. This again had 24 cylinders in H form, but the cylinders had sleeve valves and liquid cooling, and the H was lying on its side. The Sabre could be regarded as two horizontally opposed 12-cylinder engines mounted one on top of the other, with a common reduction gear.

Again, the cylinders were very small. Bore and stroke were respectively 5 in (127 mm) and 4$^3$/4 in (120 mm), so that the capacity of 2238 cu in (36.65 litres) was almost precisely the same as that of the Griffon, which had half as many cylinders.

From the double-sided supercharger, four air pipes led along the tops of the two upper rows of cylinders and to the underside of the two lower rows. The exhaust ports were on the opposite sides of the cylinders, so the exhaust could be taken out through 12 holes on each side of the engine between the upper and lower banks. Max drew and indicated just the curved exhaust ejec-

The heart of the Typhoon, the 'muscular' Sabre suffered reliability problems throughout its life

tor from the front left outlet; he also drew the rear left pair of connections, serving the rearmost upper and lower cylinders on the left side.

The foundation of the engine was the very complicated crankcase, made from two light-alloy castings joined on the vertical centreline of the engine. On each side of this was bolted a cast light-alloy block, each containing the 12 cylinders on one side of the engine. There were 48 bolts holding the engine together, and they went right across from one side to the other.

Halford did not hesitate to copy Fedden's technology in the design of the valve gear. The steel sleeves were all driven via skew gears rotated by a tubular shaft along each side of the engine, level with the exhausts but much further in towards the centreline. This shaft was driven via idler gears from the front of both crankshafts. Down the centre of each was a long torsion shaft which at the rear end drove the step-up gears to the supercharger. The drive was taken through the hydraulic oil-operated clutch at the back of the engine (far right in the drawing) which could be set to either of two drive ratios. In the Mk II engine illustrated the ratios were 4.68 or 5.83. These were modest drive ratios, because the impeller was large and the crankshaft speed much higher than in most aero engines. Conversely, because the propeller was large and the crankshaft speed so high, the propeller reduction-gear ratio was 0.2742; in other words the crankshafts rotated about four times as fast as the propeller.

The Hobson injection-type carburettor was probably the largest in any production wartime engine apart from the R-4360 Wasp Major. It had four choke tubes, all fed from the circular inlet in the centre of the radiators (see the cutaway of the Tempest). Operations from advanced forward landing grounds in Normandy threw up clouds of abrasive dust, and in 24 hours Vokes Ltd of Guildford designed and went into production with a filter specifically for the Typhoons.

The entire top of the engine was a mass of accessories. The distributor for the port (left) block looks enormous, but of course it had to serve 24 plugs. There was another 24-point distributor on the other side, just visible. The screened ignition harnesses can be seen like serpents writhing over the front of the engine. The isu (ignition servo unit) at the front automatically adjusted ignition timing. The csu (constant-speed unit) automatically controlled propeller pitch to hold engine rpm steady at different airspeeds.

All Sabres in squadron service were started by a multi-breech Coffman cartridge starter. Twice Max mis-spelt the manufacturer's name! It drove through an idler to the aft end of the upper crankshaft. Though I never got airborne in any wartime Hawker aircraft, I naturally deeply respected the

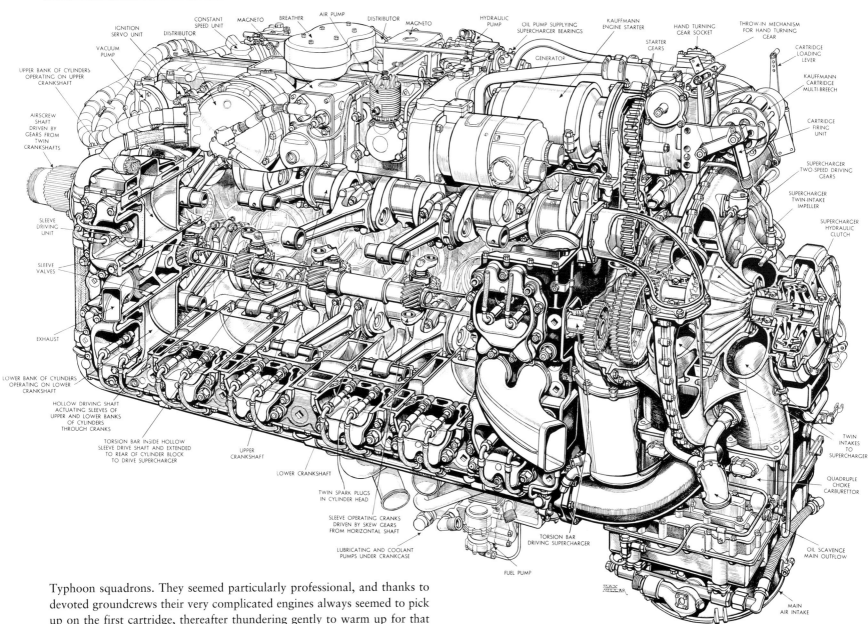

IGNITION SERVO UNIT

CONSTANT SPEED UNIT

MAGNETO

BREATHER

AIR PUMP

DISTRIBUTOR

MAGNETO

HYDRAULIC PUMP

OIL PUMP SUPPLYING SUPERCHARGER BEARINGS

KAUFFMANN ENGINE STARTER

HAND TURNING GEAR SOCKET

THROW-IN MECHANISM FOR HAND TURNING GEAR

VACUUM PUMP

DISTRIBUTOR

GENERATOR

STARTER GEARS

CARTRIDGE LOADING LEVER

KAUFFMANN CARTRIDGE MULTI-BREECH

UPPER BANK OF CYLINDERS OPERATING ON UPPER CRANKSHAFT

CARTRIDGE FIRING UNIT

AIRSCREW SHAFT DRIVEN BY GEARS FROM TWIN CRANKSHAFTS

SUPERCHARGER TWO-SPEED DRIVING GEARS

SUPERCHARGER TWIN-INTAKE IMPELLER

SLEEVE DRIVING UNIT

SUPERCHARGER HYDRAULIC CLUTCH

SLEEVE VALVES

EXHAUST

LOWER BANK OF CYLINDERS OPERATING ON LOWER CRANKSHAFT

HOLLOW DRIVING SHAFT ACTUATING SLEEVES OF UPPER AND LOWER BANKS OF CYLINDERS THROUGH CRANKS

TORSION BAR INSIDE HOLLOW SLEEVE DRIVE SHAFT AND EXTENDED TO REAR OF CYLINDER BLOCK TO DRIVE SUPERCHARGER

UPPER CRANKSHAFT

LOWER CRANKSHAFT

TWIN SPARK PLUGS IN CYLINDER HEAD

SLEEVE OPERATING CRANKS DRIVEN BY SKEW GEARS FROM HORIZONTAL SHAFT

LUBRICATING AND COOLANT PUMPS UNDER CRANKCASE

FUEL PUMP

TORSION BAR DRIVING SUPERCHARGER

TWIN INTAKES TO SUPERCHARGER

QUADRUPLE CHOKE CARBURETTOR

OIL SCAVENGE MAIN OUTFLOW

MAIN AIR INTAKE

MAX MILLAR

Typhoon squadrons. They seemed particularly professional, and thanks to devoted groundcrews their very complicated engines always seemed to pick up on the first cartridge, thereafter thundering gently to warm up for that high-pitched whining take-off.

A Sabre II typically turned the scales at 2500 lb, and was seven feet long. Take-off rating was 2200 or 2400 hp. Later versions just exceeded 3000 hp, but within a few weeks of the end of the war virtually all had been junked, leaving about a dozen engines at a Tempest armament practice camp on the island of Sylt, and scattered Tempest VI squadrons in the Middle East, making full use of those inlet filters.

# TEMPEST V

Test pilot and RAF Wing Leader R P 'Bee' Beamont reckoned the Tempest V, as drawn here, was just about perfect. He should know, because there were few significant Allied fighters that he didn't fly. The credit for the Tempest's immaculate handling was largely due to his own attentions as a test pilot temporarily detached to Hawker Aircraft at Langley. To my regret, I never got anywhere near flying either a Tempest or its predecessor, the

One of the dozen Fighter Command units to fly the ultimate wartime Hawker fighter, No 501 Sqn received its Tempest Vs at Westhampnett, in Sussex, in July 1944

Typhoon, and can only say that the sound of these Sabre-engined aircraft taking off at 3850 rpm was enough to set the pulse racing.

We have already seen, with the Typhoon, how designer Sydney Camm got it wrong and made the wing thick enough to cause high-Mach problems in fast dives. The possibility of changing to an improved wing profile was being discussed in the Kingston design office as early as April 1940, so it is rather astonishing that thick-wing Typhoons were still being built four years later. By the end of 1940 Camm's staff had finalised the design of a new wing with a so-called 'laminar' profile with the point of maximum thickness (and thus peak suction) moved back from 22 per cent to 37.5 per cent chord. Thickness/chord ratio was reduced from the Typhoon's 18 per cent to only 14.5 per cent at the root and 10 per cent at the tip. The author never asked Camm why he adopted a semi-elliptical plan shape, but there is no doubt it provided greater chord for housing the guns, as commented upon later. There is little truth in the popular story that air marshals thought every fighter had to look like a Spitfire!

In August 1941 Hawker Aircraft made a formal proposal for a thin-wing Typhoon II, and after a lot of rethinks this flew as the Tempest V on 2 September 1942. As a mere enthusiastic RAF cadet, the author was convinced that the engine should have been the Centaurus, rather than the complex and unreliable liquid-cooled Sabre. The switch did happen eventually, but not in time for the war. As it was, the engine of wartime Tempests was always the Sabre, and even with this second-generation aircraft it caused prolonged trouble.

The new wing reduced the thickness of the centre section by some 5 in (127 mm), which cut down the wing tankage. To maintain internal capacity an additional tank was put in the fuselage between the oil tank and the engine, lengthening the fuselage by 21 in (just over 0,5 m). In turn this called for extra area at the front of the fin, and this was applied in halting steps during 1943. It had been intended, in the Tempest I, to locate the radiators in the inboard leading edges. This aircraft eventually flew in February 1943, and at 466 mph it was the fastest of all the Tempests. Various problems resulted in reversion, in the Mk V, to essentially the same type of 2180-hp Sabre IIB, 14-ft four-blade de Havilland propeller and chin radiator as fitted to the Typhoon.

From the start the rear fuselage was made structurally sound, and apart from early prototypes all Tempests had the improved windscreen and sliding bubble canopy, giving a good view all round. Standard armament remained four 20 mm Hispano cannon, with belt feed, though magazine capacity went

# MERLIN XX

The biography of Sir Stanley Hooker (*Not Much of an Engineer*, written by this author) begins with the tall young 'Doc' Hooker walking into the great Rolls-Royce works in Derby for the first time in 1938. An aerodynamicist, he had never seen an aircraft engine before. How, he wondered, could he ever hope to assist the obviously brilliant designers of this great company?

Left entirely to himself, he wandered into an office and found 'a quiet grey-haired man'. Around him were lots of papers. They were the results of tests on Merlin superchargers. Hooker was elated because this involved 'the flow and compression of air', and he knew a bit about that. He asked, 'Can I borrow a set?', and was told, 'Certainly, take the lot'.

At that time the Merlin had one of the best superchargers in the world, but Hooker grew first puzzled and then astonished as he pored over the mass of graphs and charts. Nothing quite matched. The exact angle at which the hot compressed air left the edge of the supercharger impeller did not quite accord with the angle of the volute vanes ('Q' in this drawing). Everywhere he looked, things were just a bit off from the optimum design. Days later, mustering his courage, Hooker wrote a detailed report stuffed with formulae and figures. He handed it in.

For days nothing happened. Then the great Jimmy Ellor burst in to the lonely little office and barked 'Did you write this?' Terrified, Hooker admitted he had. 'Fine', said Ellor, 'from now on you're in charge of supercharger development!' Thus did Hooker put his foot on the first rung of the great ladder which was to lead to the engines of the Hunter, Concorde and Harrier, and to many honours, including a knighthood.

Not only did he redesign the Merlin supercharger, without even having touched or seen one, but he found the intake duct (on the Hurricane and Spitfire, for example) was not quite right either. This extended below the cowling and connected with the carburettor seen at bottom right. One day the 'King' of the Derby works, the future Lord Hives, came in and said 'Stanley, there's terrible pressure on Merlin production, but as soon as we can we will change both the inlet and the supercharger'.

The immediate result was the Merlin XX, drawn here so competently by Clark. Fitted in the Hurricane (which thereby became the Mk II), it raised full-throttle height from 13,500 ft to 20,500, the corresponding power from 1160 hp to 1175, and take-off power from 880 hp to 1280. In the Spitfire the same engine was designated the Mk 45, full-throttle power increasing from 1280 hp at 10,500 ft to 1315 hp at 16,000 ft, or 1470 at 9250 ft. The result was the Spitfire Mk V, of which no fewer than 6464 were built.

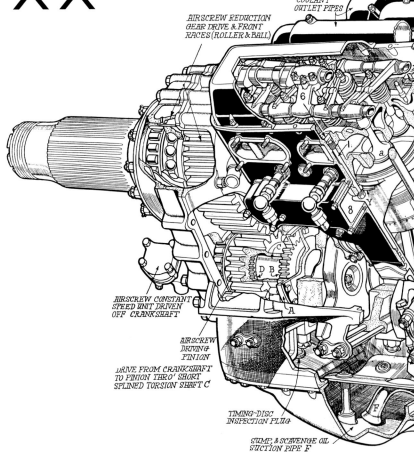

AIRSCREW REDUCTION GEAR DRIVE & FRONT RACES (ROLLER & BALL)

COOLANT OUTLET PIPES

AIRSCREW CONSTANT SPEED UNIT DRIVEN OFF CRANKSHAFT

AIRSCREW DRIVING PINION

DRIVE FROM CRANKSHAFT TO PINION THRO' SHORT SPLINED TORSION SHAFT C

TIMING-DISC INSPECTION PLUG

SUMP & SCAVENGE OIL SUCTION PIPE F

CYLINDER BOLTS 9 HC
CYL. HEAD & JACKET 2 V
LINERS BY TOP GASKE
LINERS TO HEAD . BOL
FROM PORTALS 8 & LO
BOLTS 9 ARE SEALED I
TUBES 9. NOTE LARGE

Dr

W—Splined drive from crankshaft for all auxiliaries off T.
t, t, t,—Drives for two-speed single-stage supercharger.
X—Selector forks.
L—Fork operating rod from oil operating-piston.
S—High-speed clutches.
SS—Low-speed clutch.
R—Two driven pinions solid on impeller shaft.
P—Impeller.
Q—Volute vanes.
b—Rubber sealing rings
Y—Flange on liner engages bolt and lug

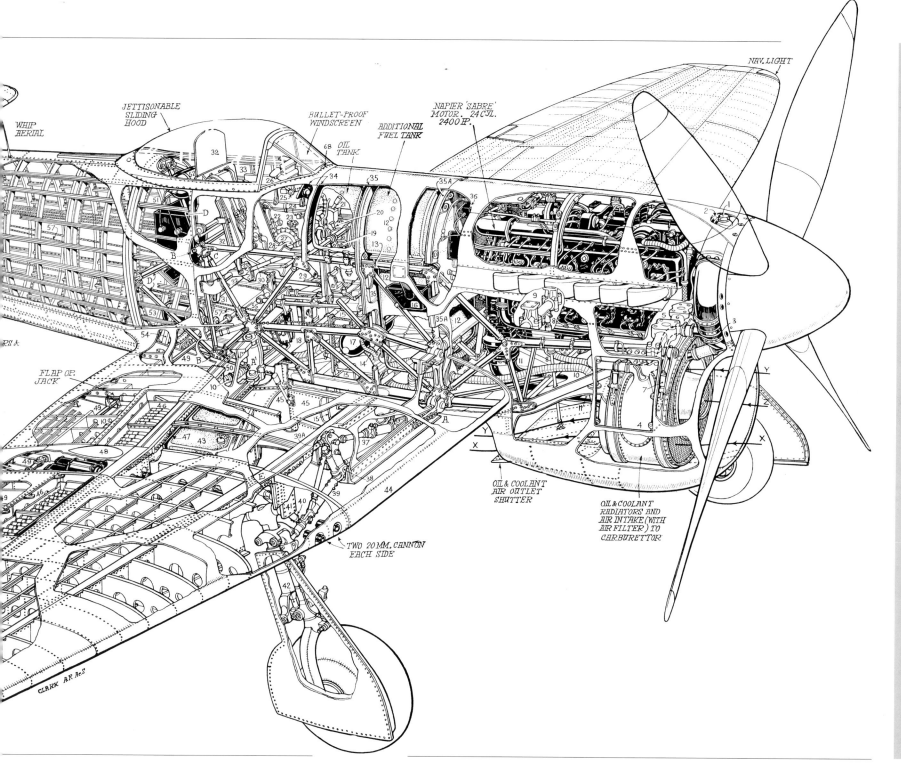

WHIP
AERIAL

JETTISONABLE
SLIDING
HOOD

BULLET-PROOF
WINDSCREEN

ADDITIONAL
FUEL TANK

OIL
TANK

NAPIER 'SABRE'
MOTOR. 24 CYL.
2400 H.P.

NAV. LIGHT

FLAP OP.
JACK

OIL & COOLANT
AIR OUTLET
SHUTTER

OIL & COOLANT
RADIATORS AND
AIR INTAKE (WITH
AIR FILTER) TO
CARBURETTOR

TWO 20 MM. CANNON
EACH SIDE

CLARK AR Ae.S

up to 200 rounds. Early aircraft had the usual Mk II gun, but (thanks to the new wing) with barrels projecting only about 18 in, the outers sticking out further, reflecting the taper at the rear of the wing. On the Tempest V Series 2, drawn by Clark, the short-barrel Mk V gun was fitted with muzzles in line with the leading edge. These aircraft also had smaller main wheels and a detachable rear fuselage. Surprisingly, because it wasn't secret, Clark did not show the possible underwing loads of two 500 or 1000-lb bombs, or eight rockets or two 45-gal (205-litre) drop tanks.

Throughout 1943 Humble, Beamont, Lucas and Seth-Smith worked every available minute on the Tempest, especially the Mk V as the only mark in production. In contrast to the disappointing Typhoon, the Tempest was good from the start. Perhaps the only feature needing a lot of 'tweaking' was the spring-tab ailerons, which were among the first on any British fighter. Once these had been got right, the Tempest V was a fighter simply without limitations, which was rare indeed. 'Bee' has recorded how, when it was as good as the Hawker team could get it, he used to 'mix it' with any fighter that happened to come by, on one occasion encountering the prototype Vampire. He said (*Fighter Test Pilot*, PSL) 'The way in which the Tempest V could intercept, out-manoeuvre and then track these evading targets accurately in the directly reflected gunsight was proof positive. This fighter was going to be a winner'.

It only had the last year of the War in which to prove itself. But, despite all that the politicians could do to play down and hush-up the RAF's contribution to defeating the V1 menace, the score of 638 bombs destroyed by Beamont's Tempest wing, based at Newchurch, Kent, speaks for itself. These targets may not have evaded, but at low level they were desperately fast and tiny targets, and you didn't want to get too close! No other aircraft got anywhere near such a score.

Another fine 'Clark', needing little comment beyond noting his omission of the key to letters: 'E', main-spar joint between centre and outer wing; 'X', engine cooling airflow; 'Y', oil cooling airflow; and 'Z', supercharger airflow with filter. Later, in the Mk VI aircraft, 'Y' and 'Z' were moved to the wing roots.

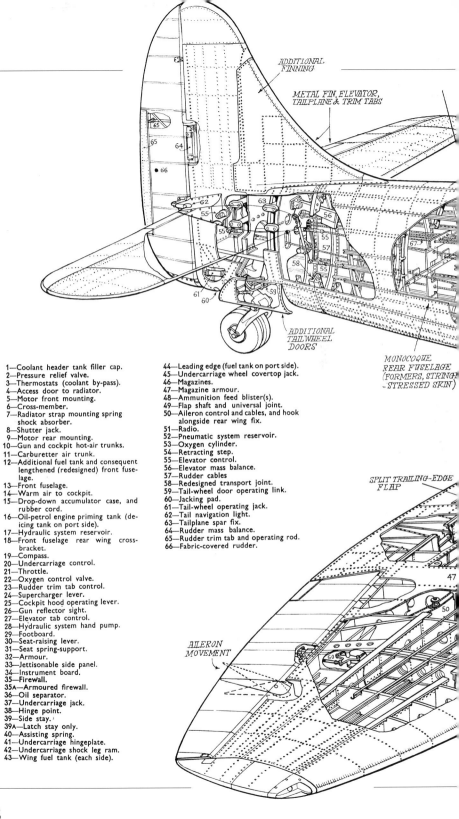

1—Coolant header tank filler cap.
2—Pressure relief valve.
3—Thermostats (coolant by-pass).
4—Access door to radiator.
5—Motor front mounting.
6—Cross-member.
7—Radiator strap mounting spring shock absorber.
8—Shutter jack.
9—Motor rear mounting.
10—Gun and cockpit hot-air trunks.
11—Carburetter air trunk.
12—Additional fuel tank and consequent lengthened (redesigned) front fuselage.
13—Front fuselage.
14—Warm air to cockpit.
15—Drop-down accumulator case, and rubber cord.
16—Oil-petrol engine priming tank (de-icing tank on port side).
17—Hydraulic system reservoir.
18—Front fuselage rear wing cross-bracket.
19—Compass.
20—Undercarriage control.
21—Throttle.
22—Oxygen control valve.
23—Rudder trim tab control.
24—Supercharger lever.
25—Cockpit hood operating lever.
26—Gun reflector sight.
27—Elevator tab control.
28—Hydraulic system hand pump.
29—Footboard.
30—Seat-raising lever.
31—Seat spring-support.
32—Armour.
33—Jettisonable side panel.
34—Instrument board.
35—Firewall.
35A—Armoured firewall.
36—Oil separator.
37—Undercarriage jack.
38—Hinge point.
39—Side stay.
39A—Latch stay only.
40—Assisting spring.
41—Undercarriage hingeplate.
42—Undercarriage shock leg ram.
43—Wing fuel tank (each side).
44—Leading edge (fuel tank on port side).
45—Undercarriage wheel covertop jack.
46—Magazines.
47—Magazine armour.
48—Ammunition feed blister(s).
49—Flap shaft and universal joint.
50—Aileron control and cables, and hook alongside rear wing fix.
51—Radio.
52—Pneumatic system reservoir.
53—Oxygen cylinder.
54—Retracting step.
55—Elevator control.
56—Elevator mass balance.
57—Rudder cables.
58—Redesigned transport joint.
59—Tail-wheel door operating link.
60—Jacking pad.
61—Tail-wheel operating jack.
62—Tail navigation light.
63—Tailplane spar fix.
64—Rudder mass balance.
65—Rudder trim tab and operating rod.
66—Fabric-covered rudder.

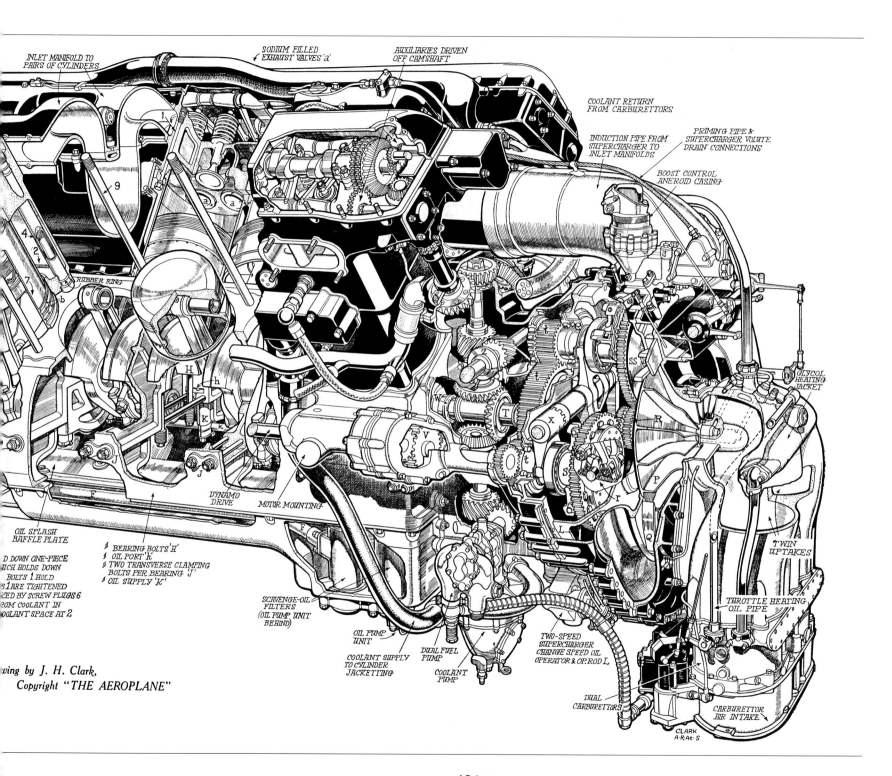

INLET MANIFOLD TO
PAIRS OF CYLINDERS

SODIUM FILLED
EXHAUST VALVES 'a'

AUXILIARIES DRIVEN
OFF CAMSHAFT

COOLANT RETURN
FROM CARBURETTORS

INDUCTION PIPE FROM
SUPERCHARGER TO
INLET MANIFOLDS

PRIMING PIPE &
SUPERCHARGER VOLUTE
DRAIN CONNECTIONS

BOOST CONTROL
ANEROID CASING

RUBBER RING

GLYCOL
HEATING
JACKET

DYNAMO
DRIVE

MOTOR MOUNTING

OIL SPLASH
BAFFLE PLATE

§ BEARING BOLTS 'H'
§ OIL PORT 'h'
§ TWO TRANSVERSE CLAMPING
BOLTS PER BEARING 'J'
§ OIL SUPPLY 'k'

D DOWN ONE-PIECE
UCH HOLDS DOWN
BOLTS 1 HOLD
S 1 ARE TIGHTENED
KED BY SCREW PLUGS 6
OM COOLANT IN
OOLANT SPACE AT 2

TWIN
UPTAKES

THROTTLE HEATING
OIL PIPE

SCAVENGE-OIL
FILTERS
(OIL PUMP UNIT
BEHIND)

OIL PUMP
UNIT

COOLANT SUPPLY
TO CYLINDER
JACKETTING

DUAL FUEL
PUMP

COOLANT
PUMP

TWO-SPEED
SUPERCHARGER
CHANGE SPEED OIL
OPERATOR & OP. ROD L

DUAL
CARBURETTORS

CARBURETTOR
AIR INTAKE

wing by J. H. Clark,
Copyright "THE AEROPLANE"

CLARK
A·R·Ae·S

136

This Merlin XX has been fitted with a Beaufighter II exhaust in the factory, which may denote where it will eventually end up

The improved engines at last got into production in July 1940. Clark showed the clutches ('S' and 'SS') which drove the new impeller at different speeds, the ratio changing (by rotation of shaft 'X') to drive it faster at higher altitudes. The carburettor float chambers incorporated the simple pierced diaphragms invented by Miss Tilly Shilling at Farnborough so that the engine kept running smoothly under negative-G (so that a Bf 109 pilot couldn't get away so easily by simply pushing the nose of his fighter over and diving for the deck – their favourite evasive manoeuvre since the invasion of Poland).

Bearing in mind that three-and-a-half years previously Clark had drawn an early production Merlin from exactly the same viewpoint, it is remarkable that he did not merely modify his earlier drawing. This one is completely new, and apart from adding the two-speed supercharger drive, contrived to show the cylinder head and valves in the far bank of six cylinders, and many other extra features. However, he omitted to explain 'A/B/C/D' in the propeller reduction gear (as he had done previously).

In his explanation of how the cylinder blocks are held down (which I think would puzzle a non-engineer) he said the bolts were sealed from the coolant space by 'tubes 9', but the number should have been 4. He also omit-

ted to add 'Z', the shaft driving the left and right magnetos, to his brief key.

Throughout the drawing he went to immense pains to improve quality. For example, compare the detail of his drive 'T' and the surrounding gear trains, with the way they were drawn in his 1939 Merlin. In many cases, of course, details of the engine, and in particular the ancillaries, had changed considerably. Here, he added the csu (propeller constant speed unit, not needed with the fixed-pitch propellers of the 1939 fighters) yet omitted the air compressor and hydraulic pump.

In the early months of the war Hooker wondered how he could possibly do any more to improve the Merlin. It was the demand for an ultra-high-altitude engine to power the pressurised Wellington VI that suddenly gave him the idea of fitting two gear-driven superchargers in series. By compressing the air twice, and then cooling it to increase the charge density, he utterly transformed the Merlin.

The first Mk 60 engine went on test 19 months before this drawing appeared on 18 December 1942, and it dramatically improved the performance of the Spitfire, Mustang III, Mosquito and numerous other Allied aircraft.

# MERLIN I

Many on the Allied side would say the Rolls-Royce Merlin was the greatest aero engine of World War 2. It was certainly the most famous. Incidentally, though in wartime RAF slang anything really good was called 'wizard', and Merlin was a famous wizard, the engine was named after a bird of prey, like its predecessors.

Also like its predecessors it had 12 liquid-cooled cylinders, each with two inlet and two exhaust valves, arranged in two cast blocks set in a 'vee' 60° apart. In the earliest drawings and a mock-up the engine was inverted, which has much to commend it (for example, in a single-engined aircraft it gives the pilot a better view when taxiing), but this arrangement was eventually considered un-British. Sir Henry Royce checked each drawing at his small design office at West Wittering on the Sussex coast. On 22 April 1933 he approved the last drawing and died later the same day.

As a result we won the Battle of Britain, and so were not conquered. The Merlin went on to play a colossal part in eventually winning the War.

At the start, however, it was one problem after another. The first Merlin had the crankcase and cylinder blocks cast as a single piece of aluminium, of course with detachable cylinder heads. This was soon dropped in favour of detachable blocks, with dry top joints. Another early change was to reject the double-helical reduction gear in favour of plain spur gears, seen in the drawing at extreme left. Prolonged trouble was encountered with the combustion

chamber and head, and after three years of toil it was decided to go back to single-piece blocks. Numerous other changes were also made.

Early Rolls-Royce engines had used plain water as the coolant, and the Goshawk (the Merlin's immediate predecessor) used steam. Early Merlins switched to neat ethylene glycol, enabling the radiator to be much smaller. By 1938 it had been decided to use 70 per cent water, with 30 per cent glycol added mainly as an anti-freeze. This was non-inflammable, gave superior cooling and needed only quite a small radiator. The efficiency of the radiator, in several different forms, was dramatically improved from 1939 onwards.

Clark's drawing has most of the features of the Merlin II, which could be called the first satisfactory version. The first production Hurricane flew on 12 October 1937 with a Mk II engine, and this was the most important version in the Battle of Britain. It had an SU carburettor with two choke tubes, simple supercharger and automatic boost control. In the form drawn by Clark it did not even have provision for a constant-speed propeller. He did not show the electric starter, nor the hand-turning gear (see his drawing of the Hurricane for this).

Take-off rating at sea level was 890 hp at 2850 rpm, but for short periods combat power at 3000 rpm reached 1030 hp at 16,250 ft. Just in time for the Battle of Britain 100-octane fuel became available, enabling boost pressure in combat power to be doubled, from 6 lb/sq in to 12 lb/sq in, raising power to over 1300 hp. This made a vital difference to the results of one-v-one combats against the Bf 109E.

Thus, just in time, the Merlin had come out of the doldrums. In 1939 Dr Stanley Hooker, an aerodynamicist who had never seen an engine, had joined the team at Derby. For a start, and entirely by chance, he was able to transform the performance of the inlet and supercharger. By 1942 he had designed a two-stage supercharger system in which the air was compressed by two centrifugal impellers in succession (as seen in the cutaway of the Griffon engine). This transformed the power at high altitudes in a way never done previously with any engine in the world. Full-throttle height nudged 30,000 ft, with the two-stage Merlin raising the service ceiling of the Spitfire by over 10,000 ft, and increasing its maximum speed by an incredible 70 mph.

Thus, by incessant development, this small engine of 1649 cubic inches (26.99 litres) displacement enabled RAF fighters to beat Bf 109s and Fw 190s with engines of from 35 to 42 litres capacity. Altogether 32,377 Merlins were made at Derby, 26,065 at Crewe, 23,647 at Glasgow, 30,428 by Ford at Manchester and 55,523 (called the V-1650) by the Packard Motor Co at

A 1936 Rolls-Royce factory shot of a prisitine Merlin I unsoiled by oil leaks and glycol smears. In the frontline powerplants were rarely cleaned to this finish once in service

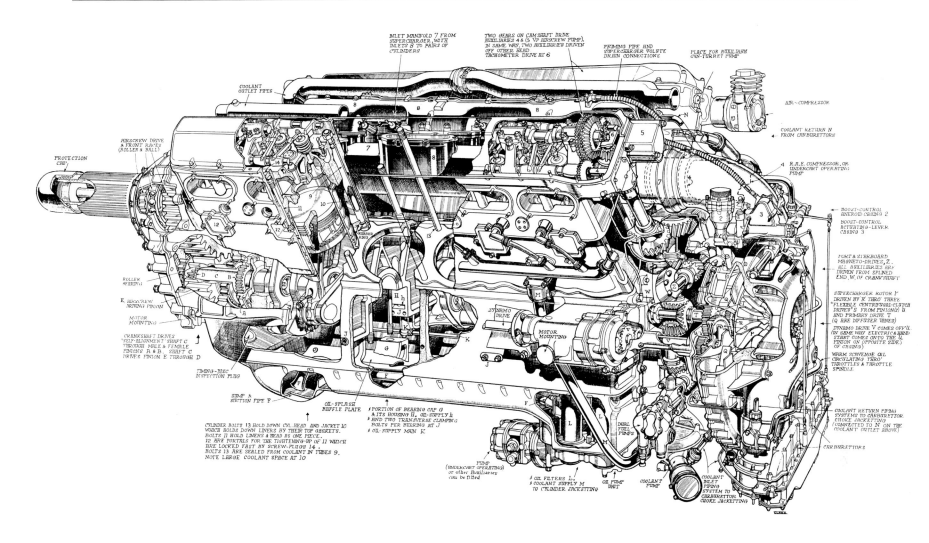

Detroit, USA. They powered Battles, Hurricanes, Spitfires and Seafires, Henleys, Defiants, Whitleys, Wellington IIs, Halifaxes, Lancasters, Fulmars, Barracudas, Beaufighter IIs, Mosquitoes, Tomahawks, Kittyhawks, Mustangs, Welkins, Yorks, Hornets and many other aircraft. Postwar, they powered the Lincoln and, in considerably modified forms requiring more development man-hours than the wartime engines, the DC-4M (Argonaut/North Star) family and Tudor.

The pilots of all these aircraft may have had plenty of problems, but these seldom involved the engine. The Merlin was, *par excellence*, an engine that could by 'flogged' for hours at a time. For example, a Lancaster pilot of No 101 Sqn found himself at 800 ft over Italy with various parts on fire, bomb doors hanging open, flaps stuck partly down and No 4 engine feathered. Nevertheless, he swung around onto a north-westerly course, climbed to 16,000 ft over the Alps and came home.

# GRIFFON

This drawing is worthy of the Royal Academy. Max Millar was always a superb draughtsman, and he loved the challenge of a complicated engine. I doubt if the Griffon could ever be more perfectly revealed in a single drawing. Yet of course, it all comes down to hours of hard work with a pen. This artwork appeared in *Flight* for 20 September 1945. Half a century later we can create marvellous drawings with electronics, and even study 3-D shapes from any angle, but I challenge anyone to re-create such a drawing on a modern graphic terminal.

Basically, the Griffon was a Merlin scaled up to the capacity (swept volume) of the Buzzard and Schneider-winning R, in other words 2239 cubic inches (36.69 litres) instead of 1649 (26.99). It obviously ought to have been larger than a Merlin in all directions (for example, cylinder bore went up from 5.4 inches to 6.0), but the amazing thing is – especially with the two-stage engines such as this Mk 65 – most Griffons were actually shorter than equivalent Merlins !

The Griffon was thought necessary to power naval torpedo-bombers such as the Barracuda. Aviation is full of ironies, and the Barracuda served all through the war powered by the Merlin, so it never really had enough power. In fact, the obvious engine for such an application was a powerful aircooled radial, such as the Hercules or Centaurus. But there was plenty of work for the Griffon, initially in the Firefly (which appeared on an earlier spread) and above all in the later Spitfires, where it was a great engine – and to the author, and perhaps others, a rather frightening one.

Though the Griffon prototype ran as early as 1934, it never really had much effort put behind it until on the first day of 1939 Harry Cantrill came from Armstrong Siddeley and was told to develop it. He did a superb job, despite being in obvious competition with the Derby 'First Eleven' led by Lovesey and Dorey on the Merlin. This competition spurred on both teams, and so was beneficial to both engines, though with Hives at the helm nobody was going to take life easy!

As in the Merlin, air was drawn in underneath at the rear, passing up through the carburettor. Unlike earlier engines, which had traditional choke-tube and float-chamber carburettors, this late-model Griffon had a very complicated injection-type unit which measured the airflow through the three induction pipes, and several other parameters, and controlled the spray of fuel from the nozzles facing the supercharger. A second nozzle sprayed extra fuel to accelerate the engine when the throttle was suddenly opened.

The mixture then passed through an aftercooler (incorrectly, as on the two-stage Merlins, called an intercooler) which in a fraction of a second cooled the rushing compressed air from about 210°C to well under 100°C to increase the charge density. Power is proportional to charge density, so it was well worth having the bulky extra cooler, plus the plumbing to an additional radiator.

These two-stage Griffons powered all the later Spitfires and Seafires, giving (in the case of the Mk 65) 2035 hp at 7000 ft and keeping maximum power near this figure all the way to 20,000 ft.

The Shackleton had the simpler Mk 58 with a single-stage supercharger giving up to 2455 hp at low level. To absorb this power in a small diameter needed a six-blade contra-rotating propeller. These were possibly the last high-power piston engines in service anywhere, keeping No 8 Sqn in business until 30 June 1991, when they switched to the somewhat different Boeing E-3 Sentry.

Max clearly showed the four valves giving good breathing through each cylinder, though some of the company's experimental sleeve-valve engines breathed even better. He drew the semi-floating coupling (with a ring of bolts round it) which ironed out torque buzz between the crankshaft and reduction gear, but did not draw attention to it. He did indicate the camshaft drive from

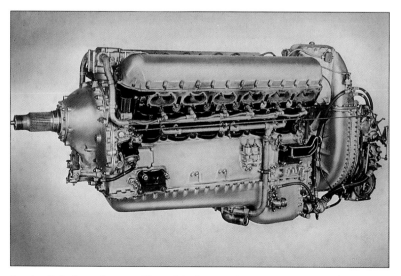

Another Rolls-Royce factory publicity shot, this time showing the definitive Griffon engine prior to installation

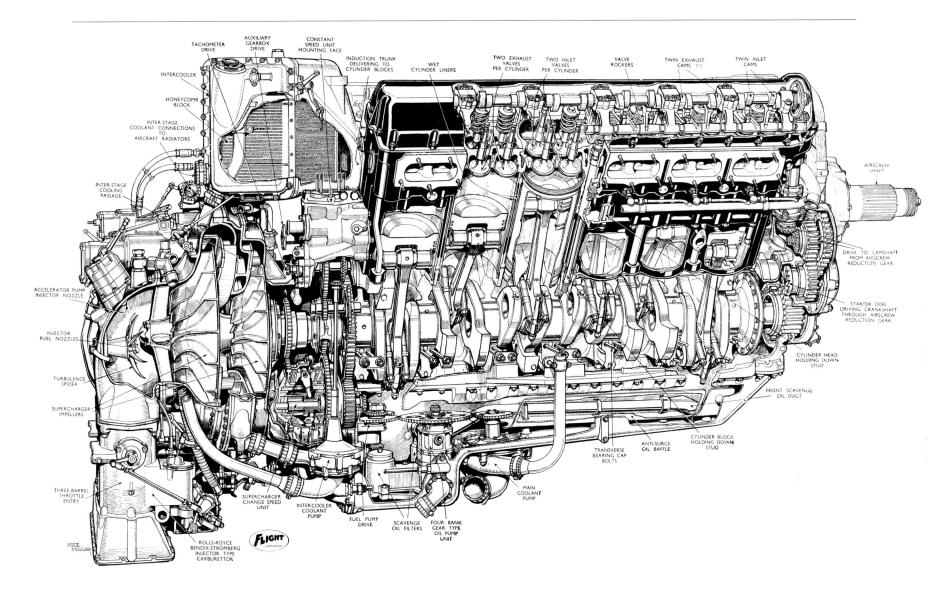

the front, which played a major role in keeping the engine short. Max drew the starter dog clutch but not the starter, which in the Mk 65 was a five-breech Coffman cartridge unit. You indexed the next cartridge, set up the throttle an inch or so open and pushed the button. There was a colossal 'CRACK'!, and in the twinkling of an eye the great engine was running.

The Mk 65 drove a Rotol five-blade constant-speed propeller. On opening up for take-off Merlin-Spitfires tried to swing to the left. As the Griffon was initially for naval aircraft it was thought better to make the propeller go round the other way (so it was better to hit the 'island' superstructure than go off the deck into the 'oggin'?). This probably caught out a few unbriefed Spitfire XIV pilots in 1944, who began to apply a little right rudder and found to their horror that the swing was in that direction, and far more powerful than with a Merlin. You needed not only a bootful of left rudder but full left rudder trim as well.

# CENTAURUS

One cannot help but have mixed feelings about Roy Fedden's development of sleeve-valve engines at Bristol. It was triggered off in 1926 by his correct belief that his basic nine-cylinder Jupiter would eventually have to lead to more powerful engines with two rows of radial cylinders. To get optimum breathing he used two inlet valves and two exhaust valves on each cylinder, and he realised that the valve gear for a twin-row radial with four poppet valves on each cylinder would be extremely complex. So he turned to sleeve valves, as explained in the drawing of the Hercules.

This work proved to be far more difficult than he expected. From the end of the Century one can see that perhaps he would have saved a lot of money and bother if he had simply settled for two poppet valves on each cylinder. Then he could easily have produced high-power engines such as the Wright Duplex Cyclone and Pratt & Whitney Double Wasp – and, in this book, the BMW 801. Having said that, Fedden's sleeve-valve Hercules and Centaurus were great engines, which seemed smoother and quieter than the poppet-valve competition.

A Centaurus engine is worked on at Eglinton in 1948. The aircraft is No 805 Sqn Sea Fury with Australian No 20 Carrier Air Group.

During the War the number of Hercules delivered exceeded 57,400, and this was about 57,000 more than the output of the Centaurus. This outrageous result was to some degree due to the fact that, when the prototype Centaurus first ran in July 1938, nobody even thought about it being useful as an engine for fighters. At this time the Hercules was becoming available at 1375 hp, whereas the Centaurus – with not 14 but 18 bigger cylinders 5.75 x 7 in, giving a capacity of 3270 cubic inches, 53.6 litres – started off at 2000 hp, with 2500 in immediate prospect.

This should have been seen as the ideal engine for future fighters. Indeed, Sydney Camm did fit one into a Tornado, and at 421 mph it was the fastest military aircraft in the world in 1941, but nobody seemed to notice. In August 1942 Camm put a later Centaurus into one of the new thin-wing Typhoon II prototypes (later called Tempest). Ministry officials had the engine taken out again! Within days the captured Fw 190 showed how stupid they were, but the Centaurus-engined Tempest was not allowed to fly until June 1943. All this seriously held back the engine which should have followed the Merlin as the most important piston engine in Britain.

At last, near the end of the War, the Centaurus V and XI began to roll off the production line in an underground factory inside a giant quarry at Corsham, not far from Bristol. Each morning there would be a waist-high mist round the long rows of machine tools, yet it was soon noticed that nobody ever reported sick! These engines powered the Tempest II, Bristol's Buckingham and Buckmaster, and the Vickers Warwick GR V. Refined versions were fitted to the Fury and Sea Fury, of which a handful are still flying.

As far as I can recall the only Centaurus installations with a cooling fan were those of the Mk 130 engines in the first prototype Airspeed Ambassador airliner and the Mks 171, 173 and 373 in the Blackburn Beverley. The Ambassador installation was troublesome, and after being completely redesigned lost its fan and emerged in a totally different form with a prominent chin inlet and cooling exit flaps at the sides only. The engine, the Mk 661, had the magnetos and ignition harness on the front. In contrast, the Beverley engines, seen in Max's drawing, had the ignition system at the rear.

Whereas earlier Bristol engines had collected the exhaust in a ring forming the front of the cowling, the Centaurus turned the twin pipes from the exhaust ports of each cylinder sharply to the rear. There was just room to get the pipes between the cylinders, with the induction pipes lying immediately underneath. The exhaust pipes emerged under the cooling gills in small groups all round, where they made the nacelle and wing hot and sooty. The propeller

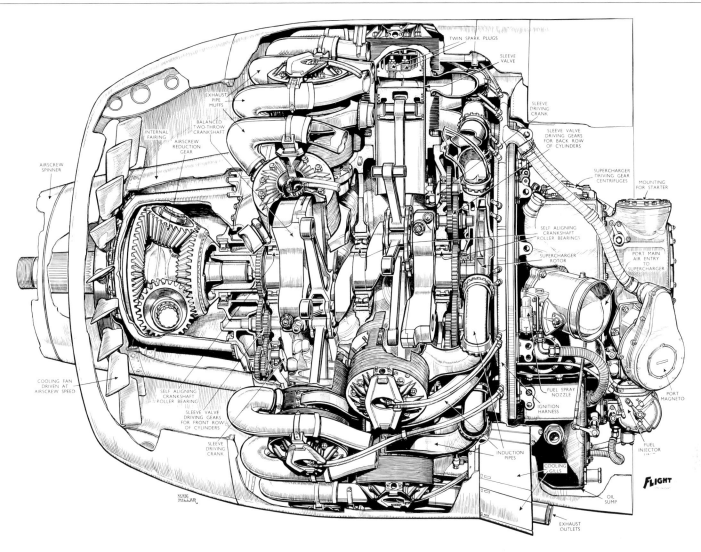

Image labels (clockwise from top):

TWIN SPARK PLUGS

SLEEVE VALVE

SLEEVE DRIVING CRANK

SLEEVE VALVE DRIVING GEARS FOR BACK ROW OF CYLINDERS

SUPERCHARGER DRIVING GEAR CENTRIFUGES

MOUNTING FOR STARTER

SELF ALIGNING CRANKSHAFT ROLLER BEARINGS

SUPERCHARGER ROTOR

PORT MAIN AIR ENTRY TO SUPERCHARGER

FUEL SPRAY NOZZLE

IGNITION HARNESS

PORT MAGNETO

FUEL INJECTOR

COOLING GILLS

OIL SUMP

EXHAUST OUTLETS

INDUCTION PIPES

SLEEVE DRIVING CRANK

SLEEVE VALVE DRIVING GEARS FOR FRONT ROW OF CYLINDERS

SELF ALIGNING CRANKSHAFT ROLLER BEARING

COOLING FAN DRIVEN AT AIRSCREW SPEED

AIRSCREW SPINNER

INTERNAL FAIRING

AIRSCREW REDUCTION GEAR

BALANCED TWO-THROW CRANKSHAFT

EXHAUST PIPE MUFFS

MAX MILLAR

FLIGHT

was a big 16-ft de Havilland with four hollow steel blades with square tips.

It may not be obvious how the Farman-type reduction gear worked. The crankshaft, turning at up to 2800 rpm, drove the rear bevel gear. This drove the three intermediate bevel gears around the fixed gear at the front, the propeller being turned at up to 1120 rpm (ratio 0.4) by the three-armed spider on which the small gears were mounted.

Each row of nine cylinders transmitted their power through one master connecting rod to which were pin-jointed the eight slave rods from the other cylinders in that row. Clearly, either the master big end or the crankshaft had

to be made in separate parts, or the engine could not be assembled. Fedden's choice was a one-piece master rod driving a crankpin on a crankshaft made in three parts. To assemble the engine the crank webs were pinched tight on the crankpins by the two large bolts. At the other end of the web was the balance weight seen behind the arrowhead from 'balanced two-throw crankshaft'.

This engine weighed about 3490 lb, and with water-methanol injection had a maximum rating of 3150 hp for take-off at sea level, and 3220 hp at 3000 ft. Very much higher outputs can be obtained from the few Centaurus installed in Sea Furies raced at Reno. I hope the owners take care of them.

# BMW 801

The author once flew a Ju 88 powered by BMW 801 engines, and was deeply impressed by both the aircraft and its engines. Later, with pounding heart, he settled into a Focke-Wulf Fw 190 and started the BMW 801, but was unable to get any further on that occasion. As in Britain, officials in Germany were steeped in the dictates of fashion and riddled with favouritism and jealousy, but this engine simply proved so good that it overcame all the political problems and by 1945 deliveries exceeded 61,000.

The famed Munich company built its aeronautical reputation on water-cooled vee-12 engines, but in order to get a new line of business in 1929 it purchased a licence from Pratt & Whitney for the Hornet 9-cylinder air-cooled radial. This had two-valve cylinders of 6¹⁄8 in (155.5 mm) bore and 6³⁄8 in (162 mm) stroke, giving a capacity of 1690 cu in (27.7 litres), and gave powers around 575 hp. BMW developed it into the BMW 132 family, of which over 21,000 had been made by 1945, among the recipients being versions of the Do 17, Ju 86 and Hs 126 seen in these pages.

By 1935 the engineers led by Helmut Sachse had done the obvious and designed the BMW 139, which was virtually a couple of BMW 132s on one crankcase. It ran in 1938 at 1550 hp, and powered prototypes of the Do 217

The BMW 801 engine in Armin Faber's Fw 190 was the subject of much attention, with engineers and scientists scrutinising it from all possible angles

and Fw 190. However, a better way of getting this power was the completely new BMW 801, with only 14 cylinders. Moreover, these were of only 156 mm (6.15 in) bore and stroke, giving a capacity of 41.8 litres (2551 cu in). The 801 was perhaps the most compact engine in the world for its power, the installed diameter being 1320 mm (52 in). Dry weight was about 1180 kg (2600 lb).

Little appreciated at the time, in the Soviet Union Arkadiya Shvetsov had used design features of the Wright Cyclone in developing a 14-cylinder engine called the ASh-82. This was in many respects exceedingly like the BMW 801. In the La-5 fighter it was beautifully installed, at a time when in Britain the idea of a radial-engined fighter was still derided. Production of the ASh-82 carried on after the War, eventually reaching 70,000.

Like the ASh-82, the BMW 801 went from strength to strength, and in various packaged installations soon became a bolt-on answer to almost any aircraft needing engines in the 1600 hp class. The most important were the two aircraft mentioned earlier, but the 801 also replaced the 139 in the Do 217E. As shown on another page, this had two BMW 801A engines, and this is the version drawn by Max. The neatness of the installation is obvious, unusual features including the cooling fan, the annular oil radiator with airflow from back to front, and the multi-fishtail flame-damping exhausts.

Like the Bristol engines, BMW used one-piece master rods driving a crankshaft assembled from four parts, each including one of the heavy balance weights. Like all the most important German high-power wartime engines, the 801 had no carburettor but injected the fuel directly into the cylinders. The Deckel pump, seen on the right, had 14 individual plungers and of course had to be made like a watch.

Most versions of the BMW 801 had single-lever control made possible by a Kommandogerät, a complex package which automatically governed rpm, boost pressure, supercharger gear ratio, mixture strength (or rather injection-plunger stroke) and ignition timing. All this high-precision trickery made life rather difficult for the Luftwaffe groundcrews, who really had to know their stuff.

At the front and rear of the crankshaft were numerous gears driving the valve gear. Whereas in Bristol's sleeve-valve engines these drove the sleeve cranks, here they rotated large gear rings (annotated front and rear 'cam gear') with cams which periodically pushed up the push-rods to open the inlet and exhaust valves. The twin 14-pole Bosch magneto was mounted vertically at the front on the reduction-gear casing, serving the two plugs on each cylinder, one inboard of each valve. The straight rods linking the tops of the cylinders

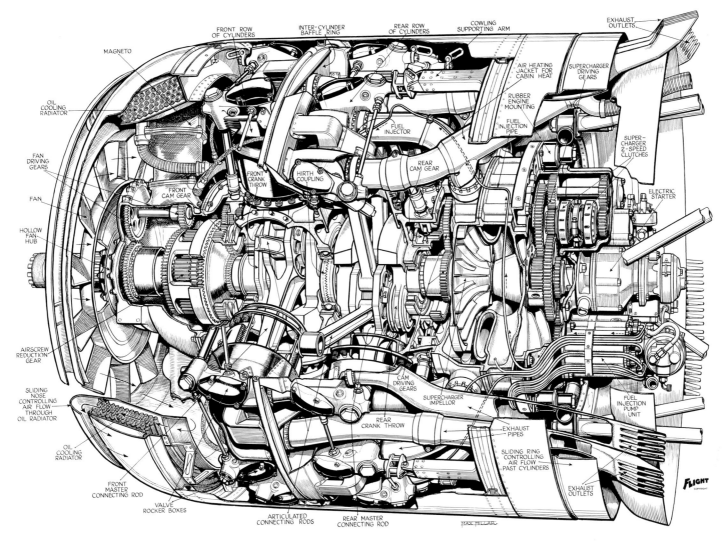

FRONT ROW OF CYLINDERS

INTER-CYLINDER BAFFLE RING

REAR ROW OF CYLINDERS

COWLING SUPPORTING ARM

EXHAUST OUTLETS

MAGNETO

AIR HEATING JACKET FOR CABIN HEAT

SUPERCHARGER DRIVING GEARS

OIL COOLING RADIATOR

RUBBER ENGINE MOUNTING

FUEL INJECTION PIPE

SUPER-CHARGER 2-SPEED CLUTCHES

FAN DRIVING GEARS

FUEL INJECTOR

FRONT CRANK THROW

HIRTH COUPLING

REAR CAM GEAR

FAN

FRONT CAM GEAR

ELECTRIC STARTER

HOLLOW FAN-HUB

AIRSCREW REDUCTION GEAR

SLIDING NOSE CONTROLLING AIR FLOW THROUGH OIL RADIATOR

CAM DRIVING GEARS

SUPERCHARGER IMPELLOR

FUEL INJECTION PUMP UNIT

OIL COOLING RADIATOR

REAR CRANK THROW

EXHAUST PIPES

SLIDING RING CONTROLLING AIR FLOW PAST CYLINDERS

EXHAUST OUTLETS

FRONT MASTER CONNECTING ROD

VALVE ROCKER BOXES

ARTICULATED CONNECTING RODS

REAR MASTER CONNECTING ROD

MAX MILLAR

FLIGHT

were the oil return pipes. Cooling airflow through the engine was controlled not by hinged gills but by a sliding ring, which was positioned by an electric screwjack linkage.

During the course of the War the BMW designers naturally strove to wring more and more power out of this fine engine. My impression was that in the Ju 88 it was fantastic at low levels, but rapidly 'ran out of steam' at over 20,000 ft. Not so for some of the later versions, notably the BMW 801TQ which had an enormous turbosupercharger and was rated at an amazing 1715 hp at an altitude of 12 km (39,370 ft)!

In 1940 the 18-cylinder BMW 802 first ran, but this was abandoned two years later. In contrast, work pressed on to the bitter end with the totally different BMW 803. This had basically the same-size cylinders as the 801, but twice as many (28), with liquid cooling. They were arranged back-to-back on a common crankcase in in-line pairs, each pair sharing a common cylinder head and camshaft. This awesome 2950-kg (6500-lb) package was rated at 4000 hp for take-off, or 2550 hp at 12 km altitude. One was recently discovered in the USA, where it took a long time to decide what it was. Then, fortunately, it was sent back to Munich, where it has been lovingly restored.

# DB 601

One of the inevitable shortcomings of a cutaway drawing is that you can't at the same time show the external appearance. Had Max instead drawn the outside of the DB 601A it would have been plain solid black, with almost no excrescences apart from the ignition harness. The Daimler-Benz engines were remarkably clean and uncluttered, and of course they were also excellent examples of precision engineering. Too bad that they utterly failed to beat the smaller British Merlin.

One of the astonishing discoveries when Allied investigating teams reached the design centre at Stuttgart-Untertürkheim in spring 1945 was the wealth of different piston aero engines that were, or recently had been, under development. At a guess I would say there were 25 distinct designs, ignoring sub-types. Some had extraordinary arrangements of multiple superchargers, in order to try to get more power at high altitude. Technical Director Fritz Nallinger appeared to have lost control, because there was no way even a small fraction of so many engines could have been developed to help the ailing Luftwaffe.

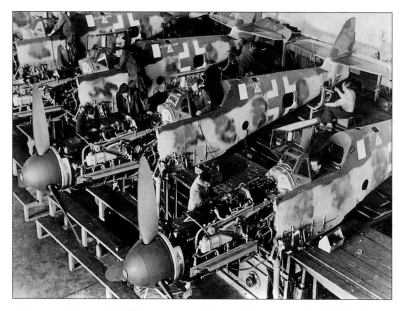

Although redisignated DB 605 to emphasise its internal changes over the DB 601, the former was externally very much the same in appearance - these aircraft seen on the production line at Messerschmitt are Bf 109G

All the original high-power production engines were similar to the 601 in being inverted-vee 12-cylinder engines with liquid cooling. A particular feature was that, whatever other superchargers might be added, the supercharger actually driven off the crankshaft was always mounted at the rear on the left side, on a transverse shaft. Moreover, this shaft was driven via a hydraulic clutch, called a "fluid coupling" by Max. This worked just like the Daimler 'fluid flywheel' seen on inter-war cars.

At sea level the input half was driven off the engine, but had no connection with the output, so the impeller stayed stationary. As the aircraft climbed, oil was progressively fed in to form a fluid link between the input and output. Thus, the supercharger spun faster and faster, until at high altitude the slip in the drive was close to zero. One drawback was that at heights between about 2000 and 15,000 ft the drive consumed power but the impeller turned too slowly to make much difference to the induction manifold pressure. Max's 'cush drive' was a spring coupling to eliminate vibration or shocks in the drive.

The first of the modern inverted-vee DB engines was the 600, designed a year after its future rival the Merlin in 1934. Cylinder bore was 150 mm (5.9 in) and stroke 160 mm (6.3 in), giving a capacity of 33.93 litres (2071 cubic inches), compared with the 26.99 litres of the Merlin. The supercharged and geared DB 600A weighed about 685 kg and was rated at 986 hp for take-off, at 2400 rpm. It powered many important prototypes, but faded before the War came in 1939.

This was because it was superseded by the DB 601. This was almost the same engine, but instead of having a conventional carburettor its cylinders received minute precisely-measured squirts of fuel from an injection pump. The drawback was that this pump demanded precision higher than anything previously seen in internal-combustion engines (if fuel consumption was not to be higher than before). This precision had to be maintained throughout arduous service in frontline squadrons. The advantages were many, notably that the induction system was no longer prone to icing, and the engine worked perfectly even upside-down or under strong negative-g. The latter advantage often decided the outcome of combats in the Battle of Britain between Merlin-engined fighters and the DB 601A-powered Bf 109E.

At the same time, I am surprised that Max decided to show the entire fuel-injection pump block, which hung under the centreline of the crankcase, because this left him with only two cylinders to draw, only one of which he sectioned. With the injection block, when you've seen one bit, you've seen all 12, whereas the cylinders could be opened up in various ways to show many

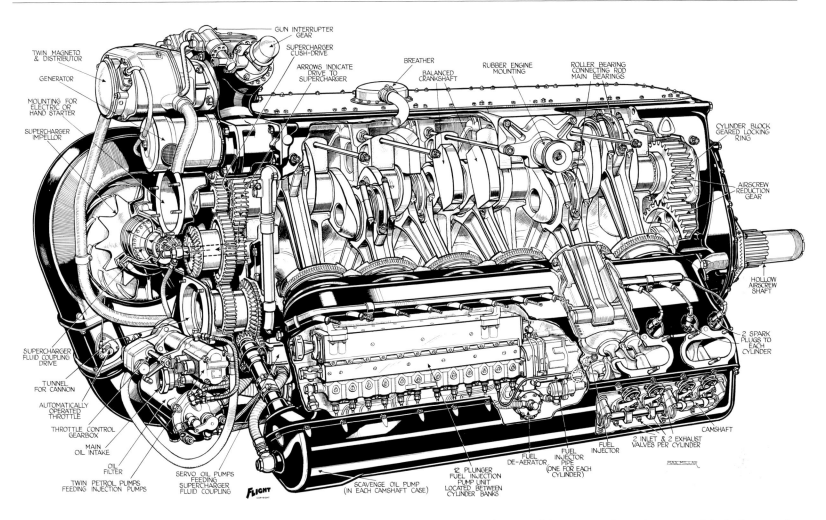

Labels on the diagram (clockwise from top):

GUN INTERRUPTER GEAR

SUPERCHARGER CUSH-DRIVE

TWIN MAGNETO & DISTRIBUTOR

GENERATOR

MOUNTING FOR ELECTRIC OR HAND STARTER

SUPERCHARGER IMPELLOR

ARROWS INDICATE DRIVE TO SUPERCHARGER

BREATHER

BALANCED CRANKSHAFT

RUBBER ENGINE MOUNTING

ROLLER BEARING CONNECTING ROD MAIN BEARINGS

CYLINDER BLOCK GEARED LOCKING RING

AIRSCREW REDUCTION GEAR

HOLLOW AIRSCREW SHAFT

2 SPARK PLUGS TO EACH CYLINDER

CAMSHAFT

2 INLET & 2 EXHAUST VALVES PER CYLINDER

FUEL INJECTOR

FUEL INJECTOR PIPE (ONE FOR EACH CYLINDER)

FUEL DE-AERATOR

12 PLUNGER FUEL INJECTION PUMP UNIT LOCATED BETWEEN CYLINDER BANKS

SCAVENGE OIL PUMP (IN EACH CAMSHAFT CASE)

TWIN PETROL PUMPS FEEDING INJECTION PUMPS

SERVO OIL PUMPS FEEDING SUPERCHARGER FLUID COUPLING

MAIN OIL INTAKE

OIL FILTER

THROTTLE CONTROL GEARBOX

AUTOMATICALLY OPERATED THROTTLE

TUNNEL FOR CANNON

SUPERCHARGER FLUID COUPLING DRIVE

MAX MILLAR

FLIGHT COPYRIGHT

different parts, such as the induction manifold, complex exhaust pipe arrangements and liquid cooling.

With inline and vee engines it is universal to make the crankshaft from a one-piece steel forging and split the con-rod big ends to fit over the crankpins. As in most wartime high-power vee engines, the DB 601 connecting rods comprised narrow blade rods from the pistons of one block (the left) sandwiched between the twin big ends of forked rods on the other side (the right). On assembling the engine all the big ends would be completed by adding the missing half and carefully tightening the bolts to a predetermined torque. The arrows from 'balanced crankshaft' point to two of the six pairs of balance weights.

Max noted a 'tunnel for cannon' down the centre of the hollow crankshaft. A 20-mm MG FF could indeed be installed, and was in fact fitted to a very few aircraft, such as the Bf 109E-3 as originally built. As noted in the Bf 109E cutaway, not many survived for long, and a better armament was two such guns in the outer wings. By 1941 the standard 109 in production was the F, also in this book, and this almost always did have a gun firing through the propeller, at first an MG FF and later the 15 mm or 20 mm Mauser MG 151. The engine by this time was the DB 605, which was almost the same as a 601 but with new blocks containing cylinders of 154 mm bore, increasing capacity to 35.7 litres. The 605 was also cleared to 2800 rpm, raising power to around 1475 hp for the Bf 109G and Bf 110.

# APPENDIX I

*The Aeroplane/Aeroplane Spotter* cutaways contained in this volume in published date order

| | | | |
|---|---|---|---|
| Short Sunderland I | January 1939 | Messerschmitt Bf 109F | 1 August 1941 |
| Napier Dagger | 11 January 1939 | Miles Master I | 7 August 1941 |
| Hawker Henley | 1 March 1939 | Bristol Beaufighter IF | 12 September 1941 |
| Rolls-Royce Merlin I | 26 April 1939 | Bristol Pegasus | 23 October 1941 |
| Handley Page Hampden I | 3 May 1939 | Bell Airacobra I | 31 October 1941 |
| Bristol Bombay I | 2 August 1939 | Short Stirling I | 27 February 1942 |
| Blackburn Skua I | 9 August 1939 | Bristol Hercules | 13 March 1942 |
| Junkers Ju 86A-1 | 19 October 1939 | Handley Page Halifax I | 24 April 1942 |
| Messerschmitt Bf 109E | 2 November 1939 | Consolidated Catalina I | 19 June 1942 |
| Henschel Hs 126 | 30 November 1939 | Focke-Wulf Fw 190A3 | 28 August 1942 |
| Dornier Do 17/215 | 22 December 1939 | Avro Lancaster I | 23 October 1942 |
| Junkers Ju 87B | 23 February 1940 | Rolls-Royce Merlin XX | 18 December 1942 |
| Supermarine Spitfire I | 12 April 1940 | Messerschmitt Me 210 | 12 February 1943 |
| Hawker Hurricane I | 6 September 1940 | de Havilland Mosquito Mk IV | 7 May 1943 |
| German 'Twins' in detail | 18 October 1940 | North American Mustang I | 5 November 1943 |
| Vickers Wellington II | November 1940 | Taylorcraft Auster IV | 21 April 1944 |
| Messerschmitt Bf 110 | 3 April 1941 | Armstrong Whitworth Albemarle I | 30 June 1944 |
| Bristol Blenheim IV | 24 April 1941 | Avro York I | 18 August 1944 |
| Junkers Ju 88 | 1 May 1941 | GAL Hamilcar | 14 December 1944 |
| Armstrong Whitworth Whitley III | 5 June 1941 | Hawker Tempest V | 9 March 1945 |
| Heinkel He 111 | 12 June 1941 | Miles Messenger | 20 April 1945 |
| Curtiss Tomahawk I | 26 June 1941 | Fairey Firefly I | 4 May 1945 |
| Fairey Battle III | 3 July 1941 | | |

# APPENDIX 2

*Flight* Cutaways 1934-45

| | | | |
|---|---|---|---|
| Hawker Hardy | 28 June 1934 | Armstrong Whitworth Whitley III | 26 May 1938 |
| Cierva C.30 Autogiro | 9 August 1934 and 23 March 1943 | Westland Lysander I | 9 June 1938 |
| Napier Rapier | 14 March 1935 and 2 December 1937 | de Havilland Gipsy XII | 23 June 1938 |
| Rolls-Royce Kestrel VI | 28 March 1935 | Zeppelin Graf Zeppelin | 10 November 1938 |
| Blackburn Cirrus Major | 13 June 1935 | de Havilland Gipsy Minor | 10 November 1938 |
| de Havilland Cirrus Major | 13 June 1935 | de Havilland Albatross | 17 November 1938 |
| Boulton Paul Overstrand | 27 June 1935 | Vickers Supermarine Spitfire I | 1 December 1938, 18 April 1940 |
| Vickers Supermarine Scapa | 27 June 1935 | | and 26 September 1940 |
| de Havilland Gipsy Six R | 12 September 1935 | Cunliffe-Owen Flying Wing | 22 December 1938 |
| Avro Anson I | 30 January 1936 | Napier-Halford Dagger VIII | 12 January 1939 |
| Zeppelin LZ 129 Hindenburg | 5 March 1936 | Short Sunderland | 26 January 1939 |
| Handley Page Heyford | 25 June 1936 | Pratt & Whitney Twin Wasp | 1 May 1939 |
| Gloster Gladiator I | 25 June 1936 | Handley Page Hampden | 4 May 1939 |
| Short Singapore III | 25 June 1936 | Blackburn Cirrus | 25 May 1939 |
| Bristol Pegasus X | 5 November 1936 and | de Havilland Cirrus Major 150 | 25 May 1939 |
| | 2 December 1937 | de Havilland Moth Minor | 29 June 1939 |
| de Havilland Gipsy Six Series II | 7 January 1937 and 2 December 1937 | General Aircraft Cygnet | 13 July 1939 |
| Armstrong Whitworth Ensign | 1 April 1937 | Short C Class Flying Boat | 20 July 1939 |
| Bristol Blenheim I | 24 June 1937 and 25 November 1937 | Miles Master | 27 July 1939 |
| Airspeed Oxford I | 1 July 1937 | Blackburn Skua | 10 August 1939 |
| Fairey Battle I | 19 August 1937 | Junkers Ju 87 | 28 September 1939 |
| Armstrong Siddeley Tiger VI | 2 December 1937 | Arado Ar 95 | 19 October 1939 |
| Short Mayo - Composite | 17 February 1938 | Dornier Do 215 | 2 November 1939 |
| Dornier Do 17 | 14 April 1938 | Fokker D.23 | 14 March 1940 |

| | | | |
|---|---|---|---|
| Hawker Hurricane Mk I | 31 October 1940 | Taylorcraft Auster III | 23 September 1943 |
| Bristol Hercules XVI | 27 November 1941 and | Avro Lancaster Mk II | 9 December 1943 |
| | 1 October 1942 | Hawker Typhoon IB | 20 January 1944 and 13 April 1944 |
| Short Stirling | 29 January 1942 | Napier Sabre II | 23 March 1944 |
| Bell Airacobra | 24 February 1942 | Boeing B-17G Flying Fortress | 4 May 1944 |
| Rolls-Royce Merlin XX | 26 February 1942 and | Lockheed P-38 Lightning | 22 June 1944 |
| | 17 December 1942 | Avro York | 17 August 1944 |
| Merlin XX Supercharger Detail | 26 February 1942 and | Fiesler V1 Flying Bomb | 5 October 1944 |
| | 17 December 1942 | Fairey Firefly | 7 December 1944 |
| Allison V-1710 C15 | 26 March 1942 | GAL Hamilcar | 14 December 1944 |
| Daimler-Benz DB 601N | 16 April 1942 | Fairey Barracuda II | 21 December 1944 |
| Handley Page Halifax III | 23 April 1942 | Hawker Tempest V | 1 March 1945 |
| Avro Lancaster Mk I | 13 August 1942 | Short Shetland | 17 May 1945 |
| BMW 801A | 13 August 1942 | Vickers Viking | 24 May 1945 |
| Dornier Do 217E-2 | 15 October 1942 | Avro Tudor I | 28 June 1945 |
| North American Mustang I | 10 December 1942 | Bristol Centaurus 373 | 5 June 1945 |
| Rolls-Royce Merlin 61 | 17 December 1942, | Boeing B-29 Superfortress | 12 July 1945 |
| | 23 September 1943 and 6 January 1944 | Rolls-Royce Griffon 65 | 20 September 1945 |
| de Havilland Mosquito II | 6 May 1943 | Blackburn Firebrand | 27 September 1945 |
| Airspeed Oxford | 27 May 1943 | Gloster Meteor IV | 25 October 1945 |
| Armstrong Siddeley Cheetah X | 24 June 1943 | de Havilland Vampire I | 20 December 1945 |
| Airspeed Horsa | 15 July 1943 | de Havilland Gipsy Queen 71 | 27 December 1945 |

All the listed cutaways are presently held by *Flight International* and are available for use. Contact;
*Quadrant* Picture Library, Quadrant House, The Quadrant, Sutton, Surrey, SM2 5AS

# INDEX